Training for Climbing

The Definitive Guide to
Improving Your Climbing Performance

"*Training for Climbing* is a great resource. Whether you're just starting out or already
ticking 5.13, you'll find valuable information here to help you climb harder. This is
the most complete and up-to-date training guide available. Better yet, it's presented
in a clean and easily understandable format, with inspiring and illustrative photos."

—MARK ELLER, ASSOCIATE EDITOR,
ROCK & ICE MAGAZINE

"Eric Hörst has taken complex scientific training concepts and integrated these with
contemporary research on climbing to produce a very readable and useful training
guide. This book will lead the climber to new heights of performance."

—PHILLIP B. WATTS, PH.D.,
EXERCISE PHYSIOLOGIST & CLIMBING RESEARCHER,
NORTHERN MICHIGAN UNIVERSITY

"Hörst is uniquely positioned to bring current methods in sports psychology and
exercise science to the world of climbing, and he has hit the mark in superb style!
If you are passionate about climbing and getting better, *Training for Climbing* will
become your dog-eared companion!"

—RICHARD K. FLEMING, PH.D.,
ASSISTANT PROFESSOR OF PSYCHOLOGY,
UNIVERSITY OF MASSACHUSETTS MEDICAL SCHOOL

"With comprehensive textbook-like descriptions of nutrition, recovery, weight training,
and structured workouts, *Training for Climbing* is a crucial addition to your climbing
library. Use this book to make 5.13 a reality instead of just a dream."

—MICHELLE HURNI,
AUTHOR OF *COACHING CLIMBING*

A FALCON GUIDE®

HOW TO CLIMB SERIES

Training for Climbing

The Definitive Guide to
Improving Your Climbing Performance

Eric J. Hörst

FALCON GUIDE®

GUILFORD, CONNECTICUT
HELENA, MONTANA
AN IMPRINT OF THE GLOBE PEQUOT PRESS

Page design: Casey Shain
Chart design: Mary Ballachino
Illustrations: Judy Newhouse
Photo on table of contents page by Stewart Green.
All other interior photos courtesy of the author, unless otherwise credited.

Library of Congress Cataloging-in-Publication Data
Hörst, Eric J.
    Training for climbing: the definitive guide to improving your climbing
performance / Eric J. Hörst.—1st ed.
        p. cm. — (How to climb series) (A Falcon guide)
    Includes bibliographical references and index.
    ISBN 0-7627-2313-0
        1. Rock climbing—Training. I. Title. II. Series. III. Series: A Falcon guide
GV200.2.H685 2002
796.52'23—dc21   2002029463

Manufactured in the United States of America
First Edition, Fifth Printing

I dedicate this book to two of the strongest, most innovative and humble men ever to pull down on rock.

The *"Master of Rock,"* John Gill and the late, great Wolfgang Güllich.

C O N T E N T S

Acknowledgments   *xi*

Introduction   *xiii*

Chapter **1** An Overview of Training for Climbing   *1*

Chapter **2** Self-Assessment & Goal Setting   *13*

Chapter **3** Mental Training   *23*

Chapter **4** Training Skill & Strategy   *41*

Chapter **5** Theory & Methods of Strength Training   *53*

Chapter **6** Strength & Conditioning Exercises   *69*

Chapter **7** Personal Training Programs   *109*

Chapter **8** Performance Nutrition   *125*

Chapter **9** Accelerating Recovery   *137*

Chapter 10 Injury Treatment & Prevention   *151*

Afterword   *171*

Appendix A Training Charts   *173*

Appendix B Self-Assessment Test Comments & Training Tips   *177*

Appendix C Fitness Evaluation & Questionnaire   *181*

Glossary   *185*

Suggested Reading   *191*

References   *193*

Index   *197*

About the Author   *207*

A C K N O W L E D G M E N T S

Writing a book is an Everest-like undertaking. It is a team effort that takes many months or years to plan and execute, but getting to the summit still takes an immense individual effort and an indomitably singular focus.

Having completed this climb, I reflect on all that has brought me to this point—the thousands of wonderful days I've spent on the rock, the countless climbers from around the world I've had the pleasure to meet, and the dozens of partners I am grateful to have shared a rope with. Learning to climb is a long, continuous process with no end, and I thank all the people who have influenced me from my days as a wide-eyed fourteen-year-old rock jock to an almost forty-year-old veteran climber. I must thank directly John Gill, the late Wolfgang Güllich, Lynn Hill, John Long, Jim McCarthy, Mark Robinson, Todd Skinner, and Tony Yaniro—all of you, knowingly or unknowingly, have inspired me and contributed to this book in some way.

Though I continue to view myself as a student of rock climbing, I enjoy more every year the role of teacher. I am humbled by all the letters and e-mails received from climbers in more than forty countries who have read my books and articles. I appreciate all the feedback, the suggestions, and, most of all, the success stories of those who have benefited from my works. Writing climbing books is certainly not a lucrative endeavor; still, knowing that I've helped thousands of people from around the planet climb better is priceless.

My appreciation extends to Jeff Serena, Shelley Wolf, and everyone at Falcon Press and Globe Pequot who have helped bring this book to fruition. I am also very appreciative of all the climbing companies that support me and my many projects, including Nicros, La Sportiva, Prana, and Sterling. Many thanks to my close friend Eric McCallister, my wife, Lisa Ann, and my family for their support and proofreading over the last six months of pedal-to-the-metal writing. I am most grateful for the encouragement and input from Mark Robinson, M.D., and Phil Watts, M.D., and I thank Russ Clune, Rick Fleming, Richard Goldstone, Jeff Leads, Keith McCallister, Travis Peck,

Barb Branda Turner, and Cliffhangers for their contributions. Mega kudos to Thomas Ballenberger, Stewart Green, Michael Landkroon, Michael McGill, Tyler Stableford, and Wills Young, whose photography is featured throughout the book. And I must thank my two beautiful sons, Cameron and Jonathan, for making this year the most exciting and wonderful in my life!

Finally, I am sincerely thankful for my original climbing partner and a real-life hero, Jeff Batzer. Minus five fingers and half a leg, Jeff recently showed me again that he still has all the moves and remains one of the most impressive climbers I've ever met. Jeff, you are a true inspiration—thanks, man!

INTRODUCTION

Twenty years from now you will be more disappointed by the things that you didn't do than by the ones you did do. So throw off the bowlines. Sail away from the safe harbor. Catch the trade winds in your sails. Explore. Dream. Discover.

— *Mark Twain*

T*raining for Climbing* is a unique synthesis of twenty-five years of studying, imagining, and experimenting with ways to increase climbing performance. Building on the foundation laid out in my first two books, *Flash Training* and *How to Climb 5.12*, and the dozens of magazine articles that I've authored, this text offers a new level of comprehensive instruction not available from any other resource.

Training for Climbing blends leading-edge sports science, tried-and-true practice strategies, and powerful mental-training techniques into a single text that will help you climb better regardless of your present ability. By faithfully applying just 50 percent of the methods contained herein, you will surely grow to outperform the mass of climbers. And if you integrate most of the material into your training, climbing, and living, you may very well progress to levels beyond your current comprehension!

Training for Climbing is as much about developing new ways of thinking as it is about engaging in new ways of training. A common thread that weaves throughout this book is that "intelligence in climbing is not measured by IQ, but instead by your thoughts and actions." The thoughts you carry and the things you do (or don't do) are ultimately what separate you from the mass of climbers. Whether you flash or fall, become superstrong or get injured, or feel happy or frustrated, springs forth from subtle differences in the ways you think, feel, and act compared to other climbers. Therefore, the primary goal of this book is to help guide you to more deliberate and effective ways of thinking and acting in your pursuit of peak climbing performance.

Since climbing is all about an intimate dance between you and the rock, it's vital to recognize that your climbing performance evolves from the inside out, and that you only trip and fall when *you* blow a move. Goethe wrote, "Nature understands no jesting; she is always true, always serious, always severe; she is always right, and the errors and faults are always those of man. The man incapable of appreciating her, she despises; and only to the apt, the pure, and the true, does she resign herself and reveal her secrets." From this perspective it becomes obvious that we must always look inside ourselves to see what's holding us back. Looking outward for the reason or to place blame is a loser's game.

This book begins with a logical progression of self-analysis, goal setting, mental training, and technique training before ever lifting a weight. Chapters 1 through 4 are focused on helping you learn, most quickly, the vital mental and technical skills that separate the best from the rest in this sport. After a brief review of the history of training for climbing, you'll get started on the road to better climbing by taking a self-evaluation test that will reveal your true strengths and weaknesses as a climber. Armed with this information, you can apply more effectively the material that follows on the subjects of training your mind and developing better climbing technique and strategy.

Chapters 5 through 7 present the most in-depth look at strength training for climbing ever published. As an intensely practical person with a background in math and science, I have always felt it important to delve into the theory and application of cutting-edge sports science. Transferring this technology to training for climbing is vital to unlocking the most effective training methods and strategies. In reading these chapters, I trust you will gain new insight into the physiology of climbing performance and thus become a more physiologically effective student of training for climbing.

The concluding Chapters 8 through 10 cover the often overlooked (or ignored) subjects of performance nutrition, recovery, and proper treatment and prevention of climbing injuries. Becoming a complete climber requires that you embrace these subjects with the same fervor as you would in executing your training program or plotting your next climb. Throughout the text, I have footnoted the relevant scientific literature so you can peruse the nitty-gritty details if you are so impassioned. These references and other useful information can be found in the back of the book.

To glean the greatest benefit in reading *Training for Climbing*, you are encouraged to employ active reading techniques such as underlining key passages, putting a star next to the most meaningful strategies, and taking notes for later review. Try lifting the most powerful phrases and posting them in places where you will see them throughout the day. Review these highlighted passages and your notes at least once a week, then reread the entire book in three months and, again, in one year. Not only will this reinforce your understanding and mastery of the concepts, but you also will gain new insight and distinctions as you become a different person at each read-through.

As you cast off into the depths of this book, I want to wish you success and happiness as you climb through this world of wonder. Though we may never meet, we are connected through our shared passion for climbing. I am grateful for you taking the time to read this book, and I hope you find the material entertaining and immensely beneficial. I welcome your feedback, and look forward to hearing from you after some grand success that undoubtedly awaits you. I wish you the best both on and off the rock.

Wolfgang Güllich on Action Directe (5.14d), Frankenjura, Germany.

An Overview
of Training for Climbing

*A man's reach should exceed his
grasp or what's a heaven for?*

— *Robert Browning*

Many words can describe the wonderful activity of rock climbing—*elegant, powerful, rewarding,* and, sometimes, *frustrating.* While there may be nothing more natural and intuitive than climbing (just watch how children climb around on everything in sight!), rock climbing is indeed a complex activity with demands unique from those of living and playing in the everyday, horizontal world.

Performing in the vertical plane requires physical capabilities such as strength, power, and endurance. It also demands the development of technical skills such as balance and economic movement while gripping and stepping in an infinite variety of ways, positions, and angles. Most important, the inherent stress of climbing away from the safety of the ground requires acute control of your thoughts, focus, anxiety, and fears. In aggregate, the above factors dovetail into what may be one of the more complex sporting activities on this third rock from the sun.

The goal of this book is to explore all the topics relevant to increasing the effectiveness of your training and the quality of your climbing. As a climber of more than a quarter century (who's been fortunate enough to meet and climb with many brilliant individuals), I feel the journey should begin with a primer on the history of training for rock climbing. Clearly, the advancements we make today are possible only because we are standing on the shoulders of the giants who preceded us. Next, we'll explore the interesting subject of genetics and the possible genetic limitations to climbing performance. This leads us into an overview of training for climbing and the things you should consider in your quest for the biggest gains in performance in the shortest possible time.

A Brief History of Training for Climbing

Compared to many other sports, the science of rock climbing is still quite young. Well over one hundred years of literature exists on, say, the technical aspects of the golf swing; the diverse array of Olympic sports have been the subject of thousands of research studies during the twentieth and twenty-first centuries. Conversely, technical rock climbing was born in the early 1900s as an offshoot of mountaineering and, as an activity far removed from the mainstream, never garnered the attention of sports scientists. What little information existed on the technical aspects of climbing was mainly passed on by word of mouth in the form of tips on technique and equipment—virtually no one considered climbing to be a sport that required training outside of climbing itself. That is, until a young man from Alabama began climbing in the early 1950s.

Now one of the legends of climbing, John Gill was the first person to experiment with sport-specific training for climbing. Unlike other climbers of that day, who were lured to climb towering cliffs and mountains, Gill was enamored with short, overhanging faces on boulders lying around the base of mountains or in river valleys. Bagging summits or climbing

big walls had less appeal to Gill; instead he sought the kinesthetic feel of gymnasticlike movement up overhanging rock.

From the mid-1950s through the mid-1970s, Gill trained on a gym rope, on the rings, and with weighted, fingertip pull-ups (often one-arm!) in preparation for his increasingly powerful ascents on boulders in the Midwest, Southeast, and Rocky Mountain states. In the early years Gill's dynamic boulder problems, use of gymnastics chalk, and amazing feats of strength were viewed, by most, with amusement. Today we acknowledge that John Gill was an innovator, a visionary, and, in fact, the father of both bouldering (as a subdiscipline of climbing) and training for climbing. His technical climbing ability was years ahead of everyone else—consider his 1961 free-solo ascent of the 30-foot Thimble, in South Dakota, now considered V5 (5.12b/c)—and, as it turns out, he was an early prototype of today's high-end climbers who possess precise footwork, intense focus, and awesome power.

By the mid-1960s a handful of climbers began to recognize the importance of what Gill was doing. Famed Shawangunks hardman Richard Goldstone met Gill during a summer trip out west, and he was enormously impressed with Gill's one-arm pull-ups, front levers, and the difficulty of his boulder problems. Goldstone returned to the University of Chicago with an enthusiasm for training and adapted the use of surgical tubing (as used by gymnasts to learn an iron cross) as a training aid for portions of his workouts.

A few years later Goldstone returned east and became a player during the golden years of free climbing at the Shawangunks. Soon, other East Coast climbers like Gunks icon Jim McCarthy began to apply some of the Gill-inspired training strategies.

Similarly, it seems that Jim Bridwell was the first West Coast climber to begin serious sport-specific training, possibly influenced by Goldstone's propensity to hang a pull-up bar in every climbers' campground, including Yosemite's Camp Four. Bridwell and others went on to develop an array of training rigs around Camp Four. Warren Harding soon dubbed the area "Olympic Training Village" due to all the training apparatti that had been installed. In the years that followed, the Camp Four workout rigs introduced countless climbers from around the world to some of the basic elements of training for climbing.

Still, sports scientists in the university community and in Eastern and Western Europe had yet to view climbing as a worthy subject of study. Though first ascents of the world's highest mountains were a source of national pride in Europe, there were no Olympic medals to be won. Therefore, research remained focused on refining the science of weight lifting, the track and field events, and other sports where world records could be broken. Still, the increasing popularity of climbing in Europe during the 1970s eventually gave birth to the first studies relating to injuries and the physiological stresses of rock climbing.

Master of Rock was published in 1977. This biography of John Gill, though not a training book, did serve to document Gill's strength-training techniques and quickly became a kind of bible for a new generation of climbers interested in pushing the physical limits of climbing. Other climbing books of the era, such as Royal Robbins's *Basic Rockcraft,* focused on climbing techniques and equipment, not strength or mental training.

From the mid-1970s through the 1980s, the worldwide growth of technical rock climbing and the first climbing competitions produced an exchange of ideas among European, Soviet, and American climbers. In Yosemite's Camp Four; Boulder, Colorado; and at the Shawangunks in New York, small groups trained and free climbed with increasing fervor as energetic newcomers like John Bachar, Jim Collins, Lynn Hill, Jim Holloway, John Long, Ron Kauk, Todd Skinner, Tony Yaniro, and others arrived on the scene. The first few articles on the subject of climbing performance were published in American climbing magazines, and numerous research studies were performed, although primarily on the subject of the unique injuries incurred by climbers. Strength-training techniques remained relatively crude, although a few innovations

John Gill on the famous Left Eliminator *(V5)* in 1968, Horse Tooth Reservoir, Fort Collins, Colorado.

such as the Bachar Ladder and the fingerboard took generic pull-up training to a higher level of intensity and specificity.

In Britain indoor climbing walls had already taken hold, but it was not until 1987 that the first commercial climbing gyms opened in the United States. Meanwhile, at the Campus Center—a weight-lifting facility at the University of Nürnberg—a strong German climber named Wolfgang Güllich invented a sport-specific form of plyometric training known today simply as *campus training*. Between 1985 and 1991 Güllich went on to establish the world's hardest climbs (he also wrote a breakthrough training book, *Sportklettern Heute,* in 1986), and campus training became a staple exercise of many elite climbers the world over. For a time campus training was viewed as the end-all in sport-specific training for climbing, but we later found that this was not quite true.

The 1990s saw climbing go mainstream with televised competitions and dozens, if not hundreds, of well-sponsored full-time climbers training year-round. At last, two books were published by American authors on the subject of training—*Performance Rock Climbing* (Goddard 1993) and *Flash Training* (Hörst 1994)—and climbing magazines began to regularly run training articles. But the proliferation of indoor walls was the real wild card that allowed the average climber to practice more frequently and climb harder than ever. All the above-mentioned factors, along with improved equipment, made what was once the maximum grade of 5.10 achievable by the masses and 5.13 quickly attainable by a handful of youngsters not even old enough to drive.

Beginning a new millennium, we find climbing as popular as ever and the benchmark of maximum difficulty at the cusp of 5.15. University researchers, awakened to the unique physiological demands of climbing, have published more than thirty studies in the 1990s and over a dozen in the first two years of this new millennium. In aggregate the body of knowledge on the science of climbing performance has grown by leaps and bounds since I entered the sport twenty-five years ago. Still, I feel we are in the adolescence stage of our knowledge on the subject.

Whereas the climbers of my generation trained largely in accordance to myth, anecdote, and trial and error, those entering the sport today have a significant amount of quality information on the subject, if they choose to use it. As I proclaimed at the beginning of *How to Climb 5.12,* "If you are reading this book, chances are you have what it takes to climb 5.12." As I complete this latest book, I maintain this same sentiment—in fact I now surmise that there's a good chance you have what it takes to climb 5.13! And if you're genetically blessed, maybe even 5.15. . . .

Genetics and Climbing Performance

Excuses are like parents—everybody has them. Ironically, your parents, or more precisely the genetic material you inherited from them, might be the best excuse why you or I may never climb 5.15. Still, your genetic makeup, which substantially determines your height, flexibility, and natural strength, among other things, is a poor excuse for not being able to climb 5.10 or even 5.12. Yes, some specific 5.12 climb might require a long reach or high step that you will never be capable of making, but numerous research studies confirm my belief that the mass of climbers have the potential to succeed at the lofty grade of 5.12, regardless of genetics.

The Role of Genetics in Sports Performance

All other things being equal, genes seem to determine the differences in performance among individuals. In a sport as complex as climbing, however, you could argue that "all other things are never equal" and, therefore, the role of genetics in climbing performance is hard to pin down. But let's try!

The role of genetics in what we become has been a favorite subject of scientists over the years—it's the old "nature-versus-nurture" argument. Certainly, genetics would seem to play an underlying role in our natural mental climate and personality. However, it's in the physical realm of strength and motor skill that genetics *appear* to play the largest role (or at least this is where genetics seem most observable and measurable for scientists). Interestingly, a review of the research on the role of genetics on performance

Figure 1.1 Relative Demands of Various Sports

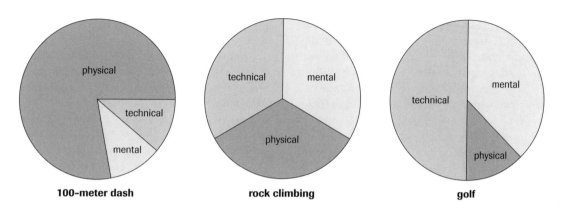

100-meter dash   **rock climbing**   **golf**

reveals an extremely complex subject with contradictory theories and findings among academics. One study (Ericsson 1993) suggests that hours of deliberate practice is the most important factor in determining performance, while another (Fox 1996) found that genes are responsible for half the variations in performance among individuals.

In the real, nonacademic world, it seems that neither of these studies is unequivocally correct. It appears that genetics play the greatest role in sports where the raw physical demands far outweigh the mental or technical requirements. For example, excelling at the 100-meter dash requires extreme explosive power but only basic mental and technical skill. Conversely, golf requires mastery of a wide range of technical skills and a well-cultivated mental calm, but the physical demands are much less noteworthy. Therefore, while genetics clearly play a major role in determining who makes it to the Olympics in the 100-meter dash, they should have much less influence in determining who plays in this year's PGA Championship.

Summing up: Hours of deliberate practice are a requisite for performing at a high level in complex (technical and mental) sports, whereas ideal genetics are a prerequisite for achieving greatness in the most physical pursuits, such as running and weight lifting. Rock climbing is unique among sports, however, in that it requires a near-equal balance of mental, techni-

cal, and physical prowess (see **Figure 1.1**). So you can argue that genetics do play a significant, though not primary, role in determining your level of performance in this sport.

Genetic Factors Relating to Climbing Performance

So just what genetic factors might be helping or hurting you? I bet they are different and more subtle than you think. Height and weight seem to be what most climbers consider their blessing or curse, but it's likely a number of less obvious attributes that help make possible the incredible 5.14/V14 ascents of climbers like David Graham, Chris Sharma, Katie Brown, and the Nicole, Huber, and LeMenestral brothers.

While the aforementioned climbers exhibit a variety of body shapes and sizes, they all possess unusually high maximum grip strength, upper-body power, and/or local (forearm) endurance—beyond that which can be acquired by the average climber training "perfectly" for many years. The genetic gifts enabling these feats probably relate to hard-to-observe factors such as tendon insertions (where they originate from and insert into the bones of the hand and arms), lever length (length of bones), muscle fiber type, and hormone profiles.

With regard to tendon insertions, a slight shift in the location compared to normal provides additional leverage that gives a few lucky folks more grip strength (off the couch!) than others could achieve through years of training. Similarly, your innate ratio of fast-twitch to slow-twitch muscle fiber determines whether your natural aptitude tends toward high endurance, high strength, or neither. Finally, we each have unique hormone profiles (testosterone, cortisol, and so forth) that vary with age and sex, and this plays an underlying role in our response to training and recovery ability (Bloomfield 1994). Because of this, some people can climb hard three days in a row or respond more dramatically to training, while most of us need far more rest in order to perform well, and our training adaptations are more gradual.

If you still aren't convinced that genetics play a role in determining who will be the very best climbers, consider the three pairs of brothers mentioned earlier. Frederic and François Nicole, Alex and Thomas Huber, and Marc and Antoine LeMenestral have all climbed at the fringe of maximum difficulty. This is not coincidence, but instead a screaming message that genetic makeup is a factor in climbing performance.

Your Genetic Potential as a Climber

If you're beginning to sense that you might lack some or all of the above genetic gifts, don't be depressed! As I stated earlier, odds are that you're "normal enough" to climb 5.12 or even 5.13. Because of the large role that mental and technical skill plays in climbing performance, you can push very high up the grade scale by maximizing your capabilities in these areas. The bell curve (see **Figure 1.2**) depicts that most of the population falls in the middle of the bell, in the area representing near-average genetic characteristics. A much smaller number of folks—call them outliers (say, one in ten)—have somewhat better or worse genetics than average. Then there are the extreme outliers (say, 1 in 1,000 or more) who have the potential to be brilliant if they discover their gift and apply themselves completely.

The fact that most of us fall somewhere in the middle of the bell curve can be uplifting or depressing, depending on your perspective. If you dream of climbing 5.15, the chart shows that even if you do every-

thing right and dedicate your entire life to it, the odds are low that have the genetic potential to make this dream a reality. But if you currently climb 5.5, 5.10, or what have you, you should be psyched that 5.12 *is* likely within your reach!

A few recent studies support this idea. One study (Barss 1997) divided a group of twenty-four recreational climbers into two groups based on climbing ability. With the exception of a straight-arm hang endurance test, there was no statistical difference in the performance of a wide variety of general and sport-specific tests between the "less skilled" group (those climbing 5.7 to 5.10a) and the "more skilled" group (those climbing 5.10b to 5.11b). Therefore, at the intermediate levels (5.7 to 5.11b), there's a poor correlation between fitness and climbing ability. The stronger climbers were not necessarily the better climbers, so mental and technical differences account for the difference in ability.

Another, more complex study (Mermier 2000) looked at a larger group of forty-four male and female climbers with a wider range of abilities (5.6 to 5.13c). The results showed that the variance in climbing performance related primarily to trainable variables, and that anthropometric variables (height, weight, arm and leg length, arm span, percent of body

Figure 1.2 Genetic Potential

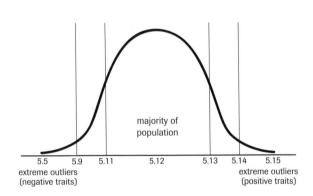

Chris Sharma and David Graham would fall into the far right portion of the curve, whereas Verne Troyer and Shaquille O'Neal would be far left.

fat, and the like) were not a statistically significant factor. So this study also supports my sense that by optimizing technical and mental skills (the trainable variables), the average climber should be able to progress to a high level of climbing, possibly even as high as 5.13c. Note that no 5.14 climbers were included in the study, so we don't know if inclusion of these world-class individuals would have yielded similar results (I suspect not).

In fact, a third, very similar study (Watts 1993) looked only at world-class climbers (those competing in the semifinals at a World Cup event). It found that these elite individuals exhibited a higher grip-strength-to-body-mass ratio, had a lower percentage of body fat, and were of a slightly smaller stature when compared to other athletic groups. This study supports the idea that those world-class 5.14 climbers are born not made in that they are extreme outliers with just the right build to be able to climb at the highest levels of difficulty.

Great Genetics Don't Guarantee You'll Be a Great Climber

Still, the premise that climbing requires equal mastery of mental, technical, and physical abilities means that good genes aren't enough to make you a rock star. Just as genetically average individual's can progress to climbing 5.12 or 5.13 by perfecting their technical and mental skill sets, naturally strong, genetic freaks who can crush bricks in their hands may forever remain 5.10 climbers due to poor technique or lack of mental skills.

Consider **Figure 1.3,** which depicts the genetic potential (solid line) and real-life ability (dashed line) of a climber with average genetic makeup versus the brick-crushing genetic freak. Through dedicated, intelligent training of all the elements under her control, the average climber has pushed her ability almost the whole way out to her genetic potential. The super-strong genetic freak, on the other hand, with his poor technique and mental control, is a complete under-achieving slacker when you compare his real-life performance to his genetic potential. Comparatively, the genetically average climber pushed the dashed line out farther and is, thus, the better climber!

Figure 1.3 Genetic Potential

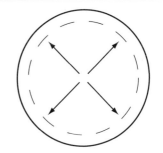

average climber performing optimally

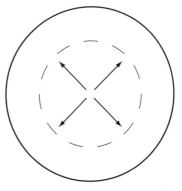

gifted climber performing poorly

Genetic potential (solid line), versus real-life ability (dashed line). Who's the peak performer?

Next time you go to the gym or crag, observe all the men and women, of all ages, shapes, and sizes, who are climbing 5.11, 5.12, and even 5.13. The vast majority of these folks are of average genetic makeup (located near the middle of the bell curve in **Figure 1.2**), but through dedication and hard work on all aspects of the climbing game, they have succeeded at pushing their dashed line out toward the edge of their genetic limitations.

Limits to Climbing Performance

The top climbing grade exploded upward from 5.12d in the mid-1970s to 5.14b by the end of the 1980s. The primary reasons for this marked improvement are equipment (better shoes, stickier shoe rubber, easy-to-place active camming devices, and bolt-protected routes), better training (indoor walls, fingerboards, and so on), and more effective practice methods (hangdogging). In 1991 Wolfgang Güllich upped the ante with his ascent of *Action Directe* (5.14d). This route went unrepeated for five years and has since only had three repeats, despite attempts by the world's best climbers.

Currently (fall 2002) *Action Directe* is still one of the world's hardest roped climbs (though a few new routes in Europe have been reported to be 5.15a), so I have to wonder if we are approaching human limitations to free climbing. While we can never rule out another breakthrough in technology (equipment), it's most likely that we will never see another grade explosion as occurred during the 1980s. Instead, slow increases will likely occur over the time scale of decades.

For a glimpse of what we might expect, let's look at several "mature" Olympic events. Over the last fifty years, improvements per decade have been approximately: sprinting—1 percent; distance running—1.5 percent; jumping—3 percent; pole vaulting—5 percent; swimming—5 percent; skiing—10 percent (Seiler 2000). Improved equipment surely contributed to the higher values for pole vaulting (fiberglass poles), swimming ("frictionless" speed suits), and skiing (ski technology seems to be constantly improving). Unfortunately, performance-enhancing drugs are also a very real factor in the improvements in many Olympic events.

Assuming no technological breakthroughs and no drugs, a good bet would be that the top climbing level would increase by just a few percent per decade. I believe these gains will result from identification of more extreme outliers as participation in climbing increases and from better matching of appropriate training on a more individual basis.

Ultimately, it appears that the achievement curve, which rose rapidly in the 1970s and 1980s, is not linear ($y = kt$), but more like a logarithmic curve [$y = aLog(1 + bt)$]: increasing, but less so as time goes on. Furthermore, our current method of rating routes may be on the verge of breaking down—the difference between 5.15a and 5.15b (or V14 and V15) may be purely a function of anatomical variation in the context of a single move or sequence. This argues for an entirely different system for assessing difficulty at the top levels, such as a scale that counts the number of climbers able to do a given move or problem. Interestingly, this is the essence of John Gill's B-scale for grading bouldering problems, developed back in the late 1950s.

Gill says, "My idea was to develop a personal system that allowed basic differentiation for difficulty, but simultaneously imposed constraints on such differentiation so that an endless, open ended stream of numbers with plusses and minuses would not result. Usually such fine differentiation would reflect merely the anatomical attributes of various climbers. B1 was to represent the highest levels of normal traditional roped climbing, and B2 was to represent a broad class of bouldering difficulty greater than B1. B3 was a (usually temporary) rating signifying a really severe route that had been done by only one person, but tried by a number of climbers. When a second climber succeeded, the route would downgrade to B2 or B1. I thought this would appeal to the competitive spirit, but avoid over-complicating the whole process and turning it into a number-chasing game" (Escalade 2001).

Training for Climbing

As discussed earlier, there are many trainable variables to work on as part of your training for climbing program. In Chapter 2 you will perform a self-assessment test to determine which of these trainable variables is most holding you back. The best training program (for you) will concentrate on the areas that can produce the greatest gain in performance output for a given training input. Of course, the goal is to train most effectively, not maximally.

A Definition of Training for Climbing

I define *training for climbing* as any practice, exercise, or discipline that increases absolute climbing performance. Clearly, this represents a broad spectrum of subjects—hence the wide range of topics covered in this book.

Through this paradigm you should recognize that

training includes a wide range of activities and practices such as bouldering (to learn problem solving and develop power); climbing on a home wall (to improve technique and strength); on-sighting, hangdogging, or for that matter any climbing (to enhance your mental and physical skill sets); and traveling to experience many different types of climbing (to gain experience and a broad range of technical skills). Training also includes efforts made in ancillary areas such as stretching (for flexibility and injury prevention), eating properly (to enhance recovery and maintain a low percentage of body fat), visualization and targeted thinking (to maximize mind programming and disconnect from bad habits), resting sufficiently and listening to your body (to optimize training results and to avoid injury), and evaluating yourself regularly (to determine your current strengths and weaknesses). Finally, training of course includes proper execution of various general and sport-specific exercises (to work toward your physical genetic potential).

For the sake of discriminating among these many types of training throughout the rest of the book, let's define several training subtypes—mental training, skill practice, fitness and strength training, and training support activities—as shown in **Figure 1.4.**

Mental training involves any thought control, discipline, or mind-programming activity that will directly or indirectly impact your climbing in a positive way. The best climbers train mentally 24/7—this is one activity in which you can never overtrain—by targeting their thoughts only on things that can, in some way, influence their climbing and by deleting thoughts and habits that might hold them back. Unfortunately, many individuals possess mental muscle that's in an advanced stage of atrophy from underuse. Visualization is just one of the many mental exercises that can improve your climbing. Chapter 3 lays out an array of practice methods and mental strategies that will have a combined effect similar to unloading a heavy weight from your back (which you've unknowingly been hauling up routes). Are you ready to spread your Mental Wings?

Practice relates to time spent learning and refining actual sport skills and strategies outside of a perform-

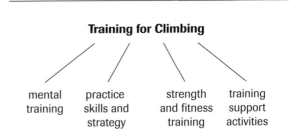

Figure 1.4 Subtypes of Training

Training for Climbing

mental training / practice skills and strategy / strength and fitness training / training support activities

ance setting. Just as baseball, basketball, and football players spend many hours practicing their skills outside of competition, climbers must practice by climbing a lot with the sole intention of improving climbing skill (and not worrying about an outcome such as a flash, redpoint, or on-sight ascent). It's my sense that many climbers' training programs are devoid of this vital subtype of training. We'll take an in-depth look at the subject of effective skill practice in Chapter 4.

Fitness and strength training covers a wide range of activities that are performed with the primary intent of improving your physiological capabilities. This includes general conditioning activities such as running, stretching, and light free-weight training as well as the more important sport-specific activities such as fingerboard, campus, and hypergravity training. Many other activities can fall under this heading, as long as they somehow help improve your climbing performance or prevent injury. It's surprising, however, how many things done in the name of training for climbing actually have a negative effect on climbing performance. Get ready to sort things out, as we take a cutting-edge look at strength training for climbing in Chapters 5 and 6. Then in Chapter 7, you will be guided on developing an effective and time-efficient long-term training schedule.

Finally, *training support activities* are comprised of a variety of crucial, yet often overlooked (or ignored), issues outside of your actual physical practice and training for climbing. Athletes in many other sports have known the vital role rest, nutrition, and recovery acceleration techniques play in their ultimate level of performance. Serious climbers looking to press out their ability level toward the genetic limit must act on these issues with utmost discipline. Chapters 8 and 9 cover these important topics—applying the material may be the key to succeeding on your own "personal Action Directe!"

The Relationship Between Skill and Fitness

While the various subtypes of training for climbing will be discussed separately, they clearly affect each other. This is especially true when it comes to skill practice and fitness and strength training, so let's dig a little deeper.

For a beginning climber in the earliest stages of learning, a low level of fitness can slow the learning of climbing skill. A certain level of strength is necessary in order to practice enough (that is, climb) to develop the basic skills of movement, hand- and footwork, and body positioning. Conversely, too much strength enables a beginner to get by on easy to moderate routes despite inefficient movement, poor footwork, and improper body position. Obviously, this will also slow (or prevent) the development of good technique—unless, that is, the strong person makes good technique the primary goal, instead of just getting up the route no matter what.

The problem is further enhanced by the fact that people tend to develop their talents disproportionately. Strong people are most likely into strength training, flexible people probably stretch, and skillful people undoubtedly climb a lot. Sure, the drudgery of working on weak points isn't fun and, at times, can be discouraging. But if you really want to climb harder, you must train smarter. That means knowing where to best invest your training time to get the most output for your input. For the majority of climbers, the best investment is on further development of climbing skills and strategy (see **Figure 1.5**).

Elite climbers may have less to gain from practicing familiar forms of climbing. These expert climbers are way out on the practice curve near their ultimate skill potential, so fitness (and the mind) becomes the crucial factor in performance. Hence, we commonly see magazine articles about these rock stars that

Figure 1.5 Relative Gains

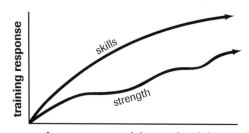

Relative gains from skill practice and strength training.

describe seemingly lethal or disastrously stressful strength-training regimes that would surely plunge the ordinary climber into despair, the doctor's office, or self-defeating over-reliance on strength training as the key to improvement.

Focused fitness training is of higher importance for all climbers after a layoff, whether due to injury, winter, or some other reason (see **Figure 1.6**). The rapid loss of strength that occurs when training or climbing ceases for a period of weeks or months is best counteracted by several weeks of dedicated fitness

Figure 1.6 Performance Losses

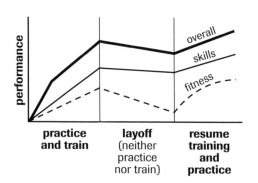

Performance losses (gains) during (and after) a layoff.

| bouldering | sport climbing | multipitch climbing | big walls | alpine |

training (fortunately, you maintain climbing skill once it's "hardwired" in the brain). While this short-term training focus helps in regaining your old form, the long-term and most significant improvements in climbing ability will still result from effective skills practice until late in your career. Only at the lofty grades of 5.12 and above does sport-specific strength become a major limiting factor.

Specific Adaptation to Imposed Demands (SAID)

Serious climbers would be wise to train and climb in accordance with the cornerstone principles of the field of exercise science. For example, knowledge of the SAID Principle (specific adaptation to imposed demands) can be leveraged to maximize the effectiveness of your training for a specific climbing goal or dream climb.

The SAID Principle explains that a certain exercise or type of training produces adaptations specific to the activity performed and only in the muscles (and energy systems) that are stressed by the activity. For instance, running produces favorable adaptations in the leg muscles and the cardiovascular system. But the muscles and systems not stressed show no adaptation, so even heroic amounts of running will produce no favorable changes in, say, the arms. Of course, the adaptations that result from running do transfer somewhat to other sports that depend on the same body parts and systems (such as mountain biking). Bottom line: The SAID Principle demands that effective training for climbing must target your body in ways very similar to climbing (body position, muscles used, energy systems trained, and so forth).

Similarly, your body adapts in a specific fashion to the specific demands you place on it while climbing. If you boulder a lot, you will adapt to the specific skill and strength demands of bouldering. If you climb mostly one-pitch sport routes, you adapt to the unique demands of zipping up, say, 30 meters of rock before muscular failure. If you primarily climb multipitch routes or big walls, your body will adapt in accordance to the demands of these longer climbs. Or if your outings are alpine in nature, your physiological response will be specific to the very unique demands of climbing in the mountains.

The vitally important distinction here is that while all these activities fall under the headline of "climbing," they each have unique demands that produce very specific physical adaptations. Therefore, the training effect from regular bouldering will do very little to enhance your physical ability for alpine climbing. **Figure 1.7** shows that the specific demands of sport climbing are much closer to those of bouldering. Consequently, the adaptations incurred from frequent bouldering will largely carry over to sport climbing (especially short sport climbs) and vice versa.

Due to the SAID Principle, your practice and training on the rocks should be spent mostly on the type of climbing in which you wish to excel. It's no mistake that the best boulderers in the world rarely tie in to a rope. Likewise, the best alpine climbers spend little time working 30-meter sport routes. Targeting your training on the specific demands of your preferred form of climbing is the essence of the SAID Principle.

In the end you must make a philosophical choice whether you want to specialize—and therefore excel—in one or two of the climbing subdisciplines, or become a moderately successful all-around climber. Certainly, there is equal merit and reward in both approaches.

Lauri Werling on Quarterback *(5.10b), Cactus Cliff, Shelf Road, Colorado.*

CHAPTER TWO

Self-Assessment
& Goal Setting

*I know of no more encouraging fact
than the unquestionable ability of
man to elevate his life by conscious
endeavor.*

—Henry David Thoreau

The first step to improving your situation—in anything—can be expressed simply as "Know thy-
self." You cannot progress beyond your current state
with the same thoughts and actions that brought you
here. Therefore, only through constant self-evaluation
will you unlock the secrets to incremental improvement. For instance, you must actively distinguish
what works from what does not work, as well as be
able to recognize what you need to learn versus what
must be unlearned. Often the key elements are not
obvious or clear, but you must accept that life is subtle and only through improving on the little things
will you succeed in the big things.

In climbing, the process of improvement begins
with getting to know your patterns at the crags, in the
gym, and in your everyday life. You must become
aware of your climbing-related strengths and weaknesses in each area of the performance triad—technical, mental, and physical—and learn to leverage your
strengths and improve upon the weaknesses. Toward
this end, your prime directive must be to train intelligently—that is, to engage in training activities that
best address your weaknesses, while not getting
drawn into the trap of training as others do.

Of course, a clear understanding of your mega
goals in this sport is equally important to the process
of succeeding. Only with a clear goal in mind can you
take consistent actions that keep you on route, as well
as have the sense to recognize when you have wan-
dered off route. Finally, at the very deepest level, you
must closely examine your level of commitment to
climbing—are you willing to make the sacrifices necessary for reaching your mega goals? This chapter will
guide you through the fundamental steps of self-
assessment and goal setting that, in turn, will initiate
your ascent to becoming a better, more successful
climber (no matter your gauge of measuring success).

Self-Assessment: Breakfast of Champions

Identifying personal weaknesses requires a paradigm
shift—a dramatic change in the way you see things—
because it's human nature to think about and practice
the things at which you excel. Consequently, your
strengths could be viewed as a weakness, because they
consume the time and energy you could be using
more productively elsewhere.

Too many climbers (myself included) have wasted precious years practicing and training the things at
which they already excel, while the ball-and-chain of
their weaknesses unknowingly holds them back. For
instance, many climbers think "more strength" is the
panacea to their climbing woes; but as shown in
Figure 1.1 on page 5, it's just one piece of the climbing performance puzzle. It requires an awakening for
most climbers to recognize the thoughts and life patterns that are really holding them back.

13

Introspection and curiosity are key attributes you must foster because, at least at the first superficial glance, your real-life experiences with failure on a climb will almost always appear to result from a lack of strength. But what about all the underlying causes that may have led to premature fatigue—poor footwork, bad body positioning, overgripping of holds, climbing too slowly, dismal focus, a botched sequence or missed rest, unreasonable fears, or a lack of energy due to poor diet or dehydration? As you can see, the other two-thirds of the climbing performance puzzle (technical and mental) determine how effectively you use the physical strength and energy reserves you possess. I estimate that average climbers unfortunately waste up to 50 percent of their strength and energy due to lackluster technique and poor mental control. It's like having a 30-miles-per-gallon car that only gets 15 miles per gallon as the result of a horrible tune-up and a heavy foot!

The moral of the story is that the best training program for climbing should include lots of climbing and constant self-evaluation. Spending three or four days a week on the rock (or an artificial wall) deliberately practicing skill and refining your climber's mindset is far more beneficial than spending those days strength training in the gym. This is not to say that you can simply climb a lot and ignore all the other facets of performance. The best climbers clearly focus on putting the complete puzzle together, and this undoubtedly includes a targeted strength-training program. Still, if you can do ten fingertip pull-ups, you are probably strong enough to climb most 5.12a routes! So search vigilantly for the true but often underlying causes of failure on routes. That's the ultimate secret to optimizing your training program and establishing new personal bests on the rock.

Objective Evaluation

The best way to identify your weaknesses is to ask yourself a series of detailed questions. To identify physical and technical weaknesses, ask yourself targeted questions like: Do I fail on a route because I'm too weak or do I overgrip and hang out too long in the midst of hard moves? Does my footwork deteriorate in the moves prior to where I fall? Do I climb too slowly through crux moves and consequently come up short on routes? Do I lack the flexibility to step onto a crucial hold or do I miss a better, easier foot placement? Am I really too short for this move or have I failed to find the body position that makes it possible for someone my height?

Some questions for identifying mental errors are: Do I fail to see the sequence, or do I fail to try something new when the obvious doesn't work? Do I sabotage myself before leaving the ground by doubting my ability or replaying past failures? Do I try too hard or give up too easily? Am I controlling my internal self-talk or is the "critic within" doing a hatchet job on me? Do I monitor and control my body tension or does my perceived pressure of the situation run the show? Am I really on a route over my head or am I overgripping the rock and losing my poise because I'm anxious or scared?

In addition to investigating yourself, consider enlisting a coach to provide an even more objective view of your performance or, at the least, have a friend shoot some video of you on the rock. These detached perspectives are especially useful in identifying obvious flaws in technique, tactics, and your overall economy of effort. For example, feet skidding or popping off footholds signals lack of attention to footwork, while constant stretching for holds seemingly just out of reach is a sign you're missing critical intermediate holds or using less effective body positions. In more general terms, evaluate whether your movement looks relaxed and fluid or appears rigid and hesitant. These outside perspectives can be a real eye-opener and you'll probably be surprised at what you find. Still, some fundamental mistakes and weaknesses are so subtle that they are not easily observed by others or by viewing yourself on video. This is where a detailed self-assessment test comes in handy.

Taking the Self-Assessment Test

A good self-assessment test takes the white light of your climbing performance and, like a prism, breaks it out into the rainbow of colors representing specific skills. The results will reveal your true (not perceived) strengths and weaknesses—and possibly even an unknown Achilles' heel that must be addressed if you are to ever reach your potential (or break through a long-term plateau). With this knowledge, you can create the most effective training program *for you!*

Take the test on pages 15 and 16. In taking this assessment, it's important to read each question once and then immediately answer it based on your recent experiences on the rock. Don't read anything into the questions or try to figure out their focus or the best answers. Instead of working in the book, consider making a photocopy of the test pages in order to maintain an unmarked self-assessment test from which to work (or copy again) in the future. Of course, it would be ideal to date your test and file it for future reference. Comparing successive self-assessments is a powerful way to track your long-term improvement in each area of the performance triad.

Exercise: Self-Assessment Test

To gauge your current climbing performance, take this test. Read each question, considering your most recent experiences on the rock, and then answer quickly by circling the number that best characterizes your performance. Don't dwell on each question or try to read between the lines. You can do that later when you analyze your final results.

For the purposes of this quiz, use the following key to your responses:

0 = almost always

1 = often

2 = about half the time

3 = occasionally

4 = seldom

5 = never

1. My footwork (use of feet) deteriorates during the hardest part of a climb.

   0   1   ②   3   ④   5

2. My forearms balloon and my grip begins to fail even on routes that are easy for me.

   0   1   2   3   ④   5

3. On hard sequences, I have difficulty stepping onto critical footholds.

   0   1   2   3   ④   5

4. I get anxious and tight as I head into crux sequences.

   0   ①   ②   ③   4   5

5. My biceps (upper arms) pump out before my forearms.

   0   1   2   3   4   ⑤

6. I have difficulty hanging on small, necessary-to-use holds.

   0   1   2   ③   ④   5

7. I blow sequences I have wired and know by heart.

   0   1   2   3   ④   5

8. I stall at the start of crux sequences. I end up having to hang on the rope and rest before I can give it a good, solid try.

   0   ①   ②   3   ④   5

9. I climb three or four days in a row.

   0   1   2   ③   ④   5

10. I get sewing-machine leg ("Elvis leg").

    0   1   2   3   4   ⑤

11. I pump out on overhanging climbs no matter how big the holds.

0   1   ②   3   ④   5

12. I get out of breath when I climb.

0   1   2   ③   ④   5

13. I make excuses for why I might fail on a route before I even begin to climb.

0   1   2   ③   ④   5

14. I miss hidden holds on routes.

0   1   2   ③   ④   5

15. I have difficulty hanging on to small sloping holds or pockets.

0   1   ②   ③   4   5

16. I grab quick draws, the rope, or other gear instead of risking a fall trying a hard move of which I am unsure.

0   1   ②   3   ④   5

17. On a typical climb, I feel like much of my body weight is hanging on my arms.

0   1   2   3   ④   5

18. I get very sore the day after climbing at the crags.

0   1   2   3   ④   5

19. I have difficulty visualizing myself successfully climbing the route before I leave the ground.

0   1   2   ③   ④   5

20. I cannot reach key holds on difficult routes.

0   1   2   ③   4   5

21. On overhanging routes and roofs, I have difficulty keeping my feet from cutting loose and swinging out.

0   1   2   3   ④   5

22. While climbing, I get distracted by activity on the ground and/or I think about whether the belayer is paying attention.

0   1   2   3   4   ⑤

23. I have difficulty reading sequences.

0   1   2   ③   4   5

24. I get a flash pump on the first climb of the day.

0   1   2   3   ④   5

25. I have more difficulty climbing when people are watching.

0   1   2   ③   ④   5

26. My feet unexpectedly pop off footholds.

0   1   2   ③   ④   5

27. I experience elbow pain when I climb on a regular basis.

0   1   2   3   ④   5

28. When lead climbing a safe route, I have difficulty pushing myself to the complete limit.

0   1   ②   3   4   5

29. I have difficulty finding midroute rest positions and shakeouts.

0   ①   2   ③   4   5

30. My first attempt on a hard route is usually better than my second or third attempts of the day.

0   1   ②   3   4   5

Looking at Your Test Results

After taking the test, record the scores from each question in the appropriate column in **Figure 2.1** (below), and then add up the scores to gain a final score for each area of the performance triad. Compare your mental, technical, and physical scores to gain a sense of which area is your strong or weak aspect of the performance triad. Your future training should be disproportionally targeted on the weak area. If all three areas are within five points of each other, congratulate yourself for being a climber of balanced abilities (something I find to be a rarity).

Figure 2.1 Score Yourself

Mental			Technique and Tactics			Physical		
1. 4	2	4	2. 4	4	4	3. 4	4	4
4. 3	2	1	5. 5	5	5	6. 4	3	4
7. 4	4	4	8. 2	4	1	9. 4	3	4
10. 5	5	5	11. 4	4	2	12. 4	3	4
13. 3	3	4	14. 4	4	3	15. 2	4	3
16. 2	5	4	17. 4	3	4	18. 4	3	4
19. 3	4	4	20. 3	3	3	21. 4	2	4
22. 5	5	5	23. 3	2	3	24. 4	4	4
25. 3	3	4	26. 3	4	4	27. 4	3	4
28. 2	1	2	29. 3	1	1	30. 2	1	2
34 34 40			35 34 30			36 30 37		
82/2								
(Total)			**(Total)**			**(Total)**		

Next, review each question of the self-assessment test and circle the ones that are a 3 or less. Each of these low-scoring questions identifies a specific element of your climbing performance that is holding you back. List on a separate piece of paper or in your training log a brief description of each problem revealed. Sort and group them according to the aspects of the performance triad. As you read through the remainder of the book, keep this list of problem areas nearby and make notes of the exercises and strategies presented that address these weaknesses. Creating such a written "mind map" that displays both the problem areas and the action-oriented solutions will keep these highly powerful keys to better climbing in the forefront of your attention. Only with this awareness will your training remain on track and effective in the weeks and months following the self-assessment.

As you move into the goal-setting exercises later in this chapter, refer back to the self-assessment test or your summary mind map. Focus your short- and medium-term training goals on the most dramatic weaknesses identified (the five or six lowest-scoring items). As you recognize improvement in these areas, shift your training focus onto other lower-scoring areas of the self-assessment or retake the entire test and develop a new training strategy based on the new results. For additional training tips that address each question of the self-assessment, see Appendix B.

The Cycle of Improvement

Your completed self-assessment is your "boarding pass" to the Cycle of Improvement. This process cycle has three stages: Set goals, take action, and make course corrections (see **Figure 2.2**).

A successful trip around the cycle gives birth to a new level of climbing performance—the Cycle of Improvement, in fact, becomes a Spiral of Improvement! Occasionally, reassessments are needed to update your goals relative to the "new you" and whatever new issues are now responsible for holding you back from further improvement. These new goals give birth to new actions and even more spectacular results.

Depending on your desires, commitment, and skill level, one trip around the cycle may take any-

Figure 2.2 Cycle of Improvement

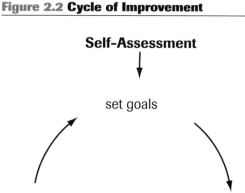

Use this three-step process to elevate your performance to the next level.

where from a couple of months to a year. Signs you are ready for a reassessment and a new cycle include a plateau in performance, training that feels flat, or a drop in motivation. If you experience more than one of these signs, take a week off then retake the self-assessment test and start a new cycle.

Remember that there is a big difference between employing the Cycle of Improvement and just going climbing year-round with your friends. The latter approach is unfocused and will yield slow results and frequent plateaus in performance. Conversely, a deliberate effort in all three stages—setting new goals, taking intelligent action, and making appropriate course corrections—keeps the spiral going upward toward your ultimate genetic potential.

Goal Setting

Defining specific goals enables you to perform a gap analysis of what actions you must take to bridge the gap (or possibly chasm) between where you are now and what you want to become or achieve. Effective goal setting begins with a pen or pencil and a calendar, training log, or climbing notebook. If you don't write down your goals, chances are they will remain intangible hopes and dreams that never materialize.

It's best to set goals in three time frames: short term (daily), medium term (weekly or monthly), and long term (multiyear or career goals). Write down the goals in precise terms and with realistic deadlines. And since pictures are even more motivating than words on paper, it's crucial to create a mental picture (representing the goal) that you can recall in your mind's eye on demand. The more precise and focused the picture and written goal, the easier it will be to zero in on the target and take actions that will someday land you right in the middle of your goal.

Next, create a purview that summarizes the overall mission for each goal-setting time frame, such as "short term, I strive for the most effective ninety-minute workout possible" or "medium term, I am committed to redpointing my first 5.11 by the end of the summer."

Finally, write down what one or two (or more) things you will give up in order to reach your short-, medium-, and long-term goals. This vital step is missing from most conventional goal-setting exercises, and it may be the number one reason why so many people fail to achieve their big goals in life. Simply put, you cannot add something new or achieve anything meaningful without sacrificing something else in its place. Ponder this powerful idea. It may explain why some of your past or present goals remain elusive.

SHORT-TERM GOALS

Short-term goals define your daily game plan. They help focus your thoughts and actions so that you are not swayed by what others are doing and don't waste precious time on less important activities (TV, partying, surfing the Net, excessive socializing). The more hectic your life, the more crucial it is that you spend a few minutes before bed or first thing in the morning doing some short-term goal setting. Folks with less difficult daily schedules may only need to set short-

term goals relating to the workout du jour. Begin by writing down the primary mission of the workout, then list the specific exercises, sets, and reps as well as the approximate amount of time you will dedicate to each part of the workout (see "An Example of Short-Term Goal Setting" on page 20). Don't forget to list what you will give up (compared to previous days or your peers) in order to fulfill these short-term commitments.

MEDIUM-TERM GOALS

Medium-term goals give shape and purpose to your schedule over the course of weeks and months. This planning is best done on a calendar so you can effectively dovetail your workouts and climbing trips with your other nonclimbing activities. Try to roughly plan things out a few months in advance (see the "Setting Medium-Term Goals" exercise on page 21).

First, block in the big events such as climbing trips, competitions, work and family obligations, and the like. Next, write in your proposed workout and climbing schedule, with special attention to maintaining enough rest days in the game plan. With the most important items now in place, you can fill in the many little, less important things in life where time allows (or this can be done on an ad hoc basis). Remember to sum up your medium-term goals with one overriding primary goal, as well as listing the activities you will forfeit in order to attain this lofty goal.

LONG-TERM GOALS

Long-term goal setting is a fun and invaluable activity in which you condense onto paper the numerous "dream" or "I wish" goals floating around in your mind. If there is to be any chance of them ever becoming reality, it's vital that they be liberated from the dreamland of your mind and put down in black and white (see the "Setting Long-Term Goals" exercise on page 21). A magical force begins to act in your life when you write down these mega goals—your subconscious mind will go to work day and night on achieving them, and your conscious mind will suddenly find them more believable (and achievable).

An Example of Short-Term Goal Setting

TODAY'S MISSION

Focus on improving my footwork and conserving energy by practicing skills and techniques.

WHAT I WILL GIVE UP TO ACHIEVE THIS GOAL

The usual bouldering games and competitions at the gym.
For today, I'll stay off all routes that are beyond my on-site ability.
I won't rush home to watch TV.

WHAT I WILL DO

1. Warm up with fifteen minutes of light bouldering, gentle stretching, and two sets of pull-ups.

2. Perform fifteen minutes of the traverse-training drill.

3. Toprope several climbs within one number grade of my limit with the focus on practicing technique, not performance outcome (whether or not I fall).
   My practice goals are: to concentrate on careful positioning and use of each foothold; to climb as briskly, smoothly, and decisively as possible between rests; to accurately read sequences before leaving the ground and while at each rest position; to remain positive, relaxed, and centered during each climb.

4. Perform three sets of ten repetitions of the one-arm lunging exercise.

5. Cool down with ten more minutes of traversing on a vertical wall.

6. Eat a good meal within one to two hours after the workout.

7. Get seven to eight hours of sleep.

Exercise: Setting Medium-Term Goals

Your medium-term goals can include both climbing and nonclimbing items; we'll focus on the climbing-related goals here. Write down your top training goals (mental, physical, and technical) for the next three months, as well as a few climbing goals such as "to-do" routes or a new area to visit. Distill these goals into a single "primary goal" for the period, and remember to list a few things you will freely give up in order to reach these goals.

_____

_____

_____

_____

_____

_____

_____

_____

_____

_____

_____

_____

_____

_____

Exercise: Setting Long-Term Goals

Go somewhere quiet, allow yourself to relax for a few minutes, and ponder what long-term mega goals are out there awaiting your best efforts. I call these mega goals because they are the few events that you most want to achieve in your life given your current perspective. For example, you might have an ultimate grade of climbing you'd like to achieve, or possibly a specific dream climb to send or mountain to summit. Think about where you'd go if time and money were not an issue—put it down on paper and the odds increase a thousandfold that you will someday be pulling down there! By all means write down a few of your nonclimbing mega goals as well, but keep the total list down to between six and eight items.

As in setting your short- and medium-term goals, it's absolutely critical that you write down a couple of major things that you will completely give up in order to reach these mega goals. Consider the activities, possessions, and people that drain your time, focus, and energy.

_____

_____

_____

_____

_____

_____

_____

_____

_____

_____

_____

Taking Action and Making Course Corrections

The Cycle of Improvement will spiral you upward in ability as long as the actions taken provide movement toward your goals. Sadly, taking consistent, disciplined action in the direction of worthy goals is very difficult for some people. The results of their misdirected actions always seem to leave them in an all-too-familiar situation. The phrase *same shit, different day* is born of this affliction.

If any of this sounds familiar (in climbing or life), it's important to begin taking notice just who is directing the actions you take on a daily basis. In many cases you'll discover that outside forces are calling the shots for you—that is, you are taking the actions someone else desires you to make, not those congruent with your goals. This is what the multibillion-dollar advertising industry is all about. Companies spend a ton of money with the sole intent of directing your actions in their favor (to make them money and drain your wallet). So while you might have a very worthy goal of, say, "getting out of debt" or "saving for a house," advertisers cleverly divert your actions in their favor. Unless you are acutely aware of what's going on (and the power they wield over you), you will veer off your course and onto theirs—and maybe never reach your goals.

This may sound negative, but the same thing often happens when you're training at the gym or climbing at the crag. Instead of doing the precise exercises and drills you need to improve your weaknesses, you end up climbing down the blind alley of someone else's agenda. Consider how many climbing days you've spent working on someone else's dream project (one that is either over your head or just not what you had planned) when you would have gained more by getting on a different type of climb. Or ponder how often you've gone to the gym and ended up socializing and just climbing mindlessly with no goal or direction. Sure, these kinds of evenings can be relaxing and fun once in a while, but on a regular basis they will not make you a better climber.

The win–win solution is to find a partner equally motivated to taking actions that will produce the fastest possible gains in ability. With this person you can evenly split the climbing time, so that you each can work effectively toward your goals. Unfortunately, in many partnerships one person makes all the calls and gets most of the benefits of the time spent training or climbing.

In summary, strive for hour-to-hour, day-to-day awareness of the "whats" and "whys" of the actions you are taking. By formulating short-term goals, as discussed earlier, you can best maintain your focus on the things you need to do to improve short term and advance toward your meaningful medium- and long-term goals. Finally, foster an acute awareness of the results you are getting from your actions. Peak performers are those who most rapidly recognize when they are off course, and respond with a reassessment of the situation and an appropriate course correction toward the desired goal.

If it's beginning to sound like becoming a better climber is a very mental thing, you are right! So let's dive into Chapter 3, "Mental Training."

3

Mental Training

The wise man will be the master of his mind. A fool will be its slave.

— *Publius Syrus*

The quickest way to enhance your performance in almost anything is to improve the quality of your thinking. This is definitely true in climbing, whether you're working a highball boulder problem, sport route, multipitch traditional line, or alpine route. All performance operates from the inside out—your beliefs, focus, emotions, confidence, preparation, and problem-solving abilities form the foundation from which you will either succeed or fail.

Great performances begin with bulletproof confidence, singular focus, positive emotions, and a bright picture of and intense belief in a successful final outcome. Conversely, setbacks and failures result from the worry, doubts, tension, and uncertainties that are born from a poorly harnessed brain running wild with fearful thoughts. It's my belief that whether you (or I) will succeed or fail on a climb is often predetermined in your subconscious (maybe even conscious) before you ever step off the ground.

While off-season strength training and year-round technique training are paramount for progressing into the higher grades, during the climbing season your biggest breakthroughs will come from toning and flexing your mental muscle. Toward this end, this chapter outlines several powerful mental strategies and skills that will help elevate your performance and enjoyment.

Practice these skills with the same dedication and resolve as you would a new strength-training program, and you'll be pleasantly surprised with the results. Obtain the greatest payoff by applying these skills 24/7, not just when you feel like it. For some, an almost instant breakthrough will follow on the rock, while others will need to persist and let these mental skills build to a critical value before they will produce a noticeable impact on your climbing. (This depends upon the current degree of tone or atrophy of your mental muscle.)

Recognize that all these mental-training skills are interlaced and can produce a powerful synergy when all are in practice. In the aggregate they may produce an effect similar to unloading a ten-pound weight (or more!) from your back that you have unknowingly been hauling up climbs. I call this using your Mental Wings.

Mental Wings for Improving Performance

The late, great Wolfgang Güllich was fond of saying that "the brain is the most important muscle for climbing." What makes this statement even more provocative is the fact that Güllich was one of the strongest people to ever pull down on stone. From the mid-1980s until his death in a car accident in 1992, he opened up several new grades of maximum difficulty by leveraging the synergy of his physical and mental fortitude. I support Wolfie's sentiment not only because the mind is one-third of the climbing performance triad (see **Figure 1.1,** page 5) but also due to the fact that poor mental control can instantly sabotage your physical and technical abilities.

Chris Sharma on High Plains Drifter
(V7), *Buttermilks, Bishop, California.*

PHOTOGRAPH **BY WILLS YOUNG**

Below are ten strategies that you can start using today in all aspects of your life. Apply them faithfully with the knowledge that most truly successful men and women in this sport possess these skills.

1. Separate your self-image from your performance.

If you are reading this book, then climbing surely plays a major role in your life. Unfortunately, when your self-image is tied too strongly or singly to this role, it translates into an overwhelming need to perform perfectly every time in order to prove your worth in that role and, thus, as a person. The subsequent pressure can become stifling and is maybe the single greatest cause of frustration in this sport (or in any endeavor).

Human beings perform best in a process-oriented, not outcome-oriented, frame of mind. Detaching your self-image from your climbing performance allows you to enjoy climbing regardless of the outcome. More important, it liberates you to try new things, take chances, or throw a dyno that might be required to get through a crux sequence. Bottom line: Self-image detachment will reduce pressure and anxiety and, paradoxically, you'll climb better by not needing to!

2. Surround yourself with positive people.

There is an aura of influence that surrounds each of us, and its effects are based on our personality and attitude toward life and its events. Your thoughts and actions will affect the thoughts and actions of those around you, and vice versa. As I see it, there are three options—either climb alone, climb with upbeat and positive people, or climb with cynical and negative people. Why would you ever want to climb with the complainers out there? Their negative aura impacts your climbing and enjoyment whether you recognize it or not. Vow to climb either with positive individuals or by yourself—both can be hugely rewarding. If pushing your limits is the goal du jour, however, then take advantage of the synergy afforded to you by having creative, motivating, and positive people by your side.

3. Stretch your comfort zone.

To improve in anything, your goals must exceed your current grasp and you must be willing to push beyond your comfort zone. In performing on the vertical plain, this means climbing onward despite mental and physical discomfort; it means challenging your fears head-on by doing what you fear; it means attempting what looks impossible to you from your current perspective. Through this process, you stretch the envelope to a new dimension and reshape your personal vision of what is possible.

4. Assess and proactively manage your risk.

Climbing is an activity with obvious inherent risks, and the desire to climb harder requires taking additional risks. These risks can come in the form of obvious physical danger such as a potentially injurious fall, or of invisible mental risks like opening yourself up to failure, criticism, and embarrassment. It's interesting to note that for some climbers the physical danger feels more benign than the aforementioned mental dangers. Consider climbers who continue upward on a horrendously dangerous route they're not prepared for because they're afraid of being dissed by those standing safely on the ground!

Make it your goal to always assess the range of possible risks before you ever start a climb. By objectively analyzing the risks ahead of time, you'll often be able to lower the risk of the climb (for instance, by taking other gear or rigging a belay differently than you normally would) and, at the least, be aware and able to respond to the most critical risks as you climb. As for the mental risks, see Mental Wings Strategy 1.

5. Fortify your confidence.

Your degree of self-confidence is primarily based on your self-image and the thoughts you hold minute by minute and day by day. Thoughts of falls or poor performance in the past and self-talk loaded with words like *I can't, don't, impossible,* and *try* lower confidence and are the seeds of failure. Conversely, focusing on past successes—by actually visualizing and feeling the process and exhilaration of positive action—leads to tremendous feelings of confidence. Using visualization throughout the day, every day, to relive great events in your past—climbing and nonclimbing—is the best way to reshape and fortify your self-confidence for success in all future endeavors.

6. Get into the peak performance zone.

"The zone" is that state where everything comes together for the perfect ascent that seems almost effortless and automatic. The trick is being able to create this state on demand and often in stressful situations, such as at a competition or before a hardest-ever redpoint. The best way to do this is by using one or more of your senses to reenact the feelings of a brilliant performance or event from your past (it doesn't necessarily have to be a climbing event). Have you ever experienced the relaxed pleasure that washes over your mind and body when you hear an old song or smell something familiar that instantly connects you to some great event in the past? That's what you're after.

If you've been climbing many years, then you surely have some "perfect" past days you can use as anchors for your peak performance state. If not, think back and identify some other event where you felt like you were in complete control and that "anything is possible." Create about a sixty-second mental movie of this past event using all your senses. Make the pictures crisp and bright, and let the feeling and state of this event take over your body. Some people find that listening to a particular song through headphones is a powerful anchor for locking in the peak performance state. Be creative and experiment in developing your own pre-performance rituals that can transport you into the zone.

7. Anchor consistent performance with preclimb rituals.

The things you think and do in the minutes and moments before you climb form the foundation onto which your performance is built. A shaky foundation generally leads to a shaky performance; a solid foundation usually gives birth to a solid performance. The nature of your foundation (sand or stone?) is a result of the quality of your preclimb rituals. These are things you do to best prepare for the ascent, including

scoping the route, visualizing the sequence, preparing your gear, warming up, and even your way of putting on your shoes. Even tiny details, such as breathing rate, posture, and final thoughts, should be programmed into the rituals that lead up to your stepping onto the rock.

Develop your rituals based on past experience. What things did you think or do before some of your best ascents in the past? What did you eat or drink, how did you warm up, how long did you rest between climbs? Awareness of all the things (little and big) that lead up to your best performances is a key to being able to reproduce similar results in the future. Once your rituals become tried and true, stick to them!

8. Control stress and tension before they control you.

This strategy is central to climbing your best, because tension kills performance. Period. Tension and stress work at you from the inside out and are revealed through your emotions. It's easy to spot the tense, stressed-out climbers at the crag by their emotional outbursts. Very few people can leverage their negative emotions to enhance performance, and odds are you can't either. Taking a deep breath and "trying softer" is almost always more fruitful than cursing and throwing a fit.

Controlling stress and tension must be an ongoing process, and practicing to control them 24/7 will go a long way toward making you a Zen master at the crags. It's a good practice to check your tension levels hour to hour throughout the day and at every rest on a climb. Here's a six-step process for controlling tension and returning yourself to an optimal performance state.

1. Strive for acute awareness of rising tension so that you can counter it before it snowballs out of control.

2. Normalize your breathing with a few deep belly breaths, then turn it over to your subconscious.

3. Scan for pockets of muscular tension, and let the tension escape from these pockets like air from a balloon.

4. Let a wave of relaxation wash over your body from head to foot.

5. Erase all thoughts of the past or future—both are enemies of competitive excellence in the present—and refocus on the process of climbing.

6. Reset your posture and flash a smile. You may now proceed to send your route!

9. Engage in positive self-talk.

Inside our heads, each of us has a "critic" voice and a "doer" voice that gab throughout our waking hours. While the critic voice can be useful in a few situations (such as evaluating weaknesses or performance errors), it's the doer voice that compels action, keeps us positive, and, in fact, helps us produce our best performances. Controlling this internal self-talk is fundamental to controlling our attitude and climbing our best.

Which voice—the critic or the doer—rules your mind? It may be that you don't know, because the chatter is so incessant that it's hard to follow. Even so, this self-talk wields a powerful influence over you, so tune in and listen for a few days, particularly while you climb.

How you were raised and whom you hang around with will help explain what you find—the complainers of the world were likely raised by complainers or hang around with other naysayers. That being said, becoming aware of this self-talk enables you to take control and give the doer voice the upper hand. When the critic surfaces to make statements, invert them into something positive. For instance, change "this route looks impossible" to "this route looks challenging"; replace "I feel nervous" with "I feel energized"; convert "I'll probably fall" into "I think I can do this, but if I fall it's okay because I'll get it next time." Constant command of self-talk is a master skill of high achievers.

10. Be happy regardless of situations and outcomes.

A superior trait of all real winners is resilience to bad results and/or criticism and unwavering belief that success will come with time, effort, and patience. Attitude is the wild card in the climbing performance equation that can often compensate for what you are lacking in strength, technique, or reach. I can't overstate the importance of always having fun. We all get into climbing because we love the outdoor experience and the feeling of moving over stone, yet in time far too many climbers become Grinches who have fun only when they are winning.

The biggest secret to better climbing is to love climbing unconditionally. Vow that any day of climbing is a great day regardless of the results, and you will usually get the results you desire.

Controlling Your Emotions

Your emotions have a direct effect on your body and mind. For example, what you are feeling exerts an influence over what you are doing or how you are thinking (see **Figure 3.1**). For instance, nervousness before a climb can derail your concentration as well as trigger preclimb jitters throughout your body. Therefore, becoming an icon of emotional control is fundamental to performing up to your potential.

Observe some of the very best climbers, like Chris Sharma and Lynn Hill, and you will see consistently positive and productive emotions. Even when they fall, you sense no anger—only love of the process of climbing, which occasionally includes falling. Now compare how your emotions change in times of frustration or failure. When the going gets tough, who runs the show—you or your emotions? A typical example of how emotions can run the show and kill climbing performance is portrayed in the story on page 28. I'm sure you've seen a few climbers act out this story line; possibly you've experienced it firsthand.

Figure 3.1 **How Emotions Run the Show**

MIND ←——→ **EMOTIONS** ←——→ **BODY**
(think)   (feel)   (act)

What you feel exerts an influence over how you think and what you do. Likewise, ways of thinking and acting affect how you feel.

1. The climber leaves the ground and moves cautiously through the initial moves. He looks apprehensive, as if he's trying not to make any mistakes.

2. As he enters more difficult moves, his breathing becomes shallow and irregular. He may even hold his breath on hard sequences.

3. Negative emotional energy rises, resulting in increased muscular tension and mental stress.

4. This building stress disrupts his coordination, balance, and footwork. Movements become tight, mechanical, and inefficient. He begins to overgrip holds.

5. He begins to hold back on hard moves, afraid to fully commit, and hangs out too long on marginal rests.

6. The fight-or-flight syndrome is triggered, adding some adrenaline to the mix. This burst of energy may help the climber thrash through a few more moves; more commonly, the jolt causes him to grab the rope or a quick draw, and retreat from the route.

7. The death grip sets in and flames out his muscles.

8. He falls and lets loose a few expletives.

Does any part of this story sound familiar? If so, I have some good news. You can learn to rein in your emotions and thus open up a whole next level of climbing performance and enjoyment. If you have good emotional control already, I bet you can still improve your climbing by optimizing your arousal and emotion. Let's explore this murky subject of emotions and discuss how you can make some immediate positive changes.

Evaluating Your Emotional State

In evaluating your emotional state, the goal is to become aware of the "sign" of your emotions (positive or negative) and the magnitude of your arousal (high or low). Obviously, positive emotions have different effects on the mind and body than negative emotions. Similarly, the intensity of these emotions (the arousal

Figure 3.2 The Energy–Emotion Matrix

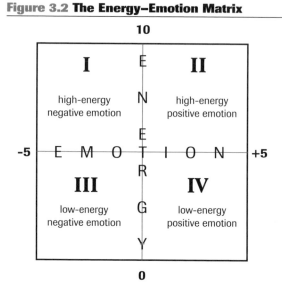

What quadrant of the matrix are you most often in?

level) plays a role in how you think and feel. To better understand this relationship, consider the Energy–Emotion Matrix (see **Figure 3.2**).

The Energy–Emotion Matrix has four quadrants: high energy, positive emotion (upper right); low energy, positive emotion (lower right); high energy, negative emotion (upper left); and low energy, negative emotion (lower left). The matrix represents a continuum of emotion and energy within these four quadrants. Therefore, you can evaluate your present location in the matrix by grading your current energy level on a scale from 0 to 10 (low to high) and scoring your current emotional state on a scale from –5 (extremely negative) to +5 (extremely positive). Knowing where you are in the matrix and having the ability to change this location if it's not optimal in the current situation is fundamental to becoming a peak performer in any endeavor.

Obviously, your energy level and emotions fluctuate throughout the day and over the course of a climb, so your place in the matrix changes hour by hour and, maybe, minute to minute in extreme situations. I believe it's valuable to study your place in the matrix in everyday, nonclimbing situations, since your most common daily state will heavily determine your disposition when climbing (it's unlikely you can be a negative person at home and work, then become completely positive when you go climbing). Use the blank E–E Timeline contained in Appendix A on page 175 to plot your changing energy–emotional state throughout the day, as shown in **Figure 3.3.** Begin upon waking in the morning, and score your state every thirty minutes, or when some event causes your emotion or energy to change in an instant.

After evaluating your emotional state for a few days, see if you can identify any patterns. What time(s) of the day is your energy high or low? What events seem to trigger you becoming more positive or negative? Recognizing these patterns / empowers you to make modifications, su_ to avoid negative triggers. Likewise, you may be a_ to see what charges up your energy level (and when) and what type of things make it tank. If you can't avoid negative triggers, it's vital that you know how to turn your states around. Below we'll discuss ways to modify your emotional state.

It's also beneficial to track how your state changes over the course of a day at the crags, and especially during an attempt at a redpoint or on-sight ascent. While you certainly can't write down your score while on a route, you can mentally score yourself by simply asking yourself "what quadrant am I in?"

Before you can change your state, you must first

Figure 3.3 **Sample Chart of Energy–Emotion Levels**

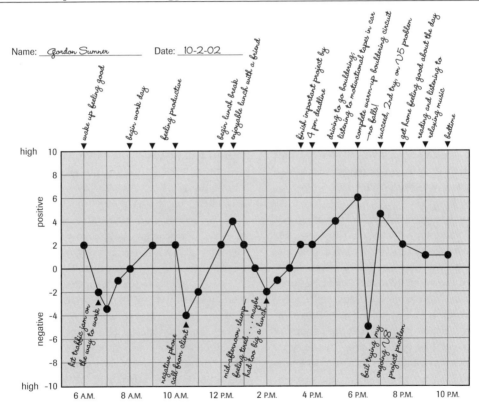

Sample chart of energy–emotion levels throughout the day, including notes of triggers or events that effected an energy–emotion change.

determine the optimal state for the present moment. Of course, beginning in a positive emotional state is always ideal, but the optimal magnitude of your arousal (energy level) will vary depending on the type of task you are involved in. For instance, a low-positive (Quadrant IV) state is ideal for taking a test or meeting with your boss, while a high-positive (Quadrant II) is best for working out at the gym or playing a high-intensity sport. In climbing, it's almost always best to be in the low-energy, positive-emotion quadrant—creative thinking, learning, and fine motor skills all demand a relaxed, positive state. The exception would be when psyching up for a vicious boulder problem or a short, powerful sport route.

Changing Your Emotional States

You can rapidly change your emotional state by leveraging the known relationships among the mind, emotions, and body (see **Figure 3.1**). Just as your emotions exert an influence over your mind and body, you can use your mind and body to influence your emotions. In negative people the process tends to be reactive and runs itself, whereas happy, productive people are skilled at using their mind and body to produce positive emotions. It may seem overly simplistic, but if you carry your body in a positive way (good posture, head up, smiling) and think in a positive way (grateful for what you have, reliving only good memories, focusing on future goals), you will feel positive and, in fact, be a generally happy person.

You should now have a good sense of the things you can do to shift into a more positive state. Physiologically, you can take on a more extended posture, you can jump up and down or do anything physical, you can pump your fist in the air and exclaim "yeah!"—even just smiling will do the trick. All these physical things will effect a rapid change in your emotions—try it now! Mentally, you can replay great events or climbs from the past, think about all you've accomplished in your life, ponder your good health or your fortune to have been born in a first-world country (where you can actually engage in a luxury activity like climbing), or visualize the medium- and long-term goals that excite you.

Hopefully, you now recognize that either your emotions are controlling you or you are in control of your emotions. Happy people and peak performers (in sports and life) are those who are able to control their emotions and adjust their arousal level on demand. In our frantic society, and when participating in a potentially high-stress sport such as climbing, these emotion-modulating skills are invaluable. Strive to monitor your position in the matrix throughout the day and optimize your state when needed, and you'll discover a new quality of climbing and living!

Dealing with Fear

As I stated in *How to Climb 5.12*, "the 'no fear' mentality is for buffoons, beer-guzzling frat boys and couch potatoes." In climbing, reasonable fears keep you alive long enough to realize your potential and to send a long lifetime's worth of stellar routes. For example, fear of taking a ground fall compels you to seek good protection on the lead and to drag a rope in the first place.

It's *unreasonable* fears that derail performance. Things such as fear of falling on a well-protected route, fear of physical discomfort, fear of failure, and fear of embarrassment must all be eliminated if you are to climb your best. There are also preclimb fears such as "I might be too tall," "too short," or "too weak" to do the climb, which—left unchecked—give birth to reality. Finally, there are subconscious, preprogrammed fears that are the root of many of the "dumb things" that seem to just happen. Have you ever fallen after the crux when the route is in the bag? Or have you slipped off a large hold or botched a wired sequence even though you felt in control? It may be that such mistakes are the result of unchallenged inner fears, not lack of ability.

Deal with your fears head-on. Start by writing down recurrent fears that regularly hurt your performance. If you can't think of any on the spot, go for a climb and pay special attention to every preclimb thought and while-you-climb concern. As the fears reveal themselves, use logic and reason to specifically counter each. This is usually pretty easy, but if no logical counter is evident, the fear may be *reasonable*.

Dealing with fear is an ongoing process—our fears are always changing. Review each poor performance and identify which fear(s) may have contributed to your difficulties. To help you with this analysis, here's a primer on four basic climbing fears: fear of falling, fear of pain, fear of failure, and fear of embarrassment.

Fear of Falling

Fear of falling is inherent to climbing. Interestingly enough, it's not really falling that we fear but not knowing what the fall will be like. This explains why your first fall on a route is the scariest, while subsequent falls are often much less stressful. Beginners probably need some hands-on proof that falls can be safe. The best way for a would-be leader to gain trust in the system is by taking some intentional falls. Find a steep climb with bomber protection, use a good rope (and double-check your knot and buckle), and take some falls. Start off with 2-foot falls and build up to 12-footers (with gear just a few feet below you). A more experienced climber fearful of falling on an upcoming on-sight climb can counter the fear during the preclimb warm-up. The tactic here is to mentally replay some past inconsequential falls and remind yourself that falls on this climb will be no different (if that is indeed the case—some falls are obviously deadly, and only a fool would ignore that possibility).

Fear of Pain

When pushing your limits, fear of pain and discomfort can become a critical weakness. This fear causes you to give up long before your body has reached its physical limitations. The pain of climbing a continuously strenuous route is akin to that of running a mile at full speed—it freaking hurts! Fortunately, the pain is brief and the challenge pays big dividends. Decide to push yourself a bit farther into the discomfort zone each time you're on a hard route. Soon your pain threshold will be redefined, as will your limits on the rock.

Fear of Failure

This deep-seated fear is often instilled during childhood when almost every action is classified by our family, teachers, and friends as either a success or a failure. We've all had childhood situations where the fear of failure was so gripping that we became immobilized and time seemed to stop. Fortunately, adults generally don't react quite this intensely, but it's still common for us to imagine all the bad things that could possibly go wrong. Once triggered, these negative thoughts can snowball and, more often than not, become self-fulfilling prophecies.

In climbing, fear of failure causes you to hold back. As your attack on a route becomes less aggressive than required, you'll find yourself second-guessing sequences in the midst of doing them, your breathing will become shallow, and your grip begins to tighten—you overgrip the rock. You may even fall prey to paralysis by analysis.

Eliminate fear of failure in one of three ways. First, focus on what is *probable* instead of what is *possible*. Sure, it's human nature to always consider the worst-case scenario, but this almost never comes true. Counter these thoughts by considering what is probable and realistic based on past experiences.

The second way to nix this fear is to focus all your attention on the process of climbing and forget about the possible outcomes. Concentrate on the things immediate to your performance—precise foot placements, relaxing your grip, moving quickly onto the next rest position, and so on. Your limited supply of energy is too valuable to waste worrying about how high you will climb or the eventual results. As William Levinson points out in his book *The Way of Strategy*, "To succeed, we must not care if we fail."

Along this same line, you must adopt the attitude that "it's okay to fall" (assuming a safe fall) and that "falling won't bother me, I'll just get back up and give it another go." By willingly accepting this fate (if it should even happen), you totally dissolve the fear of failure that handcuffs so many climbers. Therefore, by being okay with falling, it's less likely you will. This simple idea is one of the most powerful in this book.

Fear of Embarrassment

Finally, there is fear of embarrassment and being dissed. Get over this now or you'll never fully enjoy climbing, or reach your potential. Realize that occasional bad-performance days are inevitable. Instead of trying to avoid them, simply accept that they happen, analyze why they happened, then bury them. With this attitude you will be free to try chancy moves and risk an occasional mistake. In the long run you'll often look like a hero, but never like a zero. Surely this is better than embracing the critics and accepting mediocrity all the time.

Don't forget, your friends know how good a climber you are, and they won't think any worse of you because of a poor performance. Anyone else critical of you really doesn't matter. Work on improving your self-confidence and don't let the criticisms of others invade your thoughts.

In the end, embrace the attitude that there are no failures, only results. If you fall off the first move of a route, it's due to not paying attention to the move, not to being a worthless individual. The results might not be ideal, but they do contain hints for improvement. Accept that by challenging your fears and doubling your exposure to these fears, you will double your rate of achievement and maximum climbing ability.

Relaxation Training and Centering

More than ever before, there are a multitude of things in our lives that can result in high levels of stress. Our jobs, relationships, possessions, even driving to the crag can trigger a stress response such as muscular tension or negative thoughts. Interestingly, it's not the events or things in our lives that actually cause the stress, but instead our reaction to them. Knowing this, you are empowered to control your reactions to everything you experience and, in turn, regulate the total amount of stress in your life.

Recognizing that an event or situation is causing you to become stressed is the first step toward controlling its effects. Foster an acute awareness of your tension levels by regularly asking yourself things like, "How do I feel?" or "Are there any growing pockets of muscular tension?" Make such tension checks a regular part of your day. For instance, do a quick check of your tension and stress levels every hour, and especially before any type of event that requires an optimal physiological state (a big meeting or hard climb).

Keep an eye out for telltale signs of building tension such as a clenched jaw, overgripping a pencil or the steering wheel, or tightness and burning in the muscles of your neck, shoulders, or back.

On the rock, tension reveals itself in overgripping of holds, nervously muscling through a crux move, or a general lack of fluid motion. Again, your goal is to recognize and tone down the tension when it begins; otherwise it will rapidly snowball and sabotage your performance. This, in fact, is a common cause of blowing a sequence you thought you had wired, or falling off a route that should be well within your ability. By killing your economy of movement, building tension and stress may very well kill your performance. And it's probably been happening for so long you don't even recognize it's happening.

The antidote to tension is, of course, relaxation. Following are two highly effective relaxation strategies as well as a great on-the-rock centering sequence that I call the ANSWER. Experiment with all three, and try to incorporate their use throughout your daily activities. In a short time you will become a master of stress and find yourself feeling much more relaxed—and also climbing harder, thanks to an increase in apparent strength (a result of reduced tension in the antagonist muscles and elimination of overgripping).

Progressive Relaxation

In the early 1940s American physician Edmund Jacobson developed a technique known as progressive relaxation, because he felt that by fully relaxing the muscles, you would in turn relax the mind (Garfield 1984). He found that relaxation could be best learned by deliberately tensing and relaxing specific muscle groups (see the "Progressive Relaxation Sequence" exercise on page 33). This process results in a sharpened awareness of tension levels in the different parts of your body, and the ability to drain the tension like letting air out of a balloon. In time, you will be able to discern even small increases in muscular tension and act to immediately eliminate the tension before there's any degradation in performance.

Exercise: **Progressive Relaxation Sequence**

Perform the following procedure at least once a day. I find it most useful during a midday break, as part of a long rest period at the crag, or last thing before falling asleep. Initially, the process will take about fifteen minutes. With practice, you'll be able to move quickly through the sequence and reach a state of complete relaxation in less than five minutes. Concentrate on flexing only the muscle(s) specified in each step. This is an invaluable skill you will find very handy when using the Differential Relaxation and ANSWER Sequences that are discussed below.

1. Go to a quiet location and sit or lie in a comfortable position.

2. Close your eyes and begin by taking five deep belly breaths. Inhale slowly through your nose to a slow, silent count to five, then gradually exhale through your mouth to a slow, silent ten-count.

3. Keeping your eyes closed and maintaining slow, relaxed breathing, tense the muscles in your right lower leg for five seconds. Feel the tension in your right foot and calf muscles, then let go and relax the muscles completely. Compare the difference in sensation between the tense and relaxed states. Repeat this process with the left lower leg. Now, with both lower leg areas relaxed, say to yourself, "My feet and lower legs feel warm and light." Upon saying this a few times, the muscles in this area will drop into a deep state of relaxation.

4. Next, perform the same sequence in the muscles of the upper leg (one leg at a time). Tense the muscles in your upper leg for five seconds, then relax them. After doing this with both legs, finish up by thinking, "My upper legs feel warm and light." Feel all tension dissolve as your upper legs drop into deep relaxation.

5. Repeat this process in your hands and lower arms. Begin by tensing the muscles below your right elbow by making a tight fist for five seconds, then relax these muscles completely. Repeat this with the left hand and forearm, and conclude with the

mantra, "My hand and forearm muscles feel warm and light."

6. Repeat this procedure on the muscles in the upper arm.

7. Next, shift the focus to the many muscles of the torso (including the chest, abdominal, back, and shoulder areas). Repeat the process exactly.

8. Conclude with the muscles of the face and neck.

9. You should now be in a deep state of relaxation (possibly, you will have fallen asleep). Mentally scan yourself from head to toe for any isolated pockets of remaining tension, and drain them with the *warm and light* mantra.

10. At this point you can open your eyes and return to work or climbing with a renewed sense of calm and focus. Or you can leverage this relaxed state by performing some mind programming—visualization of the process of reaching some goal or the act of climbing some project route.

Differential Relaxation

Differential relaxation is used in active situations where you wish to relax any muscle(s) not needed for the task at hand. I find this skill especially useful in regaining an optimal state while hanging out and chalking at rest positions on the rock. I scan for unnecessary muscular contractions or pockets of tension and, with a few deep belly breaths, visualize the tension draining from the muscle like air escaping from a balloon. Try this next time you go climbing.

Many climbers shortchange themselves and reduce their apparent strength because of undue tension in muscles not needed for upward motion or stability. Unwanted contraction of the antagonist muscles or overcontraction of the prime movers interferes with even the simplest movements and wastes a tremendous amount of energy. Observe how climbers who try too hard or get gripped on a route become extremely rigid and mechanical, maybe even while moving through an easy sequence. Instead of using their muscles optimally, they're pitting one muscle against another, resulting in stress, fatigue, and premature failure. Conversely, the best climbers actively control undue tension (it's often an unconscious process in top climbers), move with grace and fluidity, and maximize economy of motion and energy use. As masters of differential relaxation, they can move smooth and fast like a Porsche but still get the high "miles-per-gallon" of a Honda.

Skill in differential relaxation comes with increased sensitivity to various degrees of relaxation and tension—something you will learn quickly through daily use. Practice by releasing tension in unused muscles while in the midst of common everyday activities like driving your car, sitting at your desk, working around home, or even lying down for a quick nap. Scan your body for pockets of tension or any contracting muscles that aren't critical for the task at hand. For me, it's typically tension in the shoulders, a clenched jaw (if I'm concentrating really hard), or unnecessary fidgeting by my feet.

On the rock, strive for acute awareness of tension increases so you can nip it in the bud before it results in a drop-off in performance. It's my practice to perform these "quality assurance checks" at all rest positions. Sometimes I recognize things like general tightness in my shoulders, unnecessary tension in my legs, or a little more contraction of my arm and forearm muscles than is needed to stick the grip or body position. Differential relaxation allows me to correct these problems almost instantly—although I find centering and the ANSWER Sequence to be beneficial in these situations as well.

Getting Centered

Centering is a simple, effective means of maintaining complete control of your mind and body as you head up on a difficult climb or into competition. When you're centered, you feel balanced, relaxed, and confident. Conversely, you will feel out of balance, tense, awkward, and unsure when you are out of center. And in climbing, it takes only one burst of adrenaline, one piece of gear to pop out, or one botched move to knock you way out of center.

The ANSWER Sequence, a technique detailed below, is a powerful means for returning yourself to center in just a few seconds. The ANSWER Sequence involves deliberately redirecting your thoughts inward for a moment (usually at a rest on a climb) to modulate your breathing, level of muscle tension, posture, and mental attitude. Therefore, centering goes a couple of steps beyond the use of differential relaxation, since it also addresses your posture and mental disposition. Make its use as regular and automatic as chalking up, and you'll find yourself climbing more efficiently and consistently.

Exercise: The ANSWER Sequence

Perform the ANSWER Sequence before and during each climb and in everyday situations where you need to control tension, anxiety, and focus. Initially, this six-step procedure will take a few minutes to perform. With practice, you'll be able to go through the sequence in about ten seconds—perfect for use at marginal rest positions where getting centered could make the difference between success and failure.

A - AWARENESS

1. Awareness of rising tension, anxiety, or negative thoughts.

Acute awareness of unfavorable mental and physical changes is fundamental to optimal performance. It takes a conscious effort to turn your thoughts away from the outer world toward your inner world. Peak performers habitually make these tension checks every few minutes, so they can nix any negative changes before they snowball out of control. Make this your goal.

N - NORMALIZE

2. Normalize breathing.

In climbing, your breathing should be as relaxed (basically involuntary or unconscious) and regular as it would be while on a fast walk. Unfortunately, many climbers hold their breath while in the midst of a crux sequence, then breathe heavily afterward in order to catch their breath. This process creates tension and degrades performance. Your goal is smooth, even, normal breathing throughout the climb.

S - S C A N

3. Scan for specific areas of muscular tension.

In this step you perform a tension check. Scan all your muscles in a quick sweep to locate pockets of tightness. Commonly tight areas are the forearms (are you over-gripping?), shoulders, upper back, chest, abdominals, and calves. The best way to relax a specific muscle is to consciously contract that muscle for a few seconds, then relax it and visualize the tension draining from it like air from a balloon (in other words, use the differential relaxation technique).

W - W A V E

4. Wave of relaxation.

Upon completing the tension check above, take a single deep breath and feel a wave of relaxation wash from your head to your toes.

E - E R A S E

5. Erase thoughts of past events (or the possible future) and focus on the present.

This step involves freeing your mind from the ball-and-chain of undesirable past events. There is no benefit to pondering the last failed attempt or the blown sequence you just barely fought through. Let go of the past and do not ponder the future—thoughts of the past and future are enemies of excellence in the present. Refocus on and engage the present moment.

R - R E S E T

6. Reset posture and flash a smile.

It's amazing how much positive energy you can generate simply by resetting your posture and flashing a smile. This final step of the ANSWER Sequence will leave you in a peak performance state and ready to climb into the zone. Trust your skills, have fun, and let the outcome take care of itself.

Visualization Training

Let's start off with an example of visualization. Sit back, relax, and vividly imagine the following scene as if it were a movie playing out before your eyes.

You are attempting to redpoint a route you have worked on before. You have just successfully climbed to the rest position that precedes the route's crux sequence. You are relaxed, calm, and confident as you shake out and rechalk. You feel a cool breeze blow across your body, and it seems to enhance the light, centered feeling you already possess. You gently grip the starting hold of the sequence, a sharp, positive fingertip edge. With steady breathing, you flash a smile and continue climbing.

You match hands and pull the fingertip edge to your chest. You then high-step your right foot onto a tiny crescent-shaped flake. You've hit it just right—it feels bomber. You rock over that glued right foot, spot, and then grab a matchbook side-pull edge with your right hand. You flag your left leg across and below your high right foot, then smoothly extend off the right foot. Your left hand reaches up to snag a two-finger pocket—it feels solid. You move your left foot up to a high smear on the dish hold, and, with relaxed breathing, take aim on the final lunge. Then, with your mind locked on to the next hold, you throw the lunge and easily latch on to the suitcase-handle hold that's been so elusive. You clip the anchors and feel the rush of having ticked this personal best route.

This sequence exemplifies a fundamental and important exercise used by all the world's top athletes. Although similar to the mental rehearsals performed by some climbers, visualization goes beyond the simple task of reviewing route sequences. As in the above example, visualization involves making and playing a detailed mental movie, one with touch, sound, color, and all the kinesthetic feel of doing the moves. These mental movies enhance your climbing by helping to hardwire motor skills (moves and sequences), increasing memory, and fortifying confidence. For this reason, use of visualization is as important to your success as your use of climbing shoes and a chalk bag. Don't leave the ground without doing it!

Many studies have shown that the brain is not always capable of distinguishing between something that actually happened and something that was vividly imagined (Kubistant 1986). (Déjà vu is such an experience—you can't always recall if the clear mental image that just surfaced is an actual memory or simply something you've thought about or dreamed.) Therefore, repeated visualization can trick the mind into thinking you've been there and done that before. Think of these mental movies as a blueprint for future actions—with this perspective, you should understand why visualization must be as detailed and accurate as possible. Any bad design (wrong moves) or fuzzy instructions (uncertain sequences) may lead to a building collapse (a botched sequence or fall).

Types of Visualization

There are two primary modes of visualization: disassociated and associated. Disassociated visualization provides an "on-TV" perspective, where you see yourself climbing from an observer's point of view. This mode of visualization is best for reviewing some past poor performance that you hope to improve upon. As a detached observer, you can replay the movie and objectively view the mistakes or falls without reliving the possibly unhappy emotions of the situation.

Associated visualization provides a "through-your-own-eyes" perspective and thus triggers small neurological reactions as if you were doing the climb, as well as the feel and emotion of the movie you are playing. This makes associated visualization ideal for preprogramming some future ascent. As discussed above, repeated playing of a highly detailed, positive mental movie helps trick the subconscious mind into thinking you've done the climb before. Just make sure you are using the associated, not disassociated, perspective when visualizing some future event.

DISASSOCIATED VISUALIZATION

If you are new to the practice of visualization, I suggest you begin with a simple, nonclimbing example. Go to a quiet location, sit or lie down comfortably, and relax. Using an observer's point of view (disassociated), play a mental movie of the following scene as it might appear in your apartment or home.

Visualize yourself sitting on the couch and watching TV. Note the clothes you are wearing in the scene. See yourself get up from the couch, walk over to the refrigerator, and open it up. See yourself reaching in and grabbing a can of soda, then watch yourself close the fridge. See yourself opening the can as you begin to walk back toward the couch. Note the way you are walking and observe the exact instant that you see yourself open the can. Now watch yourself sit back down in the couch.

In this disassociated example you watched the scene play out before your eyes but you did not feel or sense, in any way, what it was like to go get the soda and drink it. Reserve this perspective for reviewing negative events from the past, climbing or nonclimbing. Gather the information you need to improve your performance next time, then engage in associated visualization to preprogram the corrections into a successful future event.

ASSOCIATED VISUALIZATION

Now let's reshoot the mental movie of the at-home scene from the associated point of view. This time you will live the scene through your own eyes. Feel the action play out in your imagination just as if you were acting out the scene for real. Again, sit back, relax, and picture this scene playing out in real-life detail.

As you sit on the couch, you laugh at the closing joke of a *Seinfeld* rerun. You decide to go get a soda from the fridge, so you get up and begin walking toward the kitchen. Look around the room at the various pieces of furniture (or pictures on the wall) you pass on your way to the fridge. Enter the kitchen and open the refrigerator. Feel the cool air rush out and chill your face. As you reach into the fridge for the soda, notice the colors and design of the can, then sense the cold, damp feel of the can in your hand. Now feel your arm slam the door shut and hear the sound it makes in closing. Conclude the scene by tasting the soda as you gulp it down—what flavors do you taste?

This example reveals the explicit detail you should try to build into your associated visualization. Granted, it will take some practice to develop Steven Spielberg–like detail into your mental movies, but that's the goal. Commit to making a short film for all your project routes (or most important goals in life), and don't hesitate to reshoot or edit the film as you gain new information or beta for the route. Quality mind programming will improve the quality of your real-life performances. Guaranteed!

Uses of Visualization

I hope you now recognize that visualization is an immensely powerful tool that can be used to enhance performance in all aspects of your life. I'm sure you use simple visualization every day, maybe without even knowing it. For example, when you think about the best way to drive across town, I'm sure you see the key turns or landmarks along the way in your mind's eye beforehand. Visualization is also used "effectively" by people who worry a lot—part of their worry ritual is wild visualization of some future event that may or may not happen to them (or some loved one). This type of negative visualization is most painful and depressing when done from an associated perspective. To me, such negative visualization is insane, since you are putting yourself through the pain of some future event that may never happen.

Some climbers become consumed in the same types of negative moviemaking of future events. For instance, if you visualize yourself failing on a route or in competition, you not only preprogram this possible outcome but also destroy your self-confidence in the process. To avoid this, it's vital that you visualize only positive events and ideal outcomes when you project into the future in the associated state. Switch to the disassociated mode if you need to visualize things (from a risk-management perspective) that might go wrong—say, on an on-sight lead. See from the on-TV view the possible falls you could take and what risks might be involved in the ascent. Described below are several settings where you can use visualization to improve your safety and mind-set (among other things), as well as the chances of the ideal outcome coming true.

PREPROGRAMMING A REDPOINT ASCENT

Since you've been on the route before, you could begin with disassociated visualization of your last attempt. See yourself climbing the route and note what things need to be corrected or refined for the next attempt. Now use the associated perspective to create a movie, as seen through your own eyes, of the perfect ascent you plan to make. Imagine all the important aspects of doing the route, including the crux moves, gear placements or clips, rest positions, and such. Create all the feel of doing the moves as well as the feeling of being relaxed and centered as you move into the crux. Make the movie positive and perfect in every way, and always conclude with the feeling of reaching the top.

PREPARING FOR AN ON-SIGHT ASCENT

Visualization is invaluable when applied to a climb you've never been on before. Since you have no first-hand experience, it will be very hard to create an accurate movie from the associated perspective. Therefore, you'll want to spend most of your time visualizing from a disassociated perspective.

After studying the climb from below, create images or a movie of yourself climbing the route from the on-TV perspective. See yourself dropping in gear at the obvious placements as well as hanging out at what appear to be good rest positions. As described above, you will want to visualize any hazards unique to this climb—where a lead fall might be dangerous, what you can do to minimize the risk, and so forth. Also, if you can see enough detail from the ground, consider creating two movies of possible sequences through the crux. This way, if you get up there and find that one will obviously not work, you can call up the second movie and continue climbing without delay.

You might finish up your visualization by moving into the associated state and trying to imagine what you might feel and see as you climb the sequence you came up with from the disassociated perspective. This is not always possible, but would be beneficial.

PREPARING FOR COMPETITION

In competition climbing, good visualization skills might mean the difference between winning and finishing in the middle of the pack. Depending on the competition format, you will want to employ the redpoint and on-sight visualization strategies discussed above. Since many events allow only a brief preview period, you will only be able to create a "rough-cut" movie, including the basic route path, location of the obvious rests, and whatever you can glean about the moves or sequence. Even if you can't decipher a sequence (or if you didn't get a route preview), you can still take a mental picture of the wall and project yourself climbing with grace and confidence to the top. Most important, strive to eliminate any self-defeating images that might cross your mind in the hours and minutes leading up to your ascent of the wall.

"CLIMBING" INJURED OR TIRED

If you climb for enough years, you will at some point likely find yourself laid up due to some type of injury. Whether you are out for a few weeks due to a finger injury or out for the season with a more serious problem, you can still keep climbing inside your brain! While this may not sound like much fun, it is an effective way to maintain your knowledge of a sequence on your project route. Vivid, associated visualization has been shown to cause low-level neuromuscular activity that helps enhance motor learning (Feltz 1983) and maintain the feel of performing some skill.

You can also use this effect to your advantage next time you pump out while working a route. Instead of thrashing around on a climb for the umpteenth time (and risking injury), call it a day and spend the time pumping a few more "mental laps" on the route. This will help solidify your knowledge of the sequence without the extra physical strain and risk of injury.

Creating Laserlike Focus

The ability to narrow and maintain focus is a crucial sports skill, especially in an activity like climbing where elements of danger exert a constant pull diverting the focus from the task at hand. Widely used, but often misunderstood in the context of a climber's lexicon, *focus* is a laserlike concentration of mental energy aimed at the most important task at any particular instant. Since every movement in climbing possesses a different most-important task, it's vital to be able to redirect your focus, in an instant, to the finger or foot placement most critical at that moment.

Think of focus as a narrowing of your concentration, much like a zoom lens on a camera. At any given moment you must zoom in on the single task most critical to your performance—toeing down on a small pocket, pulling on a manky finger jam, or shifting your weight to just the right balance point. Think about anything else and this critical task may fall, resulting in a fall.

The most difficult part of focusing is learning to zoom in and out quickly from a pinpoint focus to a more wide-angle perspective. For example, a quarterback starts a pass play with a broad focus (when in search for an open receiver), but he instantly zooms in on a single player as he delivers the pass. In climbing, you have to do much the same thing—use a broad focus when hanging out looking for the next hold, then zoom in tight as you reach toward the hold and latch on to it. Similarly, you must zoom in tight when high-stepping on a dime edge, locking off and making a long reach, or floating a deadpoint. If you focus on anything else—your gear, your belayer, your pain, or spectators on the ground—you may as well add a ten-pound weight to your back. Poor focus makes hard moves harder, maybe even impossible.

Practicing Focus

Detailed on page 39 is a practice drill for developing focus and a preclimbing strategy for gathering focus in preparation to climb. The "Singular Focus Drill" exercise is best used when you are climbing on toprope and well below your maximum grade. The "Pinpointing Your Focus for a Climb" exercise can be used before attempting any climb, though it's especially effective when preparing to start up a difficult route.

Exercise: Singular Focus Drill

The best time to work on your focus is when climbing a route a couple of grades below your maximum ability. Whether you're at a gym or the crag, on toprope or lead, attempt to climb a whole route by focusing solely on one aspect of movement.

For instance, try to do a route with your complete focus on just hand placements. Find the best way to grab each hold, use the minimum amount of grip strength necessary to hang on, and feel how your purchase changes as you pull on the hold. Place as little focus as is safely possible on other areas such as your feet, balance, belayer, and the like. For now, let these areas take care of themselves—allow your sixth sense to determine where your feet go and how your balance should shift.

Chances are, you'll find this exercise quite difficult. Your thoughts will naturally wander to other tasks or even be directed to distractions on the ground. If this occurs, simply redirect your focus to the predetermined task—in this case, the handholds. It is this process of becoming aware of your lost focus and returning it to the critical task that you are after. Sharpened awareness of lost focus is tantamount to gaining control of focus.

Repeat this exercise regularly but change the focus (onto, say, foot placements or weight shifts), each time. Work on increasing the length of time you can maintain a singular focus—this helps build mental endurance. As you become more skilled, convert this singular focus drill into a dynamic focus drill where your focus constantly shifts to the most critical task at any moment. The goal is be able to shift your focus quickly among the various tasks involved in doing a route, like the flickering beams of a laser light show.

With practice, the process of directing and redirecting focus will become largely subconscious. On the rare occasions when your focus does wander away from the task of climbing, your well-trained mind will instantly recognize this loss and redirect the focus onto the climb. In this way, becoming constantly engaged and automatic on the climb helps in achieving the highly desired flow state.

Exercise: Pinpointing Your Focus for a Climb

This exercise will gather your focus into a single "beam" and quiet your mind as you get ready to cast off up a climb. Perform it after you've gone through your preclimb ritual and been put on belay.

Stand at the base of the climb, assume an extended posture (shoulders back), close your eyes, and place the fingertips of your dominant hand against the rock face. Your fingertips should be touching the wall lightly (not gripping a hold), and your hand and arm should be completely relaxed. Now take three deep belly breaths, inhaling through your nose to a count of five and exhaling through your mouth to a count of ten. Let a wave of relaxation wash across your body, and then direct your entire focus to the tips of your fingers touching the rock. Concentrate singly on the sensation of your fingertips touching the rock—you should begin to feel the thermal energy moving from your fingers to the rock (on rare occasions when the rock is hotter than your body, you will feel thermal energy conducting into your fingertips). Maintain a relaxed, singular focus on the energy exchange between your fingertips and the rock for anywhere from thirty-seconds to a minute or two. If your focus ever wanders, simply redirect it to your fingertips. Soon your mind will become completely still, as all your focus is pinpointed on the tips of your fingers. Upon reaching this state, open your eyes and begin climbing.

Roxanna Brock on **Desert Gold**
(5.13a), Black Velvet Canyon,
Red Rocks, Nevada.

PHOTOGRAPH BY
MICHAEL LANDKROON

4

Training Skill & Strategy

We are what we do repeatedly. Excellence, then, is not an act but a habit.

—*Aristotle*

Moving over stone is the essence of climbing and, therefore, no subject can be more central to improving your climbing than this chapter on training skill and strategy. Despite this, the subject of strength training tends to get all the attention and hype in conversations among climbers, and getting stronger is the most popular topic of magazine articles about climbing performance. In this book mental training and improving skill and strategy come before the subject of strength training because I feel most climbers can benefit more and improve more quickly on the rock with focused training in these areas. If you want to put yourself on the fast track to the higher grades, strive to understand and apply the information contained in this chapter as much as or more than any other chapter in the book. You won't be disappointed!

Ironically, the majority of climbers spend little, if any, time on dedicated practice of the vast spectrum of techniques inherent to our sport. With little coaching or guidance available, most climbers unknowingly service their lust for ticking routes by constantly climbing for performance. Of course, becoming proficient (or excellent) at any sport requires focused practice of new skills and work on weaknesses that need

improvement. Still, some climbers just don't want to spend time practicing on routes below their maximum grade; others avoid routes that might highlight their weaknesses. Can you imagine a baseball player who never took batting or fielding practice outside of the competition of a nine-inning game, or a quarterback who never threw a pass except on game day?

In this chapter you will learn the three stages of motor learning involved in acquiring a new climbing skill or move, as well as how the brain creates "software" to execute the move (in the future) and to make approximate solutions, on the fly, to unknown moves. This is powerful information if you understand it, because it will help compel you to leave the herd and commence regular skill practice as part of your training for climbing program.

The action portion of this chapter is a series of practice drills that you can use year-round whether you climb indoors or out. Regardless of your tenure in the sport, significant gains in your climbing technique and overall ability will result from a commitment to regularly employing some of these drills in your routine. This chapter does not instruct on any of the specific climbing techniques—crack climbing, backstepping, deadpointing, and so forth—but instead gives you the optimal methods of practice regardless of the type of move, technique, or strategy you plan to learn. Instruction on specific climbing moves can be found in a number of other books, although one-on-one personal instruction and modeling of more advanced climbers are highly recommended.

An Overview of Motor Learning

The importance of motor learning theory to optimizing training for climbing became apparent to me in the early 1990s as a result of conversations with Dr. Mark Robinson and thanks to ongoing input from my wife, Lisa Ann. As an LPGA golf pro (and climber) with an education in the field of kinesiology, Lisa Ann occasionally discussed the methods used by elite golfers to learn very difficult skills (for me, impossible!). At about the same time, Mark Robinson (former Gunks hardman and, now, an orthopedic surgeon in California) turned me on to an excellent text on the subject, *Motor Learning & Performance*, by Dr. Richard Schmidt. Robinson then penned a breakthrough piece on the application of ML&P to climbing for my first climbing book, *Flash Training* (1994). Subsequently, I've studied the subject in depth and formed a full chapter of *How to Climb 5.12* around the use of these principles for speed learning of climbing skills. Now it's time to dig even deeper.

Motor learning is the process by which we acquire some skill set of body movement. Regardless of the skill—walking, driving, climbing—learning occurs in three identifiable and overlapping stages: the cognitive, motor, and autonomous stages (Schmidt 1991).

Cognitive Stage

This stage involves thinking about the activity, listening to explanations of it or comparisons to other familiar things, imaginative projection of what it may be like to do it, visual or kinesthetic anticipation of action, and formulation of the goals or desired results for future performance.

Early attempts in this stage are clumsy, inefficient, and jerky; they expend energy and strength in wasteful ways. This is what you experience when making the first few attempts on an unfamiliar type of climbing (crack, slab, pocketed face, et cetera) or on a route that's especially hard for you. During practice sessions in this formative period, you examine the route from the ground in an attempt to figure out the moves and rest positions, then attempt to climb via toprope or, perhaps, bolt to bolt on lead. Typically, the results of such early attempts are rough and imperfect; with continued attempts (practice), however, the quality of performance improves.

The underlying capacities involved in this stage are largely intellectual and character related and, to a lesser extent, physical. Therefore, people who enjoy early success—those who appear to have natural talent—are not necessarily the strongest, but instead the most perceptive, agile, confident, and relaxed. A real-life example of this is seen daily by climbing instructors who observe a novice female climber outperform her equally novice, but stronger male partner during their first day on the rocks.

Motor Stage

The motor stage is less a product of self-conscious effort and thought than one of automatic increases in the efficiency and organization of the activity by the nervous system and brain, as a response to continued practice. A neurological "groove" develops as multiple attempts and feedback from multiple sources (internal and external) produce more reliable and effective execution. Energy expenditure decreases, and the natural inertia of the body and limbs is used to advantage—this marked increase in economy of movement is the hallmark of the motor stage of learning.

When working a climb, this stage is represented by the attempts at redpoint when the moves and clips are known, and the goals are to develop efficiency and to preserve power and endurance for the cruxes. The underlying factors involved in this stage differ from those that lead to early success. Here, they involve the sensitivity of internal movement sensors, the accuracy of limb movement, speed of detection and correction of minor errors, and the sensitivity of the performance to anxiety, doubt, and so on. These things are obviously less available to conscious awareness or control and are thus acquired only through dedicated practice and the chase of perfection.

In this stage the goal of action becomes more refined and demanding. The moves must be done well and efficiently with strength to spare, not eked out, gasping at the verge of nausea or pulped tips. Early, crude success should not be accepted since it will not lead to the best ultimate development of technique and efficiency. Having demanding goals has been shown experimentally to produce both better performance and faster gains. The goal should be to dominate at, say, 5.10a or 5.12a, not just get by at it.

Autonomous Stage

The final stage of learning is called the autonomous stage. At this point the actions are automatic and require almost no conscious attention, because movement has reached a stable and polished form. You can often do other things while in this state: For instance, you can carry on a conversation while driving a car. Or, like a chess grandmaster thinking six moves ahead, you can decipher and send a crux sequence in perfect form, on-sight. This is also the elusive flow state or zone so often touted by elite athletes. In climbing, it is reached only through dedicated, disciplined, long-term practice.

On the rock this stage can be experienced on a successful redpoint, but it more often occurs on the umpteenth repetition of a route that you have absolutely wired. You may also experience this flow state while on-sight climbing well below your maximum ability, and on rare occasions you'll feel the rapture of the zone as you send a personal-best project or float up a competition route.

Understanding Schemas: Your Climbing Software

Climbing skill and technique are specific to the kind of rock and terrain over which you move. Therefore, becoming an expert climber requires experience with a wide range of styles and rock surfaces, even if your interests are narrowly focused on one type of climbing. The reason relates to the skill programs or schemas (as sports scientists call them) that are created as you learn new moves and positions. (Some literature, mainly European, uses the term *engram* to describe such a skill program. In keeping with the American scientific literature, I use *schema* throughout the text.)

A schema is a set of rules, usually developed and applied unconsciously by the motor system in the brain and spinal cord, relating how to move and adjust muscle forces, body position, and so on, given the parameters at hand. In climbing, these parameters include the steepness of the rock, its friction qualities, the type of holds being used, and the kind of terrain (roof, corner, or the like). Therefore, if you climb at only one or two cliffs, you will develop a narrow range of schemas relative to the rock friction, hold types, and terrain of these areas. These motor programs, no matter how well learned, will work only for similar situations—and they may not apply particularly well at the outer limits of difficulty at these crags. Worse yet, should you travel to new areas, your limited schemas will leave you climbing at a much lower grade or flailing on routes of the grade you're accustomed to from your home area.

Conversely, if you become a well-traveled climber, you will in time log tens of thousands, if not millions, of different moves, positions, angles, and hold configurations into your library of schemas (see **Figure 4.1**). This huge resource will enable you to climb at a high standard on most rock types and at most areas.

Figure 4.1 Developing Schemas

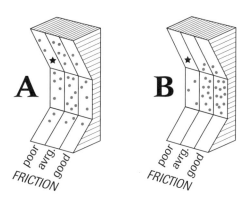

Climber A *has developed more diverse schemas (dots) and thus will be able to closely approximate the novel move (star)—and possibly on-sight it!*

Climber B *has more limited schemas, which will have him flailing and probably failing on the novel move (star).*

Furthermore, the high density of schemas will help you guess intuitively, and with surprising accuracy, the best solution to a novel move or crux sequence on-sight. Just as a highly skilled skier or surfer can "on-sight" almost any slope or wave, developing broad schemas will transform you into a climber who can on-sight at a high level at almost any crag on the planet.

Dr. Mark Robinson describes an experience he once had with a top boulderer at a local spot in California. "This man could do incredible problems in his local area that very few others could repeat; however, it was obvious that his abilities were limited because he had difficulty climbing 5.10a on his very infrequent road trips. The surprising extent of his limits became apparent one day when he went to show us one of the easier problems at his area. He twirled and pranced effortlessly up to a recently broken hold, then flew off. He had grabbed at where the hold used to be in an artful-looking blind move, only to land on his butt. By the next week, most other local boulderers, some of only average ability, had worked out a new sequence. But not our hero. His limited number of schemas had limited him once again."

Developing Schemas (Learning New Skills)

Learning a new skill requires a progression through the three stages of motor learning before you will be able to use the new skill efficiently and intuitively. Depending on the difficulty of the skill, this process may be slow, awkward, and frustrating. Therefore, discipline and an intense belief that you will become excellent in the skill (with effort) are fundamental to the process of learning difficult skills. You must not try to shortcut the process and get around having to learn it by relying on your strengths in other areas.

Unfortunately, many climbers do exactly this when they lunge, swing, or scum wildly through a sequence that could be done more efficiently by learning a new move, technique, or body position. Another example plays out when a competent gym or face climber first attempts to learn crack climbing. The common tendency is to avoid the awkward—and possibly painful—jams and pawl up the face on either side of the crack. Typically, climbers pump out and exclaim

that the route felt way harder than its grade—which, of course, it did, since they weren't using the techniques required to climb the route most efficiently.

The moral of the story is that you must convince yourself that no matter how hard a new move feels at first, it will become easier to execute—and maybe even intuitive—as the result of focused practice. Also, keep in mind that you will become most competent at a new skill by practicing it on as many different rock varieties, angles, and settings as possible. So in the crack-climbing example above, you'd want to practice on cracks of all widths, depths, and lengths, as well as on as many types of rock and rock angles as possible. Surely climbing a slick, parallel-sized sandstone hand crack will feel different than jamming up a gritty granite crack that features slight variations in width. This difference in feel is evidence that somewhat different schemas are called upon in climbing these similar routes. Consequently, to perform optimally in both settings requires prior practice on both types of cracks.

Another important principle states that learning becomes slow and difficult in states of fatigue, fear, and urgency, whereas a fresh, relaxed, and confident approach yields rapid acquisition of new skills. Consequently, it's best to practice new skills (and develop solid schemas) early in your training sessions and to employ liberal hangdogging when working on hard routes. Both approaches will enable you to learn most quickly.

Despite this, there is no single best way to train or practice for any particular kind of climbing. It seems that as people learn any new skill, even babies learning how to walk, the brain generates numerous different solutions. These solutions are tried, the successful ones are retained, and the unsuccessful ones are discarded. This process—neural Darwinism—is constantly at work as you learn a new climbing move or attempt an unfamiliar style of climbing or a hard route.

Furthermore, original and creative solutions to problems of movement are routinely created as part of the learning process, and they may be recognized and learned by others. Until a certain point in time, unique moves like the heel hook, deadpoint, backstep, or Figure 4 simply did not exist and could not be learned. Somebody or perhaps many people created them in the course of learning to climb, and now these moves are commonplace. In the end, the most important prerequisites to becoming a skilled climber may be an open mind, curiosity, and a willingness to learn new techniques no matter how unimportant, unexciting, and awkward they may seem.

Transference of Skill

In motor learning the idea of transference relates to how practice or skill in one activity accelerates or improves learning of another, different activity. One startling, but apparently consistent, result in this field of study is that transfer is usually either absent or small, even between seemingly similar activities (Schmidt 1991). The complexity, coordination, and integration of skilled movement are so specific that they derive very little help from other skilled movements. Therefore, practice at climbing will improve climbing skill, balance, and technique, while playing around on a slack chain, kicking a Hacky Sack, snowboarding, or what have you are wastes of time for the purpose of improving climbing performance.

This helps us understand why the old assumption that gymnasts, with their incredible strength and motor skills, would instantly and effortlessly become excellent climbers has not proven true. Although climbing and gymnastics obviously share certain physical requirements, the motor skills are largely unrelated and they are based, in part, on markedly different underlying capacities.

Rate of Improvement and Your Ultimate Skill Level

According to the Law of Practice, performance improves rapidly from its baseline level when the activity is first practiced and continues to improve in slowly decreasing amounts as ability approaches some ultimate (personal) skill level (see **Figure 4.2**). In learning a simple task, like driving a car, it only takes a few weeks to become fairly skilled. Beyond this, all the thousands of hours you spend driving over the rest of your life will yield only a small amount of improvement.

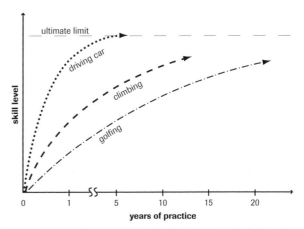

Figure 4.2 Rate of Skill Acquisition

Performance improves rapidly from its baseline level when the activity is first practiced and continues to improve at a slower rate as ability approaches some ultimate personal skill level.

The learning curve for complex activities, like golf or climbing, also rises rapidly upward as a result of the initial practice sessions. Because of the high complexity and wide range of skills inherent to these sports, however, you can continue to improve for many years, even decades. In fact, golf is clearly the more technically difficult sport of the two, since several gifted climbers have reached world-class status in less than five years, while the best golfer ever, Tiger Woods, took fifteen years to ascend to that level—and that was unusually fast!

As discussed in Chapter 1, you can maximize your rate of improvement in a specific style of climbing by focusing your practice and training in that one area. It's increasingly common to observe climbers who quickly progress to a high level of ability in one type of climbing—say, indoor bouldering competitions or flashing overhanging crimpfest routes. Since both these endeavors require only a small subset of total climbing skills, it's possible to focus your practice on developing the small set of schemas necessary to excel on said terrain. The trade-off, of course, is that your limited schemas will make climbing other types of routes very difficult, if not impossible.

The bottom line: Becoming a proficient, all-around

climber is a long-term proposition. Developing wide-ranging schemas will take you at least five to ten years of climbing at many different areas, and you can still continue to improve your skills even after twenty or thirty years in the sport. Consequently, the most intelligent approach to training for climbing would be to emphasize learning skill over getting wickedly strong during your first few years in the sport, and even likely beyond that. If you hope to become a tiger on the rocks, be prepared to invest many years of dedicated practice and strive to become a solid all-around technician.

The Keys to Effective Practice

Effective skill practice requires knowledge of your technical weaknesses on the rock (skill and strategy), liberal amounts of dedicated practice time, and an arsenal of Smart Training Drills for enhancing the learning of new skills.

Your completed self-assessment from Chapter 2 should have helped identify some of your technical weaknesses. Still, it will be beneficial to perform a more focused assessment that will highlight specific flaws in your technique and strategy. Take a few minutes and work through the following exercise.

Exercise: Uncovering Technical Weaknesses

Think back over the last few occasions that you really struggled on the rock or even at a particular climbing area. Close your eyes and replay the routes and sequences where you became frustrated, fell, or were completely shut down by the route. Also, review the moves and situations where you became anxious, tight, and felt like you were close to losing it, even if you didn't fall. Reliving the situation in vivid detail will help you get to the heart of the matter.

Take out a sheet of paper and write down all the things that seemed to contribute to your struggle or frustration. No doubt you will list numerous mental and physical issues, but it's important to dig deeper and discover the underlying technical weaknesses that caused you to get physically pumped or mentally stressed. When you've run out of reasons, cross out all the physical and mental issues and distill only the technical issues onto a new list on a separate piece of paper. Finally, order the technical reasons into a "top ten list" of sorts, with the most critical technical flaws heading the list. For example, the list might read:

1. My footwork deteriorates on difficult moves.
2. I climb way too slow over steep, pumpy terrain.
3. I always seem to miss key holds.
4. I often miss rest positions.

Now put a star next to your top three technical flaws—these are the items on which you must focus your skill practice in the weeks to come. Once you recognize significant improvement in these areas, begin practice on correcting the next three problems on the list. You may want to perform this exercise again in case new technical problems have moved into the "starred positions."

• • •

Now that you have a clear picture of your technical weaknesses, you must dedicate a portion of two practice sessions per week to correcting them. Whether you plan to practice in a climbing gym or at the crags, it's important that you make the distinction between practice and performance days. Most climbers handicap themselves by constantly focusing on performance during weekly visits to the cliff or gym. Even if you don't have a specific tick list, it's easy to succumb to the natural tendency to climb as close to your limit as possible—this can be most gratifying, but it's not the most effective use of practice time.

As you can see, this inclination to perform all the time conflicts with the processes required for improving technical problem areas. We've all seen climbers with horrible footwork flailing repeatedly on a steep route so that they can eventually tick some impressively difficult route. While they may ultimately succeed at sending their "5.hard" climbs, they gain little in technical ability from this exercise—and in fact they further groove their bad habits and poor technique. I call such practices "stupid training."

Conversely, intelligent climbers will dedicate a block of practice time early in the workout when they're mentally and physically fresh. During this practice period or day (if at the crags), the goal is to seek out routes that will target the technical weaknesses. Since performance is not a goal, there is no hesitation to hang on the rope and experiment with moves, body positions, and sequences that feel awkward or difficult.

For example, if backstep and drop knee moves are a weakness, you'll want to dedicate some time during each workout to getting onto steep routes that demand these moves if you're to climb them most efficiently. Chances are, the type of route you must get on will be intimidating, since up to this point it's probably been your tendency to climb routes that favor your strengths. If you are poor at drop-knee moves, for instance, I'll bet you avoid steep routes because they feel especially hard and look overly intimidating to you. The same goes for any style of climbing—slab, thin face, cracks, roofs, what have you. You must partake in regular practice on the terrain and type of routes that target your top three technical weaknesses. Excellence comes no other way.

Finally, I want to touch on a few practice drills and games that can enhance your rate of learning new skills and correcting weaknesses, as well as making the process a little more fun. More examples of such speed learning practices can be found in my book *How to Climb 5.12*.

Smart Training Drills for Enhanced Learning of Motor Skills and Strategy

Bouldering

Bouldering is often touted as the supreme method for developing sport-specific strength, but it's even more effective for learning climbing skills and acquiring new schemas. For proof of this, consider a recent bouldering session in which you worked a difficult problem a few times before eventually succeeding. Did you ultimately succeed because your strength increased after each attempt, or did each successive attempt result in learning of the body positioning, feel, and hand- and footwork necessary to do the moves most efficiently and successfully? I think the answer is obvious.

With all the restraints of roped climbing removed, bouldering allows you to narrow the focus and partake in relaxed, repeated attempts at learning a specific skill

or sequence of moves. Sports scientists call this blocked practice, because the fixed moves can be practiced over and over again until they are successfully acquired. Once a skill is perfected, however, there is little benefit to additional blocked practice of that skill. Further learning demands that you either move on to practicing a new skill via blocked practice (say, a new boulder problem with new moves and positions) or modify the original problem so that some element of it has changed (say, angle, hold size, hold position or spacing, or the like). This latter strategy is known as variable practice, and it's the gold standard for learning a skill that must be performed in a variety of positions or settings: hitting a golf ball from an infinite variety of lies, shooting a basketball from anywhere on the court, floating a deadpoint from any one of a million different body positions.

Indoor walls and home gyms are the ideal setting for variable practice. Supposed you want to gain skill at, say, using undercling holds and hip turns on overhanging cliffs. To begin, set a problem with a relatively easy sequence of underclings and hip turns. Practice the sequence several times until you feel it's 100 percent wired. Now redesign the problem with slight changes in the hold positions and locations, and repeat the practice drill until this, too, is wired. Next, reduce the hand- and foothold size and repeat the drill. Keep repeating this process until you've exhausted the possibilities.

Completion of this variable practice drill might take anywhere from a single evening to a couple of weeks. Regardless, the end result is comprehensive schemas surrounding this type of movement, and rapid recall and execution of the skill in some future performance setting. So, while bouldering outdoors on a wide range of move types and angles is best for building a diverse library of climbing skills, using the variable practice strategy on an artificial wall enables comprehensive learning of a new type of movement in a wide range of configurations. Clearly, there is great value in both formats, so get busy!

Traverse Training

Like bouldering, traverse training is a no-frills activity that affords focused practice on numerous technical aspects of the climbing game. Although some people find "ad lib" traversing along a cliff base or at a climbing gym boring next to climbing boulder problems, this drill does have some major benefits when compared to working a known, graded boulder problem. When working the graded boulder problem, it's natural to want to succeed at any cost, even if your technique is sloppy and inefficient. As discussed earlier, it's difficult to develop new skills in such a performance setting.

Conversely, traversing for the sake of practicing technique and movement eliminates the pressure to perform. You can experiment with new grip positions, gentle and precise foot placements, and various body positions with no concern about whether or not you step off the wall. Maximize the benefit of this drill by carefully spotting each foot placement, concentrating on keeping your weight over your feet, relaxing your grip as much as possible, and learning to move quickly and confidently through thin, tenuous sequences. Finally, strive to remain calm and relaxed at all times, and refocus on your feet anytime you sense you're losing control.

To mix things up and increase the intensity and benefit of traverse training, you can also play around with various elimination or focus drills. For example, try doing a complete traverse using only two fingers (index and middle fingers, for example, or middle and ring fingers) of each hand. This drill forces you to maximize the weighting of your feet (a good thing); it's also an excellent way to increase your finger strength. As another variation, challenge yourself to do a complete traverse using only open-grip finger positions. (This will be especially difficult and beneficial if you naturally favor the crimp grip.) Be creative and make up other drills, such as "side-pull only," "undercling only," or "cross-through only" elimination traverses. Beginner and intermediate climbers have much to gain from performing these drills on a regular basis.

Toproping and Hangdogging

Toproping and hangdogging are the ideal formats for practicing difficult moves near your limit or when diving into unfamiliar terrain like pocket or crack climbing. As discussed earlier, a relaxed, low-stress environment is critical to rapid learning of new skills.

Obviously, climbing on toprope or on lead, bolt to bolt, represents a low-stress setting where you can experiment with tricky, awkward moves without the risk of a serious fall and injury.

When attempting a route that is continuously hard or with multiple cruxes, it's best to break down this route into smaller sections or chunks. This reduces the mental burden by allowing you to view and solve the route in parts. Much like working a boulder problem, you can employ blocked practice to work a sequence repeatedly. Once a problem is solved and programmed to a high likelihood of success, you can move on and begin work on the next chunk. Upon solving all the chunks (and after a good rest), your next goal should be to combine chunks. For example, on a route that you had broken down into four hard sections, you would try to link the top two chunks, and then move down and link the top three chunks. Such incremental learning will wire you for a successful redpoint or toprope ascent after another rest or on your next outing or day at that area. (*Note:* See Chapter 5 of *How to Climb 5.12* to learn many more strategies for working and sending project routes.)

The Stick Game (aka Send Me)

This popular game is great for learning to quickly assess and execute a novel, unknown move on-sight (a vital skill when on-sight climbing at the crag or in competition). Best played on an indoor wall, the drill requires at least two players who take turns pointing out (with a broomstick) impromptu boulder problems. Begin by identifying the starting hand- and footholds for the "victim"; then, as the climber pulls up on them, the course setter points to the next hold to be used. Continue in this fashion until the climber falls or the problem is done. Commonly, the game is played with open feet—while the climber can use only the handholds that the course setter specifies, all footholds are on route.

First Touch

First Touch is a great practice drill for would-be competition and on-sight climbers—though anyone can benefit from its use. An indoor facility with a wide range of toprope routes is the ideal setting for this drill. As the name implies, you must climb a route by using each handhold in the exact way that you first grab it—no readjusting or changing your grip after you first touch it. By climbing many routes in this fashion (and, of course, obeying the guidelines completely), you will learn to examine holds more closely—both from the ground and while climbing—and thus increase the likelihood you'll use them optimally from the first touch. On lead, this skill saves you time and energy, both of which increase your odds of on-sighting a route.

Tracking and Elimination

This drill can be used indoors when bouldering or on toprope. The goal is simply to climb a route by tracking your feet on the exact same holds used by your hands. It's kind of like climbing a ladder, where you press down on a rung with your right hand and make room to step on that same rung with your right foot. As a type of elimination drill, this will make a climb much harder than it would be if climbed with all the holds on route. Therefore, if you normally practice skill by climbing 5.10 or 5.11 routes, you'll want to do this drill on routes in the range of 5.7 to 5.9.

If you climb indoors a lot, exercise your creativity and develop other elimination drills that might improve your skill, strategy, and strength. For instance, begin eliminating certain hand- and footholds from the routes you have ruthlessly wired. There's little to be gained from blocked practice of the same tired routes over and over again. So challenge yourself by eliminating the five biggest holds from the route, or by limiting yourself to grabbing the holds only as side pulls or underclings, or with only two fingers, or what have you. Not only can this make for some good fun for you and your friends, but it's also an excellent way to enhance your skill practice and overall ability.

Downclimbing Routes

When leading or toproping indoors, it's rare that I climb a route to the top and lower off without trying to downclimb as much of the route as possible. There are many benefits to this practice beyond the obvious one of doubling the pump. If you know you are going to downclimb a route, you become a more observant and focused climber on the way up. What's more, since poor footwork is a leading handicap for many climbers, there's a lot to be gained from this practice, which demands intense concentration on footwork!

At first you will find downclimbing to be difficult, awkward, and very pumpy. But that's the M.O. when first attempting anything new that's worthwhile (read *challenging*). As your hold recognition improves, however, and as you learn to relax and fluidly reverse the route, you'll find that downclimbing a route often feels easier than sending it in the first place. This is because your eccentric (lowering) strength is greater than your concentric (pulling) strength, and due to the fact that by leading with the feet while downclimbing you learn to maximally weight them and conserve energy. All of the above make downclimbing a killer drill—one not to be overlooked by any serious climber!

Speed Training

When the rock gets steep and the moves hard, there's no more important weapon to have in your arsenal than being able to climb fast and precisely. Climbing quickly is primarily a function of skill, not strength or power (I'm not talking about lunging wildly up a route). In fact, the less strength and endurance you possess, the more important this skill becomes.

To begin with, it's important to note that there is no benefit to climbing faster if you begin to botch sequences or if your technique degrades. Therefore, you want to practice speed climbing on routes you have completely wired and, likely, at a number grade or two below your personal best. Climb several laps on the route (rest between attempts), each incrementally faster than the previous. Attempt to climb about 10 percent faster on each successive lap, but back off the accelerator at the first sign that your technique is suffering.

Perform this drill a few times a week for several months, and you'll find yourself naturally moving faster when climbing on-sight or redpoint at the crags. This new skill alone could push your redpoint ability

...her over the course of a single season—
...r gain than you'd achieve from strength

Mental Wings Strategies to Enhance Problem Solving and Learning

I conclude this chapter with six mental strategies to enhance your skills at on-the-spot problem solving and learning of a difficult sequence or complex route. Being able to quickly decipher perplexing cruxes while conserving mental and physical energy is a master skill in our sport. Learn to utilize these skills effectively and you're on your way to becoming a grand master at flashing.

Focus on Problem Solving, Not Performance

One thing I love about working a hard boulder problem or project route is the challenge of studying a complex problem and gradually seeing a beautiful, unique sequence take form. Just like piecing together a puzzle when you were a kid, you can best solve a rock puzzle by remaining focused on the task and having fun regardless of how the long the puzzle takes to complete.

For instance, when working a boulder problem or crux sequence, ponder the beauty of this rock puzzle and feel the joy of being engaged in this challenging process. This disposition will shift you out of the can't-fail mind-set of frustration and help turn your focus away from the problem and onto finding a solution. Remember, the brain naturally magnifies whatever you focus on. Obviously you want to magnify the possible solution, not the problem, so always be solution oriented.

Relax and Remain Positive

Both problem solving and motor learning occur most rapidly in a stress- and anxiety-free state. Therefore, controlling tension through deep breathing, positive visualization, and remaining process oriented is crucial for accelerating these processes.

It's also fundamental that you eliminate thoughts of "needing to flash the route" or "having to redpoint the climb this attempt"—these are both positions that work against you. By entertaining such needs, you create stress and anxiety that may prevent the very thing you desire. Instead, acknowledge that falling is part of the learning process and accept each fall as a personal clue from the route (don't ignore it!) instructing you on what needs to be done differently or better. Predetermine that you will accept a fall (the clue) if it happens and believe completely that success will come with creativity, effort, and patience. In doing so, you create the optimal state for learning and succeeding most quickly.

Chunk Down the Route

As mentioned earlier, chunking down a long, hard route into a series of short problems makes the climb less overwhelming and easier to learn. Furthermore, these short problems or chunks can each be viewed as a short-term goal to be reached or accomplished. So, while you may fail for several days on the project as a whole, you will experience short-term success as you solve each of the individual chunks. This sense of success helps keep you energized, positive, and on track to eventually succeeding on the route.

When working through the individual chunks, avoid becoming obsessed on any one of them. Beating yourself up on, say, the second chunk of a six-chunk route is self-defeating, since even if you eventually solve this chunk, you'll be too mentally and physically wasted to put in meaningful work on the other chunks. Therefore, it's best to move on to working the next chunk upon the onset of frustration or any judgmental self-talk, such as "I can't do this" or "I'll never figure this out." If allowed to burrow into your subconscious, such judgments form the basis for reality. You are much better off solving the rest of the route before returning to the problem section.

Long-term achievement of a formidable goal (where short-term failures are inevitable) demands mental agility as well as the ability to trick yourself into persevering in the face of adversity. Breaking a climb into a series of more manageable chunks and setting yourself up for several small wins is a most effective strategy.

Engage Both Sides of the Brain

You may be familiar with the fact that the brain has two hemispheres—the left hemisphere, which presides over logical, practical, language, mathematical, and related matters, and the right hemisphere, which dominates in creative, artistic, intuitive, situational, and imaginary matters. The majority of people are "left-brained" and, even if you aren't, intense situations with lots of information—like climbing—tend to bring the left brain into command. The result is that many climbers leave their right brain on the ground and therefore handicap their problem-solving ability, big time! I can think of countless times I've fallen on routes because I was thinking in a linear fashion and with blinders on that prevented me from finding a key hold, sequence, or rest. (Cut me a break, I'm a scientist, not an artist!)

The right brain is best accessed when you are in a relaxed state (another reason some climbers have a tough time freeing it up). Thus, bringing it into play requires that you resist the Type A behavior of rushing up to a route and quickly going for the send, and instead get comfortable at the base of the climb, warm up slowly, and make a relaxed study of the climb before tying in to the rope. Some severely left-brained people will need to force themselves to think out of the box. Seeing the big picture and imagining all the possible approaches and sequences on a climb is a habit you may need to foster through your own initiative. Your goal should be a balanced approach to problem solving in which you can think logically and practically as well as intuitively and creatively. Being able to create (on demand) and leverage this state is one of the hallmarks of brilliant climbers such as Lynn Hill and Chris Sharma, who can perform at an exceedingly high level in a wide range of styles and settings.

Employ Multisensory Learning

Everything we learn comes through one of our five senses, and the more senses we use in learning, the faster and easier it becomes. Climbers tend to use primarily the sense of vision before they leave the ground, and feel once they begin to climb. While the senses of smell and taste can't contribute to performance in this sport, the auditory sense can also be a powerful learning tool (Knudson 1997), particularly when faced with a tricky boulder problem or when working to memorize a difficult sequence. Climbers who give names to key holds and moves and then create verbal beta are using this trick. Remembering an obscure sequence of tiny holds by feel or vision can be enhanced with descriptive verbal beta like "high-step to the dime edge, then deadpoint to the potato chip flake." It may sound funny, but it works.

Multisensory learning is a sign of the intelligent climber, so begin to talk through your sequences in addition to visualizing and feeling the moves. By talking the talk, you make it easier to climb the climb!

Try Something Ridiculous

The biggest block to learning is judgment. Self-talk like "Others use this sequence, so that must be the best way," or discounting a novel or improbable sequence that flashes into your mind without trying it first, is a form of self-sabotage. It's vital that you don't limit yourself this way—your brain doesn't know what you can or cannot do until you tell it. Don't prejudge sequences or your capabilities!

The best problem solvers are both creative and uninhibited. They never hesitate to try a novel solution that's entirely different from the known sequence. You can foster these skills by ignoring the obvious solution—the one that's not currently working for you—and attempting a few completely different, even ridiculous sequences.

Regardless of how improbable a given technique looks—heel hook, undercling, high step, kneebar—don't pass judgment on it until you make a few attempts with that technique. Try a variety of body positions, foot flags, lunges, and don't ignore the nonpositive holds like gastons, side pulls, and pinches. Eliminate the seemingly must-use hold—or at least try using it with the opposite hand. Search for unchalked holds that might unlock the sequence, and keep a constant watch for footholds that are off the main line of the route—a single missed foothold or high step can make the difference between "impossible" and "possible."

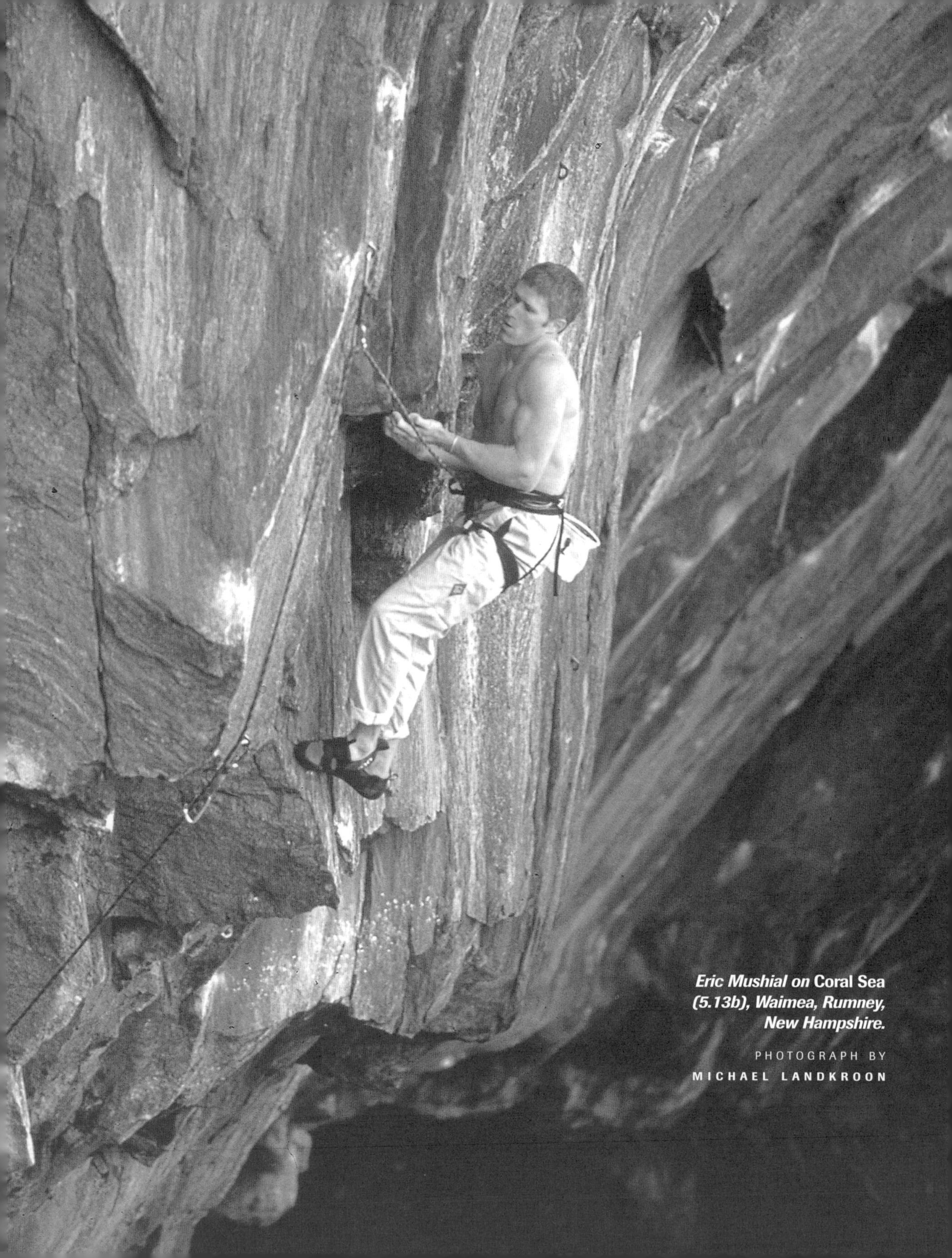

Eric Mushial on Coral Sea *(5.13b), Waimea, Rumney, New Hampshire.*

PHOTOGRAPH BY
MICHAEL LANDKROON

CHAPTER FIVE

Theory & Methods of Strength Training

Man is in a position to act because he has the ability to discover causal relations which determine change and becoming in the Universe.

— Ludwig Von Mises, "Human Action"

Perhaps no sport can match rock climbing for the dramatic increase in the mean level of performance of its participants in recent years. Today's average climber is capable of a standard that few climbers dreamed of achieving when I began climbing in the mid-1970s. Furthermore, many weekend warriors are able to progress to the lofty levels of 5.12 and 5.13—grades that hardly existed two decades ago. The reasons for these incredible improvements include sticky-soled shoes, sport-climbing tactics, and, more than anything else, the advent of climbing gyms and a growing focus on sport-specific strength training.

Still, there are many arguments among climbers about the best way to train, and people frequently tell me that they are confused by the often conflicting training information published in the climbing rags. Surely an article or book describing the training practices of some 5.14 climber is of little help for average climbers—it might even get them injured. Alternatively, joining a health club and performing the typical weight-lifting workout would be of little benefit

for most climbers; in fact, it may even hurt their climbing performance!

As a result of all the confusion, numerous climbers have quipped to me that they have decided to "just climb, as training for climbing." While this is an excellent strategy for a novice climber, intermediate and advanced climbers definitely need to partake in some sport-specific strength training if they want to continue to improve and, hopefully, someday reach their genetic potential.

The goal of this chapter (as with this whole book) is to help you avoid—or step out of—the muck and mire of confusion that surrounds so much information on strength training for climbing. Toward this end, I will arm you with a basic understanding of the theory and science of strength training. I have always felt that the theoretical person is a practical person. Therefore, gaining knowledge of training theory will enable you to act and train more practically and effectively. Furthermore, you will be able to evaluate more critically and effectively what you read elsewhere.

Overview of Strength and Fitness Training for Climbing

One reason that climbing is not the best training for climbing is because the ultimate goals of these two activities are very different. For instance, when rock climbing it's your goal to avoid muscular failure at all costs—ideally, you want to reach the top of a boulder problem or climb before the muscles of your arms and forearms pump out. Conversely, when training for climbing you

53

want to exercise at the highest possible intensity and produce muscular failure in a few minutes, if not a few seconds. In other words, when climbing, you avoid failure; when training, you pursue failure.

Another example that underscores the difference between climbing and training for climbing is the way in which you grip the rock. In climbing, the rock dictates a random use of many different grip positions; at times you may even deliberately vary the way you grip the rock. As a result it's unlikely that any single grip position will ever get worked maximally, and therefore the individual grip positions (crimp, open hand, pinch, and so forth) are slow to increase strength. This should help you understand why a full season of climbing will indeed improve your anaerobic endurance (endurance of strength), but do little to increase your absolute maximum grip strength. Therefore, varying grip positions is a great strategy for maximizing endurance when climbing for performance, but it stinks for training maximum grip strength. Effective finger-strength training demands you target a specific grip position and work it until failure.

On the following pages, we'll delve into the science of strength training and reveal some of the other secrets to highly effective training for climbing.

Primer on Exercise Physiology

While there is no need to get into an advanced-level discussion of exercise physiology, I feel it's beneficial to have a basic understanding of some functions involved in strength training. For instance, understanding how different types of muscle fiber become "recruited" into action and how the muscles adapt to training stress are key distinctions in how you might best go about training your upper body. Furthermore, knowledge of the body's energy systems and why muscles fail can give clues as to how you might modify your climbing to maximize power or endurance. Let's get started.

Muscle Movements and Roles

In producing movement, there are three different muscular actions as well as three basic roles they can play during a sports performance.

- **Concentric contraction:** Muscle action in which the tension developed produces a shortening of the musculature, as in the biceps during the upward phase of a pull-up.

- **Eccentric contraction:** Muscle action in which the muscle resists as it's forced to lengthen, as in the biceps during the lowering phase of a pull-up.

- **Isometric contraction:** Muscle action resulting in no shortening of the muscle (no movement), as in musculature of the forearm while gripping a handhold.

- **Agonist:** The muscle or muscle groups causing an action to occur. For instance, the biceps and the latissimus muscles of the back are some of the prime movers in the pulling motions common to climbing.

- **Antagonist:** The muscle or muscles providing an opposing force to the primary muscles in action. For example, the muscles on the back of your forearm oppose the forearm flexor muscles when squeezing a rubber doughnut.

- **Stabilizer:** The muscle or muscle groups that help stabilize the skeletal structures so that tension of the agonist (prime movers) can effectively produce movement. In climbing, there are many small and large stabilizers that come into play, from the arms to the core muscles of the torso and down through the legs.

Muscle Fiber Types

There are two distinct types of muscle fiber: slow twitch and fast twitch. Fast-twitch fibers are further subdivided into two main subcategories: Type IIa and Type IIb. A third subcategory of Type IIc fibers has been identified, though they only exist in very small numbers.

- **Slow Twitch (ST):** These Type I fibers comprise approximately 50 percent of total skeletal muscle, though genetic variation can range from about 20 percent to 80 percent (Bloomfield, et al., 1992). They are recruited primarily during low-intensity, aerobic endurance activities.

- **Fast Twitch (FT):** These fibers are recruited during high-intensity movements or activities. Type IIa (FTa) fibers are energized through both aerobic and anaerobic processes and are, therefore, fatigue resistant. These fibers excel at longer-duration high-intensity activity, and they would be most active when climbing long, hard routes. Type IIb (FTb) fibers have the fastest contraction time and generate energy almost entirely through the anaerobic system. These fibers are recruited during brief, maximum movements such as a difficult boulder problem or a powerful crux move.

Your relative percentage of FT and ST muscle fibers is genetically determined and varies little in response to training. Naturally strong climbers are likely gifted with a higher-than-normal percentage of FT fibers (among other things), whereas gifted mountaineers, who can keep on going like the Energizer Rabbit, are likely have a higher percentage of ST fibers. Fortunately, ST fibers can be taught to act like FT fibers through use of certain training protocols (Chu 1996), which I will introduce later.

RECRUITMENT

Muscle fibers of the same type are organized into motor units. ST motor units innervate between 10 and 180 fibers, while FT motor units innervate up to 800 fibers (Bloomfield, et al., 1994). When a muscular contraction is triggered, motor units are recruited on an as-needed basis beginning with the smaller ST motor units. As muscular tension increases, a greater number of ST motor units will join in, and if the tension grows further, the larger FT motor units will begin to fire. Maximum muscular force is eventually achieved if all motor units (ST and FT) are recruited into action (see **Figure 5.1**).

Knowing this physiological process should help you understand why it's important to train with high intensity and with maximum weight (resistance) if you want to recruit, and make stronger, the FT fibers. Compare this to "just climbing a lot of routes" for training: That way you would recruit primarily ST fibers on the many moderate moves and only occa-

Figure 5.1 Muscular Force Production

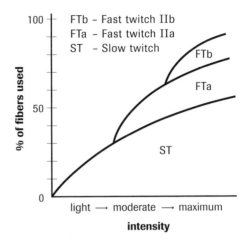

Maximum muscular force eventually can be achieved if all motor units (ST and FT) are recruited into action.

sionally recruit the FT a fibers when you encounter hard moves. The high-threshold FT b fibers would seldom be called into action—only when a move or sequence requires explosive power or application of maximum strength.

Muscular Adaptations to Strength Training

Two primary adaptations occur in response to strength training—adaptation of the neural system and adaptation of the muscular system.

ADAPTATION OF THE NEURAL SYSTEM

The nervous system adapts to strength training in three ways: motor learning, motor unit synchronization, and disinhibition.

- **Motor Learning:** The first neural adaptation, motor learning, should sound familiar after reading Chapter 4. During the initial work at a new exercise (say, uneven-grip pull-ups or even campus training), your primary limitation will be a lack of coordination and feel for the exercise. The first few weeks should yield rapid improvement as a result of motor learning and improved coordination among the prime mover, stabilizer, and antagonist muscles. Beyond this point, further strength gains will depend on other adaptations taking place.

- **Motor Unit Synchronization:** Motor unit synchronization is the second neural adaptation that increases strength. Suppose you have acquired the coordination and motor skills needed for performing a given exercise—or perhaps you're adding a new exercise that requires no learning (such as hanging on a fingerboard). Initial training triggers motor units to fire in a rather random, asynchronous manner. However, continued training enhances motor unit synchronization and, eventually, most of the motor units will fire in unison, resulting in more strength and power.

- **Disinhibition:** The final neural adaptation, disinhibition, is most important (and exciting) for intermediate to advanced climbers in search of gains in maximum strength and power. The neuromuscular system has a built-in feedback mechanism that acts as a safeguard during times of increasing force production. The Golgi tendon organ, located in the musculotendinous junction, is sensitive to the level of tension in the muscle, and in situations of high force it sends inhibitory signals that prevent further motor units from firing. In most individuals this protective response limits force production to some amount far below your absolute maximum-force-producing potential. It's like putting a restrictor plate on the engine of a race car to limit its top speed to 150 miles per hour, even though it's capable of 225. Fortunately, regular high-intensity training reduces the sensitivity of the Golgi tendon organ (disinhibition) and thus opens up a new level of maximum strength.

The difference between your maximum voluntary force and the absolute maximum capacity is called the strength deficit. Research has shown that significant gains in strength are possible by training to reduce these neural inhibitions. One study (Tidow 1990) showed that untrained individuals possessed strength deficits of up to 45 percent; that is, neural inhibition was reducing their maximum strength to almost half of their absolute capacity. The study also revealed that targeted training by elite athletes reduced strength deficits to only 5 percent. Therefore, large gains in strength are possible without ever growing a larger, heavier muscle!

As a final note, the best type of training to produce disinhibition depends of the magnitude of your strength deficit. Intermediate climbers, who likely have larger strength deficits, would benefit most by training with heavy loads (heavy pulldowns, hypergravity training on a fingerboard or HIT system, and so forth). Elite climbers with smaller strength deficits might realize further improvements only through a combination of heavy loads (hypergravity training) and high speed (plyometric training).

ADAPTATION OF THE MUSCULAR SYSTEM

Long-term gains in muscular strength result from increases in the size of the individual muscle fibers (see **Figure 5.2**). This process of growing larger muscles is known as hypertrophy. Since there is a strong relationship between the size and the strength of muscles, your ability to grow stronger, long term, will somewhat depend on hypertrophy.

Certainly large muscles in the wrong place (such as legs, chest, and shoulders) are a liability to climbers. Even overdevelopment of the all-important pull muscles can be a bad thing if it's the result of exercising in a nonspecific way (such as free-weight or circuit training). For example, baseball-sized biceps that result from doing heavy biceps curls will not only underperform on the rock but also get in the way and prevent you from locking off effectively while you are climbing.

Still, any muscular hypertrophy occurring in the forearms, arms, and back resulting from sport-specific training should be viewed as a good thing. In fact, an experienced climber who has been training for a long time and doesn't realize a little hypertrophy probably isn't training effectively. Since most hypertrophy occurs in response to high-intensity, heavy-load train-

Figure 5.2 Muscular Adaptations

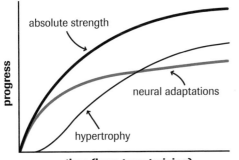

time (long-term training)

Initial gains in strength result mostly from neural adaptations, whereas long-term gains will somewhat depend on hypertrophy.

ing, you would want to train with higher resistances (weighted pull-ups or hypergravity) to trigger this adaptation.

It's interesting to note that a well-developed neuromuscular system is not absolutely necessary for being a strong climber. As mentioned in Chapter 1, a small number of individuals possess tendon insertion points at a larger distance from the joint (axis of rotation) than the rest of us with average genetics. These gifted people will exhibit what seems to be amazing strength given their modest body builds. Other genetic factors, such as having a slight build or an unusually high percentage of fast-twitch fibers, may further enhance their physical prowess. With this in mind, you can see why these rare climbers will be incredibly strong regardless of the type of training, if any, in which they engage. Hence, it would be a mistake to copy their training methods, and you should question the advice of anyone who instructs you to train like "such-and-such a 5.14 climber does."

Energy Systems

In climbing, energy production in the crucial pull muscles most often comes from the ATP-CP system

and the lactic acid system. The lactic acid system can function both in the presence (aerobic) or absence (anaerobic) of oxygen.

ATP-CP

The ATP-CP system provides rapid energy for brief, intense movements such as a vigorous boulder problem or a few maximal crux moves. In training, the ATP-CP system is the primary fuel source for brief, intense exercise lasting less than fifteen seconds—for example, campus training or doing a one-arm pull-up. ATP and CP are high-energy phosphate compounds resident in all muscle cells in small amounts; intense exercise, however, will exhaust the supply in a matter of seconds.

LACTIC ACID

Consistent, high-intensity exercise lasting up to three minutes calls the lactic acid energy system into play. This is the primary energy system that fuels your climbing through the long crux section of some heinous route. Carbohydrates, in the form of glycogen, fuel the lactic acid system, which can operate in either the presence or absence of oxygen.

- **Anaerobic:** High-intensity exercise forces the muscles to create energy in the absence of oxygen (anaerobic) and at the expense of lactic acid production. The resulting accumulation of lactic acid leads to fatigue, muscular pain, and, quite soon, muscular failure. This limitation of anaerobic energy production helps explain why sustained climbing on maximally difficult moves is limited to about three minutes or less (if there are no rests). Consequently, climbing as quickly as possible from rest to rest is the best strategy on hard, sustained routes.

  The *anaerobic threshold* is defined as the workload or oxygen consumption level at which lactate production by the working muscle exceeds the body's ability to remove lactate. Therefore, once you cross this threshold level, the net amount of lactic acid increases, and muscular failure soon follows (see **Figure 5.3**). Depending on your level of conditioning, the anaerobic threshold may be

Figure 5.3 Anaerobic Threshold Level

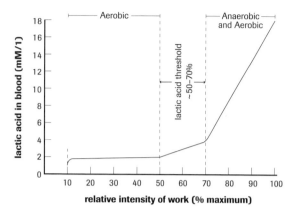

Once the anaerobic threshold level is crossed, the net amount of lactic acid increases, and muscular failure soon follows.

Figure 5.4 Muscular Energy Production

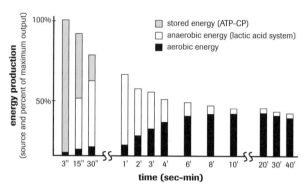

Brief, maximal muscular action is fueled by ATP-CP. After about fifteen seconds, anaerobic energy production becomes the primary energy source. Exercise lasting longer than three minutes depends mostly on aerobic energy production, though muscular output is only a fraction of maximal.

crossed at an exercise intensity of anywhere between 50 percent and 80 percent of maximum. Becoming winded and burning muscles are two signs you have crossed the anaerobic threshold.

The above knowledge underscores the importance of using an interval approach to high-intensity climbing. In sending a hard route, you want to avoid crossing the anaerobic threshold for as long as possible and, once you do cross it, climb as quickly as possible to a rest or easier terrain. Only then will you get back down below the anaerobic threshold and allow your body to begin lowering blood lactate concentration. Depending on the amount of lactic acid in your system, it could take twenty minutes or more to return to a baseline level of blood lactate (Watts 1996).

- **Aerobic:** Muscular action lasting longer than three minutes demands use of oxygen to produce energy. With ATP-CP reserves depleted and high muscle and blood lactate levels (from anaerobic energy production), exercise can continue only if the intensity of movement is reduced (see **Figure 5.4**).

Anaerobic energy production is limited to an amount proportionate to the liver's ability to remove lactic acid (and convert back to glucose) from the blood. Therefore, aerobic energy production takes over and powers most of the muscle action by means of a breakdown of carbohydrates, fats, and (if exercise continues long enough) protein in the presence of oxygen. Since aerobic energy production does not produce lactic acid, low-intensity movements may continue for up to an hour or two without cessation (as in hiking or climbing over easy terrain).

Training Principles

Possessing a basic understanding of relevant training principles empowers you to make the most of your time investment in training. Without getting too deeply into sports science, let's examine the important principles of specificity, individualization, progressive overload, variation, rest, and detraining.

Specificity

The principle of specificity of training may be the most important of all. It simply states that the more specific a training activity is to a given sport—velocity of movement, pattern of movement, body posture, range of motion, and type of contraction—the more it will contribute to increasing performance in that sport. Therefore, for an exercise to be effective at producing usable strength gains for climbing (such as grip strength, lock-off strength, or lunging power), it must be markedly similar to climbing in many ways. The more specific the training activity or exercise, the greater the benefit to your climbing performance. Let's look at a few examples of how this rule applies to training for climbing.

Circuit training or pumping iron does not train the muscles in the slightest way similar to their use in rock climbing. Consequently, health-club-style weight training is basically a waste of time for all climbers, except those possessing unusually poor levels of general fitness. Some intermediate climbers have disputed me on this, since they have noticed improvement on the rock while participating in weight-training regimens. Since gains in climbing skill and strategy produce most of the increase in overall ability during the first few years in the sport, however, these folks would have improved regardless of the type of training they participated in. They probably would have improved as much with a training regimen outside of climbing itself consisting of ice skating and poker playing.

Squeezing a rubber hand doughnut (or other similar spring-loaded device) is likewise unproductive for improving your finger strength for climbing. Grip strength shows a remarkable amount of specificity depending on the grip position (crimp, open hand, pinch), the positions of the wrist and elbow, the intensity of the contraction, and even the type of contraction (isometric, concentric). Furthermore, since your grip tends to fail while you are pulling down on it with near maximum load, it must be trained in much this same way. Consequently, squeezing a rubber doughnut is basically useless as climbing training, though it may have some merit as a warm-up exercise or in injury rehabilitation.

What about the basic pull-up (palms away), a most popular exercise among climbers? Obviously the motion is similar to climbing, but your posture, your degree of body tension, and the exact position of your hands and arms do not vary randomly as they do on rock. What's more, the ability to stop or lock off your arm in some novel position is often more vital in climbing than is the simple act of pulling. Therefore, to produce the most transfer of your pull-up training to the rocks, you want to alter the pull-up in a variety of ways with every set. For example, you might change the distance between your hands, stagger one hand lower than the other (use a webbing loop), and include some lock-offs or stops in the motion at a variety of arm angles. This approach would be much more advantageous than just doing pull-ups in the same fixed position.

Finally, let's consider the concept of cross-training as some individuals try to apply it to climbing. Clearly, the idea that performing any other sports activity might improve climbing performance is in blatant conflict with the principle of specificity. In fact, the only sports in which cross-training seems to be practical are the aerobic endurance sports, as popularized by the triathlon phenomenon.

Individualization

No climber on this planet is quite like you; therefore the most effective training program for you will be different than that of any other climber. This might sound obvious, but many climbers copy the training program of their peers or, worse yet, imitate what some elite climber does. I consider this a rather stupid approach to training.

The most intelligent training program (for you) would take into account your strengths, weaknesses, and previous injuries, as well as your goals and the amount of time you have available to work out. Furthermore, since you may recover from training at a faster or slower rate than others, your optimal amount of rest may dictate a different workout frequency. Consequently, it would be wise to develop and execute what seems to be the best program for you and ignore how others train.

Progressive Overload

This granddaddy of strength-training principles states that in order to increase muscular strength, it is necessary to expose the musculature to a level of stress beyond that to which it is accustomed. You can achieve this overload by increasing the intensity, volume, or speed of training, or by decreasing the rest interval between successive sets. While it's probably a good idea to vary the method of overload from time to time, increasing intensity (using a higher training load) appears to be the most important in triggering long-term muscular adaptations.

In training for climbing, you should look for ways to incorporate (and alternate) all the above methods of overload, especially the practice of increasing intensity through greater training loads. This is best achieved through a variety of hypergravity exercises such as weighted pull-ups and fingerboard hangs, or the HIT workout. All will be discussed in depth later.

Variation

One of the most common training errors among all athletes is the failure to regularly change their training program. This principle states that the body becomes accustomed to training stimuli that are repeatedly applied in the same way. Therefore, if you go to the climbing gym and engage in the same basic routine every time, your strength and climbing gains will eventually plateau despite what feel like good workouts. Strive to vary your training by manipulating the type of overload (per above) as well as mixing up the type and order of climbs and exercises performed.

Periodization, another form of variation, involves alternating the overall workout intensity and volume from session to session. For example, with indoor training you might alternate workouts among "high volume" (doing many moderate routes), "high intensity" (hard, powerful bouldering), and "high, high" (climbing as many hard routes as possible). You could also vary your workouts every few weeks as in the 4-3-2-1 training schedule described in Chapter 7. Bottom line: Make the principle of variation a cornerstone of your training for climbing program and you will get uncommonly good results!

Rest

The muscular adaptations discussed earlier occur between, not during, workouts. Sufficient rest and healthy lifestyle habits (including proper nutrition and adequate sleep) are fundamental to maximizing the strength gains that result from training stimuli. As a rough guideline, complete recovery (supercompensation) takes anywhere from twenty-four to seventy-two hours depending on the intensity and volume of the stimulus (see **Figure 5.5**). For example, it might only take one day to recover from a high volume of low-intensity activity like climbing a bunch of really easy routes or just hiking, whereas it would probably take three or more days to recover completely from a high volume of high-intensity exercise, such as climbing a bunch of routes near your limit, or performing hypergravity and campus training in a single workout.

The importance of this principle cannot be overstated, since training too often (or resting too little) will eventually lead to a decline in performance and/or injury (see **Figure 5.6**). This is known as the overtraining syndrome, and it's surprisingly common

Figure 5.5 **Supercompensation Cycle**

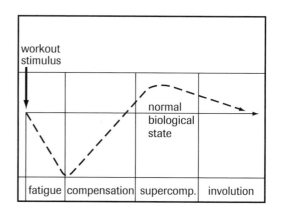

Complete recovery (supercompensation) takes anywhere from twenty-four to seventy-two hours, depending on the intensity and volume of the training stimulus.

Figure 5.6 Long-Term Training Response

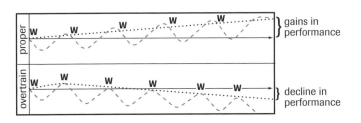

Adequate rest between workouts allows full supercompensation and long-term gains in performance. Conversely, workouts too close together result in a long-term decline in performance.

among climbers—observe how many climbers out there are whining about their nagging injuries or complaining that they are "not getting stronger" despite their dedication to hard training.

Another factor leading to overtraining or unusually long workout recovery is the mistake of placing too much training stimulus on the neuromuscular system. As shown in the Supercompensation Cycle (**Figure 5.5**), the workout stimulus results in neuromuscular fatigue and a temporary degradation in functional ability. With adequate rest, the system regenerates to a level higher than before the workout. Interestingly, working out beyond a certain point provides no additional stimulus for growth, though it does make further inroads (muscular breakdown) from which you must recover. This is an important concept to keep in mind when performing high-intensity training. Doing ten sets of campus training probably provides no more stimulus for growth than five sets, but by doing ten sets you dig yourself a deeper hole from which it will take longer to recover. The same argument could be made against doing twenty sets of pull-ups or spending sixty minutes training on a fingerboard. Summing up: In high-intensity training, less is usually more.

Detraining

Upon cessation of strength training (or frequent climbing), recent gains in strength begin to erode slightly in just ten to fourteen days. A more significant decrease in strength will occur in the weeks that follow if training

or climbing does not resume. While some downtime is a good thing each year (mentally and in the case of nagging injuries), frequent breaks in training make it very difficult to acquire long-term gains in strength.

If you are someone who travels a lot on business, or for some other reason frequently misses a week or two of training, you can temporarily delay the detraining by leveraging your knowledge of the lengthened supercompensation period after high-intensity workouts. Since we know that it can take three or more days to recover from an intense workout, performing such a workout the day before the beginning of your break would delay the beginning of detraining by a few more days. Therefore, you might return from the break and be at peak strength even after ten or more days off. This long period of supercompensation after extremely strenuous training or climbing explains why the many enthusiastic climbers who are unknowingly overtraining discover a new level of strength after taking a week or two off.

Training Methods

Detailed below are the concepts and methods central to effective strength training for climbing. Since the pull muscles are most often the limiting physical factor in climbing, examples of how this information applies to climbing will focus on training these body parts.

Strength Training versus Endurance Training

Strength training results in neural and muscular adaptations that eventually enable muscle action at higher loads. Meanwhile, strength-endurance (aka anaerobic endurance) training produces different adaptations, such as increased capillary and mitochondrial (little ATP "factories" inside cells) density, that enable greater volumes of exercise (see **Figure 5.7**). Certainly climbers would benefit from enhancement in both areas; gains in strength training, however, are more vitally important. As climbing icon Tony Yaniro astutely points out, "If you cannot pull a single hard move, you have nothing to endure." So strength training is paramount.

Figure 5.7 Physiological Adaptations to Training

Structure, System or Energy Source	Adaptations from Strength Training	Adaptations from Endurance Training
Muscle fiber size	Increase	No change or decrease
Capillary density	No change or decrease	Increase
Neural disinhibition	Increase	No change
Mitochondrial density	No change or decrease	Increase
Muscle glycogen	Increase	Increase
ATP-CP	Increase	No change

Adaptations from strength versus endurance training.

This notion is supported by the fact that strengthening a muscle also improves its endurance, because a stronger muscle can use a smaller percentage of maximum strength to execute a sequence of nonmaximum moves. What's more, a stronger muscle will have a higher relative anaerobic threshold than a weaker muscle with higher endurance capabilities. Conversely, endurance training will not increase maximum strength one iota.

In the final analysis, the best all-around climbers will exhibit prowess at muscular strength and endurance of strength as a result of long-term training of both systems. Individuals who focus on training just maximum strength (and power) will excel mainly on boulder problems and short routes, while those climbers who emphasize high-volume training will be best at climbing much longer routes. As discussed in Chapter 1, you must always consider your climbing goals when deciding on the best form of training.

Muscular Strength versus Muscular Power

Strength is defined as the force a muscle group can exert in one maximum effort. Your ability to pull a single hard movement or grip a small, difficult handhold is a function of your maximum strength. Muscular *power* is more complex, because it is the product of force and the distance through which the force acts.

Therefore, power is the result of strength and speed. This would be expressed as: power = strength x speed (where speed = distance/time).

So while strength and power are clearly related, they differ in the rate at which a force is applied. A real-life example that helps clarify this distinction relates to your ability to grip a tiny hold versus your ability to quickly stick (draw in) a small handhold at the end of a lunge. Figure 5.8 shows hypothetical force–time curves for three climbers. Climber A possesses the strongest grip strength and can hang on the smallest holds, but he is not very powerful. Climber B has less absolute strength than Climber A, but she is more powerful. Consequently, she can summon her strength more quickly (that is, she has greater contact strength), and she will be more successful at throwing dynos and quickly latching on to holds. Climber C is neither strong nor powerful—he'd better stick to climbing slabs.

Obviously, it's ideal to maximize your strength and power, much like Climber B. This can be achieved

Figure 5.8 Rate of Force Production

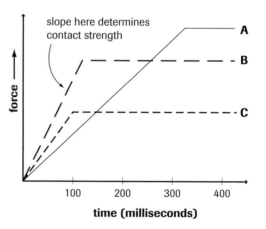

Hypothetical grip strength of three climbers. Climber A has the greatest absolute grip strength, while Climber B has the best contact strength.

by partaking in a variety of exercises that train both strength and power.

Training for Strength

Rate of strength gains, as a result of training, decreases as a function of your current level of strength. Therefore, initial increases in strength will result from even a poorly conceived and executed training regimen. Adaptations in stronger, more advanced climbers occur more slowly—and possibly not at all unless they are using the best training methods. This helps explain why so many intermediate to advanced climbers feel they are no longer getting stronger: For them, further gains require advanced training techniques and the discipline to apply them precisely over a long period of time.

In terms of training maximum strength—your ability to pull a single maximum move or grip a small edge or pocket under full body weight—it is widely accepted by sports scientists that exercising at high intensity and heavy loads is the most important factor. Furthermore, the muscles must be progressively loaded beyond the point to which they are accustomed. In the weight-lifting world, this is achieved by performing five to ten repetitions at some high load, which is increased over time. Unfortunately, this is a difficult protocol to create for the purpose of developing finger strength for climbing. For instance, what do you do to create progressive overload of the fingers (forearm muscles) once you are strong enough to handle your own body weight over steep terrain? The obvious answer is to "climb longer," which is exactly what many climbers do. This strategy, however, develops endurance of strength (anaerobic endurance), not maximum strength.

BOULDERING AS STRENGTH TRAINING

A better strategy is to seek out progressively more strenuous boulder problems that seem to require near-maximum strength. The drawback here relates to the fact that it's very difficult to say if you fell off a move because of muscular failure or because you performed the movement poorly (bad technique).

Further diluting the training effect is the random and shape of handholds, which dictate use of different grip positions—we now know that varying grip position is a good endurance strategy, but it's poor for building maximum grip strength. Consequently, while you may notice some gains in strength and power from bouldering, you can assume that it's not providing you with the greatest strength gains possible. There are just too many variables involved.

Bouldering on a steep artificial wall represents a better format for upper-body strength training, because you can control the size and distance between holds and minimize the technical aspects that might spit you off before muscular failure. Still, there are practical limits to how far you can increase hold spacing and decrease the size of the handholds—beyond a certain point the moves will become overly technical or the tiny holds too painful to climb on. As described above, it's necessary to perform five to ten maximum repetitions before reaching muscular failure (for the purpose of developing maximum strength); in the case of climbing with both hands, you would need to perform ten to twenty total hand movements before failure.

HYPERGRAVITY TRAINING

Once the above strategies have been exhausted for the purpose of developing further gains in maximum grip strength, you need to up the ante by employing hypergravity training. At advanced levels of training for climbing, the importance of training at progressively higher intensity and with heavier loads cannot be overstated. This is best achieved by adding extra weight to your body while performing certain controlled, sport-specific movements. As a result, your fingers (and other upper-body pull muscles) are exposed to a load and intensity not previously experienced at normal body weight. The extra weight simulates a greater-than-normal gravitational pull (hence the name I coined for this technique—*hypergravity*). After a period of hypergravity training, you will return to the rock and feel like you are climbing on the moon!

The dramatic gains in strength produced by hypergravity training are the result of neural and muscular adaptations (discussed earlier). In particular,

'gher degree of disinhibition and
v never result from climbing at
of body weight. I also suspect
...ng may trick ST muscle fibers
...f fiber—more on this later.

...a disclaimer, it must be pointed out that
hypergravity training is an advanced strength-training
method to be used only by well-conditioned and
advanced climbers with no recent history of injury.
Chapter 6 discusses the four best applications of
hypergravity: weighted pull-ups, weighted fingerboard hangs, weighted bouldering, and Hypergravity
Isolation Training (HIT).

FUNCTIONAL ISOMETRICS

Functional isometrics involve superimposing one or
more isometric contractions within the concentric or
eccentric phase of an exercise motion. This strategy
has been shown to provide significantly greater
strength gains (16 percent more in one study) than
those achieved by doing the same exercise without
intermittent isometric contractions (O'Shea 1989).
Greater overload during the isometric contractions is
what stimulates the muscle for enhanced strength
gains. The overload is created by removing the load-
lightening effects of momentum and use of stored
potential energy (a benefit of the elastic properties of
muscle and tendon).

You can best leverage this method when training
to strengthen your pull-up and lock-off strength.
Superimposing numerous lock-offs (isometric contractions) within a set of pull-ups will produce surprising
gains in absolute strength. And unlike hypergravity
training, even novice climbers can safely incorporate
this strategy into their training regimen. The exercise
known as Frenchies (described in Chapter 6) represents an optimal use of functional isometrics.

Power Training

As I discussed earlier, power is the product of strength
and speed as expressed by the equation: power =
strength X speed (where speed = distance/time). Since
you have just learned several leading-edge methods
for increasing strength, we now need to consider ways

to effectively train the other factor in the power equation, speed.

First, you must recognize that there is an inverse
relationship between force and velocity—creating
maximum force, as in high-load strength training, can
only be done at relatively slow speeds (see **Figure
5.9**). Conversely, performing an exercise at high speed
demands use of relatively light weights (low force production). Therefore, you could conclude that there are
a number of effective ways to train maximum power:
Use a high force and low speed, use a low force and
high speed, or use a moderate force and moderate
speed. Research has shown, however, that the latter
method of training—moderate force at a moderate
speed—is best for developing power (Kaneko 1983).

BOULDERING TO TRAIN POWER

No doubt there are some boulder problems that
demand the moderate force production and faster-
than-normal (for climbing), moderate-speed movements required for optimal power training. Unfortunately, the typical boulder problem might only
include one or two such moves, and as such it lacks the
repeated movement ideal for training. This is, again,
where indoor walls are preferable to outdoor boulder-

Figure 5.9 **Force Versus Velocity Curve**

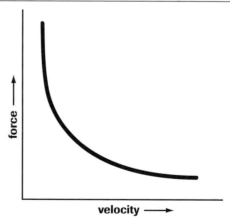

**Creating maximum force, as in high-load strength
training, can be done only at relatively slow speeds.**

ing, since you can design a problem up a steep wall that requires several moderate-force, moderate-speed movements. Power gains realized from this strategy will come primarily to the larger pull muscles of the upper arm and back.

PULL-UP POWER TRAINING

Another good power-training strategy would be to perform pull-ups at a faster-than-normal-rate—but not at ballistic speed. After a thorough warm-up, you would perform these "power pull-ups" in sets of six to ten repetitions, with a change in arm position or spacing for each set. This strategy only works, however, if you are already a moderately strong climber—able to do at least fifteen pull-ups at normal speed. In this case you should try to simulate hypogravity (reduced gravitational force) so that you are executing the correct number of pull-ups at a resistance less than body weight. You can achieve this by using a Gravitron (or some other pull-down machine) or by standing in several loops of thick elastic cord, surgical tubing, or a cut bicycle inner tube.

PLYOMETRIC FINGER TRAINING

Plyometric training involves a dynamic coupling of explosive eccentric and concentric muscular contractions, such as in doing consecutive vertical (leg) jumps without hesitation. First used by Russian athletes in the 1960s, the method was originally applied to climbing by the late Wolfgang Güllich with the advent of campus training. Before we get into this and other types of plyometric training for climbing, let's first look at the unique stimulus (and results) created by these powerful movements.

First, consider that since plyometrics are performed at relatively high velocity, the resistance used (training "load") will be significantly less than in the maximum strength-training exercises above. For this reason, the adaptations that result from plyometric training are primarily neural, not muscular. This explains why plyometric training alone produces little in the way of hypertrophy or gains in maximum strength. Still, the numerous neural adaptations resulting from plyometric training will indeed produce noticeable improvement in your ability to make powerful lunging arm movements or stick (like Climber B in **Figure 5.8**) a fast grab at a difficult handhold.

It should be noted that the dynamic, high-velocity nature of plyometric training makes it one of the most stressful and dangerous training exercises. Impact forces can become dangerously large; injury may result from improper execution or overuse of plyometric training. Fortunately, there are several plyometric exercises—with a range of potential risks (and benefits)—that are applicable to climbing. Campus training is by far the best known (and most dangerous), but Chapter 6 will outline other, somewhat diluted (and safer) methods such as one-arm lunging, one-arm traversing, feet-off climbing, and feet-on campus training.

Anaerobic Endurance (A-E) Training

Anaerobic endurance training is of high importance if your goal is sending difficult rope-length routes or long, sustained boulder problems. Think of A-E as your ability to maintain a high level of strength output over a relatively long period of time. As shown in **Figure 5.4,** true maximum strength output (near 100 percent intensity) can only be sustained for a few fleeting moments. Anaerobic endurance relates to how long the muscle can function above the anaerobic threshold—that is, at a level not far below the absolute maximum. Of course, muscle action above this threshold generates lactic acid faster than the liver can metabolize it. Inevitably, blood lactate concentrations become so high that the working muscle fails or functions only at a much lower aerobic intensity (below the anaerobic threshold).

The goal of A-E training is to produce muscular adaptations that will enable you to climb above the anaerobic threshold for as long as possible. Through repeated exposure, the muscles adapt by developing a higher tolerance to elevated blood lactate, enhanced lactate removal (due to increased capillary density) and metabolism, and other increases in cardiovascular efficiency. If you regularly climb to the point of getting a Hindenburgian forearm pump (muscle failure), you have already acquired some of these adaptations. You can also pat yourself on the back if you sometimes climb several hard routes in a row with only brief rests in between—this is one of the best A-E training methods.

HIGH-REPETITION TRAINING

High-repetition training involves performing a relatively high number of muscular movements at an intensity above the anaerobic threshold. Although the exact level of this threshold varies according to your conditioning, 70 percent of maximum intensity is the average threshold value commonly quoted in scientific literature. In high-repetition training your goal is to climb or exercise for as long as possible at an intensity level above this threshold. Gauging the proper intensity for A-E training is a sense you will develop with practice. As a rule you are training at too high an intensity if muscular failure occurs in less than one minute, whereas your intensity is too low if you are still climbing and feeling good after four or five minutes. Anaerobic endurance training creates a rapid lactic acid buildup and thus represents one of the more uncomfortable, often painful, types of training.

If you don't have access to a climbing wall, you can train A-E in a somewhat sport-specific way using a pull-up bar, fingerboard, or pulldown machine. In each case, you want to reduce the resistance to a level that allows you to exercise for one to three minutes. For the forearm muscles, you might simply try to hang on a pull-up bar or fingerboard for as long as possible. After muscular failure, rest for a minute or two and repeat. Since only a small amount of lactic acid will be removed during the brief rest period, you will find each set more difficult and painful. Repeated long-term training will produce adaptations that transfer favorably to the rock. Similarly, you could perform several sets of high-repetition pulldowns or pull-ups at less than body weight. The goal should be thirty to fifty repetitions at a moderate weight and speed.

INTERVAL TRAINING

Interval training is the gold standard when it comes to A-E training, because it's so similar (specific) to how we climb on hard routes. That is, most difficult climbs (except one-move wonders) feature several sections that will work you pretty hard (high-intensity movements) as well as intermittent sections of easier terrain—and maybe even a couple of rests. In the gym you want to simulate this exact scenario by alternately climbing above your anaerobic threshold for one to three minutes, then backing off and climbing easier moves (recovery period) for one to three minutes. This, in fact, mirrors the way serious runners (and other athletes) perform interval training—runners commonly alternate fast and slow intervals in 100-, 200-, or 400-meter increments. Interval climbing is just another one of the ways we can successfully transfer to climbing the training methodology used in other sports (though more often than not this isn't possible). You will learn several applications of interval training in Chapter 6.

Training Pure Endurance

Pure endurance and maximum strength are at opposite ends of the muscular strength spectrum. Therefore, you cannot optimally train for both maximum strength and maximum endurance—nor can you expect to become excellent at both. Just as no one has ever won an Olympic gold medal in both the 100-meter dash and the marathon, it's highly unlikely we'll ever see a climber who boulders V14 and summits Mount Everest without oxygen. The mental and physiological requirements are just too different.

Chapter 1 introduced the SAID Principle, which explains that training time should be invested in a way most specific to your primary focus in climbing. If your focus is bouldering, sport climbing, or multipitch free climbing, then training maximum strength and anaerobic endurance must be at the center of your fitness-training program, whereas serious alpine climbers would want to spend much of their time training for pure endurance.

It's well known that the best method for developing pure endurance is long, slow distance aerobic training. Applying this method to climbing involves performing a high volume of low- to moderate-intensity exercise lasting at least thirty minutes, though one to two hours is ideal. While climbing many pitches on easy to moderate terrain would produce some stimulus for increasing endurance, this is generally neither practical nor most effective. Developing pure endurance requires numerous adaptations within the cardiovascular system such as increased heart stroke volume, lung capacity, and intramuscular capillary density. In the aggregate these adaptations will improve pure endurance as well as the ability to function at altitude.

In the final analysis, the average rock climber will not benefit from large amounts of endurance training. With the exception of the overweight climber (wanting to lower percentage of body fat), any aerobic activity beyond a few twenty-minute sessions per week would not be advantageous. As stated above, endurance and strength training are opposites, so excessive aerobic training should be viewed as an enemy of anyone pursuing maximum strength.

Complex Training

I'll conclude this section on training methodology by introducing you to the exciting concept of complex training. Complex training represents the leading edge of strength and power training, and it's now in use by elite athletes in numerous sports. Applied to climbing, the complex training protocol described below may represent the most powerful training concept known to climbers at this time.

Complex training involves coupling a high-intensity, low-speed exercise with a moderate-intensity, moderate-speed exercise. Of this pair, the first exercise caters to developing maximum strength, while the second exercise zeros in on developing power. Research has shown that performing these two very different exercises back to back (and in the order of strength first, power second) produces gains in strength and power beyond that achieved by performing either exercise alone. While no studies have been done with climbers, there is compelling research in the use of complex training to increase vertical jump that shows phenomenal gains in absolute ability (Adam, et al., 1992). In this study six weeks of strength training produced a 3.3-centimeter increase in the vertical jump, compared to a 3.8-centimeter increase after six weeks of plyometric (power) training. The group performing complex training (strength and plyometric) for six weeks experienced an incred-

ible 10.7-centimeter increase in jumping ability.

To understand why a coupling of these two exercises produces such a synergistic gain in strength and power, we must examine the unique ways in which the neuromuscular system is stressed. This two-step process begins with high-intensity strength training that excites the muscle to near-maximum motor unit recruitment. The second step takes the already excited muscle and challenges it to function at higher speed. In this way complex training stimulates the muscle fibers in conjunction with the nervous system in such a way that slow-twitch fibers are taught to behave like fast-twitch fibers (Chu 1996). Consequently, complex training could be viewed as the "magic bullet" exercise for the average climber born with an average percentage of fast-twitch fibers (approximately 50 percent).

Incorporating the complex training method into your program could be done in several ways. Remember, the key is a back-to-back coupling of a maximum strength exercise and a power exercise. Intermediate climbers might couple light hypergravity training with dynamic one-arm traversing. Or they could perform a few maximum boulder problems that are really fingery and, upon getting pumped, immediately crank out a few sets of one-arm lunges.

A more advanced protocol would begin with some heavy Hypergravity Isolation Training (HIT), then immediately turn to a few maximum sets on the campus board. This latter strategy of combining HIT and plyometrics should be a staple technique of elite climbers: It may represent the single best training protocol for fulfilling genetic potential in finger strength and upper-body power.

Obviously, complex training is an advanced technique that produces both high passive and active stresses—it should be used only by well-conditioned climbers with no recent history of injury. Furthermore, its use should be limited to once every four days, and it should be cycled on and off about every two weeks. Finally, complete recovery from a complex workout could take as long as three to five days. Any other strenuous training or climbing during the supercompensation period would tend to negate its benefits.

Lisa Rands on White Arete (V7), Ibex, Utah.

PHOTOGRAPH BY
WILLS YOUNG

6

Strength & Conditioning Exercises

What lies behind us and what lies before us are tiny matters compared to what lies within us.

— *Oliver Wendell Holmes*

The previous chapter provided an overview of the principles and methods of strength and fitness training for climbing. With this understanding, we can now take a more purposeful look at the dozens of conditioning exercises that are of value to climbers. Of course, the exercises holding the most value for you are those that target the specific physical weaknesses you identified in Chapter 2's self-assessment test or from your on-the-rock experience.

Another key factor in exercise selection is your current level of fitness and climbing ability. Obviously, novice and moderately out-of-shape climbers would not want to perform the same strength-training exercises as a well-honed climber with a few years of experience on the rock. Similarly, a wickedly strong, elite climber would gain little by performing the same training exercises used by the aforementioned intermediate climber. Therefore, I've graded the exercises in this chapter on an A through C scale similar to that used to classify gymnastics moves.

A exercises are the most basic, and they can be used by all climbers regardless of ability. B exercises are more difficult, requiring both a base level of fitness and a year or more of exposure to the unique stresses of climbing. This period of exposure is crucial for allow-

ing the body to adapt to the sport-specific stresses placed on the fingers, arms, and the joints of the upper body. Finally, the C exercises are for advanced climbers who no longer benefit from performing A and B exercises (though these exercises might be excellent as part of a warm-up or cool-down) *and* who have acquired high levels of mental and technical mastery. For these elite climbers, further gains on the rock demand that they push their absolute level of strength, power, and anaerobic endurance up another notch. This can be achieved only by exposing the body to the "shock" of the high-force, high-stress C exercises.

The format of this chapter is not one that makes for a smooth, entertaining read from beginning to end. Instead, you may want to initially skim through the pages, paying special attention to the type of training and grade of exercise that best matches your ability level (A for beginners, B for accomplished, C for advanced). Then in Chapter 7 you will be guided in developing an effective training program given your current weaknesses, ability level, and available time.

Matching Exercises to Training Goals

When it comes to physical conditioning for climbing, most people are interested in strengthening the all-important pull muscles of the upper body. While many of the exercises in this chapter are central to this theme, there are several other important goals of conditioning for climbing. Chapter 5 introduced you to five such goals, and this chapter will detail at least a few exercises and strategies useful for improving in each of these areas (see **Figure 6.1**).

Optimizing Body Composition

As stated earlier, climbers with less-than-ideal body composition can increase their strength-to-weight ratio most quickly by decreasing weight, not by increasing strength. Knowing your approximate percentage of body fat is the best way to determine if you need to work on this area or if you would be better off placing your training focus elsewhere.

Measuring Your Percentage of Body Fat

Most health clubs and some universities have the equipment necessary to measure your percentage of body fat, so getting your body fat measured may be just a phone call and a few miles away. A study of athletes in a variety of sports reported that males possessed body fat ranging from 4 percent in wrestlers to 8–12 percent in runners and 16 percent in football players, with an elite average of below 12 percent (Wilmore 1983). The same study showed that female athletes possessed body fat between 8 and 25 percent, with an elite average of 15 percent. Therefore, a percentage of body fat near (or slightly below) these elite average levels (12 percent men, 15 percent women) would seem to be a good goal for most climbers.

Figure 6.1 Training Goals

An ideal training program will optimize conditioning in these five areas.

If you are unable to get a professional body fat measurement, you can always employ the highly economical, at-home method—that is, pinch a fold of skin just above your hip. If you can pinch an inch or more (thickness of the fold), you definitely need to drop some body fat. A fold between ½ and 1 inch thick indicates you may be slightly overweight for a climber. If you pinch less than ½ inch of fat, then your body fat is likely at or below the target averages stated above.

In addition to optimizing your percentage of body fat, you should consider the size and location of the muscles you carry. For instance, it is indisputable that possessing hulking leg muscles is as bad or worse for a climber than carrying a spare tire around the waist (especially since muscle weighs more than fat per unit volume). Since the legs muscles are never the weakest link while climbing, you should say good-bye to any training practices that might increase the size of your legs. The same goes for any weight-lifting exercise or practice that produces a bulking-up effect in any other part of the body. This subject has been discussed earlier in the book, but it's worth pointing out again that strength training must be extremely specific in order to transfer to climbing. Squats, heavy bench presses, and other traditional muscle-building exercises are of little benefit for many high-level athletes since they lack absolute specificity (Bell 1989). And for climbers, these exercises may be counterproductive since they will likely result in weight gain.

Strategies for Optimizing Body Composition

Certainly there are genetic limitations to how much you can change your body composition through training and diet. Some people are naturally going to carry a little more body fat; others naturally have a larger frame and bulkier muscles. Still, many novice climbers can improve their body composition significantly in a way that will benefit their climbing. The two key strategies are improved dietary surveillance and increased aerobic training.

Performance nutrition will be discussed in depth in Chapter 8, but for now let me state the obvious—reducing body fat is possible only if you create a net calorie deficit over the course of several days and weeks. Simply put, burning more calories than you consume causes the body to tap into and burn fat reserves. Crash dieting is unhealthy and dangerous, especially for a serious athlete. Instead strive for, at most, a 500-calorie deficit per day. Over the course of a week, this would add up to a 3,500-calorie deficit and equal the loss of one pound of body fat. Surely the bathroom scales will indicate that you've lost more weight, but this additional weight loss is all in the form of water and glycogen. This nonfat weight loss will return next time you eat a surplus of calories that can replenish the muscle glycogen stores.

Your daily calorie deficit is best created by a combination of reduced calorie intake and increased calorie expenditure. For burning fat, nothing beats aerobic activities such as running, biking, and swimming. Given a healthy back and knees, select running as your choice activity since it will not result in muscle hypertrophy (larger muscles) in the legs. Relaxed swimming and biking on relatively flat terrain are the next best alternatives. Unfortunately, mountain biking over rugged terrain is a leg-muscle builder. No matter what you choose, make it your goal to perform a minimum of thirty minutes of sustained moderate-intensity aerobic activity at least four days per week.

If your schedule is too busy to accommodate this two-plus hours of aerobics per week, recent research indicates you can get a similar (and possibly better) fat-burning effect from shorter, high-intensity interval training (King 2001). For instance, after a three-minute slow warm-up jog, alternate a minute of sprinting with a minute of jogging for an additional twelve minutes. This vigorous fifteen minutes of interval training may burn less fat during the actual training than the slow thirty-minute run, but its metabolism-elevating effect will have you burning more calories for the rest of the day. Regardless of your chosen mode of aerobic training, you can maximize the fat-burning effect by doing it first thing in the morning and before eating breakfast.

Upon reaching your desired percentage of body fat, cut back somewhat on the aerobic training and refocus your efforts elsewhere. Slowly reintroduce more calories incrementally and watch your waistline and body weight. The goal is to find a level of calorie consumption equal to your daily energy use and thus maintain a steady body weight.

Summing up: The subject of body composition is most important for sports that require a high strength-to-weight ratio—but it's not everything. Some climbers obsess over minimizing percentage of body fat to the point of starving themselves. A few of these anorexic-looking climbers may climb at an exceedingly high level (due to their finely tuned mental and technical skills), but their malnutrition is certainly holding them back from climbing even harder. We'll talk more about the subject of nutrition and performance in Chapter 8, but it's important to note here that extreme dieting and excessive aerobic activity are not good training strategies for rock climbers.

Flexibility Training

There is little need for extraordinary flexibility in climbing—in fact, some of the best climbers I know are about as flexible as a 4-by-4! While there are, no doubt, a few routes out there that require some extreme stemming or some Cirque du Soleil body contortion, the vast majority of climbs do not. Therefore, the primary goal of stretching is to help prepare the body for training and climbing, and to aid in the recovery process (to be discussed more in Chapter 9). The secondary goal of stretching is to enhance your lower body's range of motion. Still, simply climbing a lot is an excellent active stretch for the lower body and will, over time, produce noticeable gains in functional flexibility (high-stepping and stemming). As for the upper body, some gentle stretching exercises are excellent as warm-up and cool-down activities, but excessive stretching and loose joints may actually open you up to injury.

Detailed below are fourteen stretches that are ideal for fulfilling the above-stated goals. Certainly, there's no need to spend an hour stretching each day; in fact, that could be viewed as a poor use of your training time. Instead, commit to about ten minutes of gentle stretching as part of your warm-up for climbing and strength training. Some additional stretching on rest days may be beneficial, especially if you indeed feel a need to improve your lower-body flexibility.

It's important to point out that stretching as a

Front of shoulders, chest, and biceps.

Finger and Forearm Flexors

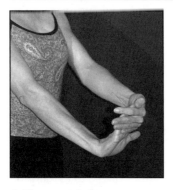

1. Fingers pointing up.

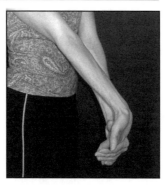

2. Fingers pointing down.

Finger and Forearm Extensors

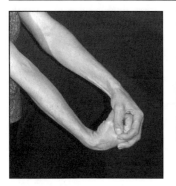

1. Fist pulled inward.

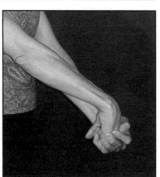

2. Forearm rotated to work the stretch.

warm-up for training and before climbing should always be gentle and nonpainful. While stretching does increase blood flow to the muscles and help them warm up, forceful stretching of a cold muscle could be disastrous. Consequently, it's best to perform some light aerobic or other exercise activity for a few minutes before stretching. For instance, a few minutes of jogging or even some jumping jacks will increase your heart rate and noticeably warm the muscles. When climbing outdoors, the hike to the cliff base often provides the perfect lead-in to your preclimb stretching.

Upper-Body Stretches

FRONT OF SHOULDERS, CHEST, AND BICEPS

Sit on the floor with your arms just behind your hips, elbows straight, palms flat, and fingers pointing back. Slowly walk your hands away from your hips until you feel tension in your chest, shoulders, and biceps. Hold for ten to twenty seconds and repeat.

FINGER AND FOREARM FLEXORS

Before doing this stretch, perform twenty "finger flexors" (quickly open and close your hand as if you were flicking water off your fingers). Now straighten one arm and place the fingers (arm to be stretched) into the palm of the opposite hand. Pull back on the fingers/hand of the straight arm until you feel the stretch begin. Perform this stretch in two positions—fingers up and fingers down. Hold each stretch for ten to fifteen seconds.

FINGER AND FOREARM EXTENSORS

Straighten one arm and make a fist (arm to be stretched). Place the fist in the palm of the other hand and gently pull the fist inward so as to stretch the back of the forearm. Hold the

T R A I N I N G *for* C L I M B I N G

stretch for fifteen to twenty seconds, during which time you rotate your forearm so as to work the stretch with your fisted hand turned upward, inward, and downward. Repeat this stretch two to three times with each arm. It's a vital stretch for preventing elbow tendonitis.

SHOULDERS AND UPPER BACK

Pull your elbow across your chest toward the opposite shoulder. While still pulling, slowly move the elbow up and down to work the complete stretch. Hold for ten to fifteen seconds and repeat.

TRICEPS, SHOULDERS, AND UPPER BACK

With your arms overhead and bent at the elbows, grab one elbow and pull it behind your head until you feel a stretch in your triceps and shoulder. Finish by slowly leaning sideways in the direction of the stretch to extend it below the shoulder and into the back muscles. As with previous stretches, remember to work both sides.

ARMS AND UPPER TORSO

This is a great "finish" stretch because it revisits many of the muscles isolated previously. Begin with your arms overhead, crossed at the wrists, and with palms together, and stretch upward as if reaching for the sky. Repeat several times, moving your hands slightly forward or backward to vary the stretch.

Lower-Body Stretches

The legs, hips, and lower back are areas where many climbers benefit from improved flexibility. While your ultimate degree of flexibility is largely a function of genetics, dedicated daily stretching will produce some gains in functional flexibility. You will need to decide if performing twenty minutes of lower-body stretches is a good use of your training for climbing time (is lack of flexibility holding you

Shoulders and upper back.   *Triceps, shoulders, and upper back.*

Arms and upper torso.

back on the rock?). If so, spend quality time each day working through each stretch using the five-phase procedure described below (adapted from *The Book About Stretching* by Sven Sölveborn).

Phase 1: Wake-up stretch. Perform a gentle stretch with only light tension. There should be no pain involved.

Phase 2: Building stretch. Apply more light tension to the active muscles, but begin to "try" the muscle a bit more than in the first stretch.

Phase 3: Work stretch. Hold steady muscular tension for a few breathing cycles (about twenty to thirty seconds).

Phase 4: Gain stretch. Work the stretch even more. You should feel some discomfort, but not pain. Again, hold each stretch for three to five breaths.

Phase 5: Another gain stretch. Focus on making an advance, even if small, beyond prior sessions.

KNEE TO CHEST

This stretch feels good because it loosens the often tense muscles of the lower back. Pull one knee toward your chest while keeping your other leg straight and flat on the floor. As a variation, you can pull your knee slightly across your body toward the opposite shoulder to stretch the outside of the hip.

WALL SPLIT

This is an easy stretch that is very effective at stretching the legs and groin area. Start with your legs elevated and together, and your butt no more than a few inches away from the wall. Slowly separate your legs—heels resting on the wall—until you feel the stretching begin in your groin. Hold for up to one minute, relax, and repeat. Maintain a flat lower back (not arched) and consider wearing socks to reduce the friction between your heels and the wall.

STRADDLE SPLIT

This one is another good stretch for the groin, hips, and legs. Sit with your legs split in a V position and slowly lean forward. Bend at the hips and keep your spine straight—do not lean forward with your head and shoulders! To stretch one leg at a time, turn to face one foot and bend forward from the hips. Hold each stretch for twenty to thirty seconds.

Knee to chest.

Wall split.

FROGGIES (AKA BUTTERFLY)

Lie on your back with your knees bent and soles of your feet together. Relax and let gravity pull your knees down. Hold for one to two minutes. Keep your spine straight and flat on the floor.

The sitting butterfly is a variation performed in a sitting position with just a *slight* bit of added pressure applied with your elbows. Keep your spine straight, lean forward at your hips, and gently press down on your legs (a few inches above the knee) with your elbows. Perform this stretch with your feet together but at varying distances from your groin. Hold for twenty to thirty seconds.

DOUBLE STAG

Safer than the infamous hurdler's stretch for working the quadriceps muscle. With one knee on the floor, step forward so your forward knee is directly over the foot (the knee should never pass forward of the foot). Now reach back with the hand opposite the rear leg, and pull that foot gently toward your buttocks.

SPINAL TWIST

Sit with one leg flat on the floor and the other bent and crossed over the flat leg. Place the elbow opposite the bent leg on the outside of the bent leg. Turn gently at the hips as if to look over your shoulder. Hold for ten to twenty seconds and repeat. *Note:* Do not force this stretch beyond the point of mild tension.

Straddle split.

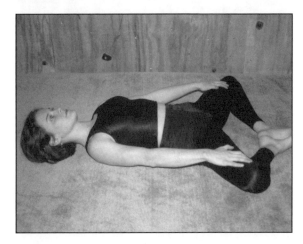

Froggies.

Double stag.

Spinal twist.

ABDOMINAL SEAL STRETCH

Perform this stretch carefully, particularly if you have lower-back problems. Lying flat on your stomach, press your shoulders away from the floor while keeping your legs and pelvis in contact with the floor. Relax and allow the curve of your spine to extend up through your upper back and neck. *Note:* Contract your buttocks to maintain a "grounded" pelvis—this will help reduce the stress placed on your lower back. Hold the stretch for ten to twenty seconds, relax, and repeat.

Abdominal seal.

Calf stretch.

CALF STRETCH

Start on all fours and walk your hands and feet together until the angle formed at your hips is about ninety degrees. Relax one leg, moving it slightly forward while keeping the rear leg straight. Hold the rear heel to the floor and move your hips forward and backward to regulate the tension of the stretch. Hold for twenty to thirty seconds and repeat. Alternatively, you can perform this stretch by leaning forward against a wall or rock face.

Overview of Sport–Specific Strength Training

When it comes to training for climbing, increasing sport-specific strength is what most climbers wish to accomplish. To this end, the following pages will serve up a veritable cornucopia of exercises that will increase your functional strength, power and anaerobic endurance on the rocks. Be forewarned, however, that all the exercises are not for all people. As discussed at the start of the chapter, each exercise is graded on an A, B, or C scale for beginner, accomplished, and elite climbers, respectively. Furthermore, determining which exercises to do on what days is also a matter of your day-to-day training and long-term travel schedule. Suggestions for developing a comprehensive training schedule are forthcoming in Chapter 7.

Finger Positions

Before we get to the actual exercises, it's important to recognize the basic finger positions we use when climbing. According to the Principle of Specificity, gains in strength from training will transfer favorably to climbing only if the exercise is extremely similar in motion, body position, and functional use. Therefore, it would be best to incorporate these finger positions, whenever possible, as you perform the exercises contained in this chapter.

The basic finger grip positions are full crimp, half crimp, open hand, and pinch. Of course, there are many variations of the above positions—for instance, a one-, two-, or three-finger pocket can be gripped with a half-crimp or an open-hand position.

CRIMP GRIP AND HALF-CRIMP GRIP

The full-crimp and half-crimp grips are favored by many climbers, especially beginners. Although this grip feels extremely natural to use, it's the most stressful on the joints and tendons. Orthopedic surgeon Dr. Mark Robinson says, "The crimp grip places high passive (uncontrolled) forces on the first joint of the finger, which in time may result in swelling and even arthritis." He also points out that use of the crimp grip sacrifices the full force potential available in the flexor tendons.

Consequently it would be best to limit your use of this grip to the occasional hold that requires its use (such as small edges, flakes, or incut holds). It's also good not to overuse this grip when training. A limited amount of crimp training (less than one-half of total) is necessary since grip strength is specific to the position of the fingers. The goal would be quality training of the crimp positions while avoiding the most tweaky, painful handholds.

OPEN-HAND GRIP

The open-hand grip, also known as the extended grip, has distinct advantages over the crimp grip. Most important, it's the safest grip due to reduced tendon strain and because the joints receive some support from the rock. Furthermore, the flexor tendon can be used to its full advantage, allowing you to train closer to your absolute maximum grip strength.

This grip is most effective on rounded or sloping holds, and particularly when pulling on pockets. If you're unfamiliar with the open-hand grip, it will feel quite awkward and unlikely at first. But rest assured that your open-hand grip strength will improve markedly with targeted training. As Dr. Robinson points out, "The open-hand grip is so effective that it's also the grip preferred by arboreal apes for locomotion!"

PINCH GRIP

The pinch grip is vital for latching on to protruding holds such as pebbles, rock ribs, or opposing edges. Though used less frequently than the crimp and open-hand grips, the pinch grip is still worthy of training. Possessing viselike crimp grip strength does not guarantee you'll be equally strong on pinch holds. Specificity of training demands you train all grip positions, including a variety of pinches (different widths).

Full-crimp grip (with thumb lock).

Half-crimp grip.

Open-hand grip.

Pinch grip.

Arm Positions and Movements

The three basic arm positions are down pull, undercling, and side pull. As with finger positions, it's advantageous to incorporate the arm positions you actually use in climbing when doing these exercises.

DOWN PULL

Pulling down or locking off on a horizontal handhold results in what's called the down-pull arm movement or position, respectively. This is the most common position and movement in climbing, of course, and it's typified by the arm-bent, elbow-out position.

UNDERCLING PULL

An inverted, downward-facing handhold demands gripping the

Down pull.

Undercling pull.

hold with the palms up (crimp or open hand) and contracting the arm muscles with the arm bent in an elbow-down or elbow-back position. In a fashion opposite to using a down-pull movement, the undercling pull is, in fact, usually released slowly in an eccentric contraction as you move up the rock. Though many of the muscles used seem the same as in the down-pull movement, your level of strength in the undercling position is not directly related to your proficiency in the down-pull position. You must train both positions to be proficient in both.

Side pull.

SIDE PULL AND REVERSE SIDE PULL (AKA GASTON)

The more difficult a climb is, the more likely you'll need to use side pulls. As the name implies, these positions and movements are used to leverage off holds that face primarily to the side, not up or down. Most people are naturally stronger and more comfortable using a standard side pull: Grab a hold off to your left or right and pull inward toward your body. Still, the more difficult reverse side pull must be used on many side-facing edges that are located in front of your body. For instance, imagine a left-facing vertical edge in front of your face. The best use of this hold would often be to grab it with your right hand (thumbs down) and pull outward to the right. This is the classic Gaston move.

Gaston/reverse side pull (right hand).

Finger and Forearm Training

Climbing is obviously very stressful on the joints and tendons of the fingers, so efforts put into training the fingers outside of climbing itself should be designed to limit the additional stress. While *effective, low-stress finger training* could be viewed as an oxymoron, a prudent approach to finger training would incorporate the following strategies.

- Perform a progressive warm-up that gradually builds from easy full-body activity to difficult, sport-specific exercises.

- Make a conscious effort to avoid the most painful and stressful holds (such as sharp, small-radius edges and pockets that feel tweaky).

- Eliminate redundancy by using a few different exercises each session. Don't just train for an hour on a single apparatus (like a fingerboard or campus board) or on one type of problem (such as an overhanging crimp ladder).

- Immediately stop training at the first sign you may be injuring yourself.

- Avoid overtraining and overuse injuries by getting plenty of rest between sessions. A high-intensity workout may require seventy-two hours (or more) of recovery time.

A comprehensive warm-up of the fingers and arms is paramount prior to beginning any serious finger training. A cold muscle, tendon, or ligament can be easily injured, whether training or climbing. Conversely, well-warmed-up tissues are stronger, more flexible, and less inhibited. Begin your warm-up with twenty finger flexion/extensions and some gentle forearm stretching (see "Flexibility Training"). Now perform a couple of minutes of massage on each hand and forearm—this is excellent for increasing circulation in even the most catatonic hands, like mine.

Rest and recovery time is ultimately as important as training time. A full day off is the minimum requirement between intense finger workouts, and as a general rule the fingers should not be seriously weighted more than four days a week. Some elite climbers train fingers on two consecutive days, though this strategy is not recommended for recreational climbers.

As a final note, many of the following exercises involve the use of straight-arm hangs or one-arm lock-offs. Add these exercises gradually, decreasing the number of sets at the first sign of pain in the elbows or shoulders. Beginners should stand in loops of bungee cord or on the edge of a chair (displaced forward) to reduce resistance, while overweight climbers should avoid these exercises entirely. Conversely, advanced climbers may need to progressively add weight to their body (hypergravity training) in order to maintain the proper resistance needed to trigger further strength gains.

Straight-Arm Hangs (A)

Though it's a very basic exercise, novice climbers can find it quite challenging to attempt to hang from a pull-up bar for a minute or two. An untrained forearm muscle will typically begin to burn from lactic acid accumulation after the first minute, making the second minute an exercise in stretching both the physical and mental boundaries. While you would rarely have to hang out on a single hold this long on a route, this exercise does seem to benefit beginner climbers by increasing forearm endurance and through the developed sense of just how long the forearm will perform while in the burning mode. Remember to cease doing these straight-arm hangs at the first sign of any shoulder pain. Persistent hanging in a single position can cause injury in a small number of individuals with loose shoulders as well as in those who are significantly overweight.

There are two possible training strategies for straight-arm hangs performed on a pull-up bar (or the bucket hold of a fingerboard). Many people simply time how long they can hang until muscular failure, then rest for five minutes and repeat for a total of five sets. A better approach would be to employ an interval-training strategy in which you end each interval before reaching muscular failure while decreasing the rest interval. In effect, this will increase the total amount of time you will be hanging and likely produce a better training effect. A true novice would

Straight-arm hang.

want to do brief intervals—say, hang for twenty seconds then rest for forty seconds, and repeat ten to twenty times. As endurance improves, increase the hanging time to approximately one minute, with a one-minute rest. Again, strive for ten to twenty sets. Finally, maintain tension in your shoulders by consciously contracting the muscles surrounding the joint—this will help protect the shoulder from injury.

In the end, this exercise has many limitations as a sport-specific exercise. Beyond the initial months of training, it would be best to progress to some of the more specific exercises described below, such as fingerboard training and bouldering.

Fingertip Pull-Ups (A+)

When I first began climbing in the mid-197 tip pull-ups on a doorjamb were the main form of home training for climbers! All these years later, performing these crimpy pull-ups on ½- to ¾-inch-deep edge is still good for a quick training fix if you have no access to a climbing gym or other equipment. Perform two to three sets of pull-ups using each of the three primary grip positions: full crimp, half crimp, and open hand. You could also perform some straight-arm hangs and Frenchies (as described below). For a rude awakening, attempt a few one-arm fingertip pull-ups a la John Gill!

Training Maximum Grip Strength Using a Fingerboard

Since its advent in the mid-1980s, the fingerboard has become the standard apparatus for performing pull-ups and straight-arm hangs. What's more, the fingerboard is economical (less than $80) and can mount in just about any apartment or home. So if you don't have the space or resources for a home climbing wall, consider a fingerboard mandatory. In fact, even those with home walls find the fingerboard an excellent tool for warm-ups and the many pull-muscle exercises to be discussed later.

The obvious strengths of fingerboard training are its ease of access and the ability to isolate a wide variety of grip positions. Its limitations relate to lack of specificity—other than the way you grip the board, hanging on the board isn't very similar to the way you climb (body position, movement, and the way your forearms and arms contract when climbing). Therefore, the best strategy is to circulate your grip around the board in a manner as similar to climbing as possible. There are a couple of different methods of doing this.

The more fundamental is what I call the grip–relax repeating sequence (GRRS). Consider that it's a good climbing tactic to move quickly through cruxes and to get on and off difficult holds (the grip–relax) as fast as possible. This conserves energy reserves and even allows for brief, but invaluable steps in recovery between each grip. The physiology behind this process relates to the fact that blood flow is occluded (closed off) in a hardworking muscle (that is, during periods of high-intensity contraction) and resumes only when the muscle relaxes. Inevitably, if you have to grip a hold maximally to stick it, then the blood flow in your forearms is occluded and your grip will ultimately fail in a matter of fifteen seconds or less. With brief relax periods between each maximum grip (the few seconds while your other hand grips), however, you can climb on for a surprisingly long time. Top climbers use the GRRS to keep them going and going up the most improbable-looking routes. It's also the secret to effective, low-risk fingerboard training.

Of course, a complete warm-up is imperative. Ideally, perform some light general exercise to elevate your heart rate and muscle temperature. Proceed to crank out a few sets of pull-ups along with gentle stretching of your fingers and upper body. Complete your warm-up with some self-massage of the fingers, forearms, and arms. Finally, consider reinforcing the tendons at the base of your fingers with a few tight turns of tape (especially if you plan to train with added weight), and stop training at the first sign of pain in the joints or tendons.

The best strength-training routine is a series of brief, high-intensity hangs on small- to medium-sized holds. Use one of the two protocols outlined below: repeaters and pyramids.

REPEATERS (B)

Perform five maximum-intensity hangs on the same pair of holds. Each hang should last just three to ten seconds, with just a five-second rest between each hang (hence, the GRRS). Take a one- to two-minute rest upon completing the set of five hangs, then begin another set of five repeaters on a different pair of holds. Train your most problematic grips first, then work successive sets on gradually larger and easier holds as you tire. Also, attempt to order the grip positions trained for maximum variety: for instance, shallow two-finger pocket, small crimp, narrow pinch, small sloper, shallow three-finger pocket, medium crimp, deep two-finger pocket, medium sloper, medi-

um crimp, and large sloper. Working a set of repeaters (five repetitions each) for each of these ten grips would result in a total of fifty near-maximum contractions—a pretty good finger workout! A more advanced climber could take a fifteen-minute rest and then do a second and third series of repeaters.

In training repeaters, it's obviously fundamental that each grip is trained at high intensity. Intermediate to advanced climbers will need to add weight in order to work the muscle at near-maximum intensity. (As a gauge, you need to add weight if you could have maintained a grip on the holds used for more than ten to fifteen seconds.) Start with a five-pound weight belt or a similar amount of weight clipped onto your harness or in a backpack and build toward 20 percent of your body weight over the course of years.

Conversely, less experienced climbers may need to train at body weight or less for the first year or two. Standing in a few loops of thick bungee cord is a popular means of lowering resistance, though "standing" (actually, just weighting a bit with your toes) on the edge of a chair placed a foot or two behind the fingerboard is equally effective. Using the latter method, you can easily vary the resistance by shifting your body weight forward (more on the chair and less on the fingers) or back to a position directly below the board.

PYRAMIDS (B)

Per the Principle of Variation, it's beneficial to vary your fingerboard-training protocol. The pyramid method is one such alternative method of training maximum grip strength. Progress through the full seven-step pyramid using a single set of holds (see **Figure 6.2**). After a one-minute rest, perform another pyramid on a different set of holds. Ideally, you want to work all the primary grip positions (as in doing repeaters) over the course of seven to fifteen full pyramid sets. Limit yourself to only a one-minute rest between sets. Use smaller holds or add weight to your body if this regimen seems less than maximum (the last few steps of each pyramid should be difficult to execute).

Figure 6.2 Fingerboard Pyramid Training

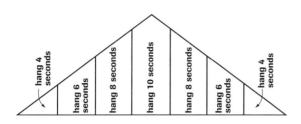

hang 4 seconds | hang 6 seconds | hang 8 seconds | hang 10 seconds | hang 8 seconds | hang 6 seconds | hang 4 seconds

Using the same pair of holds, follow each step precisely with just a five-second rest between each step. That is, hang four seconds, rest five seconds, hang six seconds, rest five seconds, hang eight seconds, and so on.

Endurance Training Using a Fingerboard

There are two main methods of training endurance on a fingerboard: straight-arm hangs and what I call moving hangs. Using comfortable holds, execute the straight-arm hangs exactly as outlined earlier in this chapter. Moving hangs are more effective and certainly less boring, however, so make these the method of choice given your fingerboard setup allows it.

MOVING HANGS (B)

This protocol allows you to work the board continuously for several minutes, much like climbing a long sustained sequence on the rock. Doing this requires somewhere to place your feet while your hands circulate around the board using the grip–relax repeating sequence (GRRS). One possible setup would be to mount your fingerboard so it's set out a foot or two from a wall onto which you mount numerous small footholds. If your fingerboard is mounted above a doorway (quite common), simply place a chair or stool a couple of feet behind the board. "Resting" your feet (actually, use only your toes) on the edge of the chair will simulate the body position of a steep route and allow you to move your hands from hold to hold on the fingerboard.

Either way, develop long sequences of ten to twenty hand movements on difficult holds, then move on to a bucket for a brief shakeout. After a ten- to twenty-second rest, continue moving around the board for another ten to twenty hand movements before taking to another large hold for a rest. Continue in this fashion for a total of three to ten minutes, then take about a ten-minute rest. Repeat the process for a total of three to six sets.

Bouldering (A)

Bouldering is arguably the best all-around training method for climbers, since it can produce improvement in all three areas of the performance triad: physical, technical, and mental. Without the constraints of belaying and placing gear, bouldering allows you to narrow your focus onto the mission of climbing the hardest moves you are capable of doing. Add the camaraderie of a few friends and bouldering becomes one of the most gratifying training and climbing experiences around.

On the flip side, bouldering as training does have some limitations. Obviously, it's difficult to train endurance unless you have a cliff base that you can traverse for long periods. Effective training of maximum finger strength is also quite difficult since the technical difficulties of a given problem may prevent you from pushing your muscles in the way best for developing strength. Finally, the wide range of different finger positions you might use in cranking a boulder problem means it's unlikely you will ever train a single grip position to failure. Of course, most of these flaws can be corrected for when bouldering on an indoor wall. Designing routes to isolate a specific arm position, move, or grip position is the most effective training strategy. This flexibility of being able to set isolation problems is one of the many good reasons for building a home wall.

Clearly, steep boulder problems are excellent for developing upper-body power as well as strengthening the full chain of stabilizing core muscles that translate leverage and force between the hands and feet. For this reason alone, every serious climber should partake in some bouldering on overhanging terrain.

OUTDOOR BOULDERING

As a rule of thumb, consider outdoor bouldering a valid method for training upper-body power, technique, and a variety of mental attributes including tenacity, focus, and the "killer instinct." Begin each bouldering session with a purpose—whether it be to work just a few hard routes (train power and maximum strength), to send a slew of more moderate routes (anaerobic endurance), or to climb specific routes that will train known technical and physical weaknesses (skill practice). Each approach is equally valid, though most climbers go bouldering with the first purpose, of working maximum routes, in mind—these individuals would definitely benefit from greater diversity in their bouldering sessions.

Another key distinction for maximizing the training effect of time spent bouldering outside is to focus on quality over quantity. Beating yourself up with a rapid-fire succession of attempts on a problem or thrashing up a large number of known routes can be counterproductive. With this approach, you won't perform at your best on most routes, you'll tend to hardwire inefficient moves, and you risk getting injured. Instead, force yourself to rest more than you think you need to, and attempt each problem with the goal of putting out your best effort—physically, mentally, and technically. As a rough rule of thumb, rest for three to five minutes between attempts of short bouldering problems (six hand moves or less), five to ten minutes for medium-length problems (seven to fifteen hand movements), and about fifteen minutes or more between attempts at long problems.

Finally, keep the session reasonable in length so as to not dig yourself too deep a hole to recover from (or risk injury). Two to four hours of bouldering (using the above rest guidelines) is plenty, though advanced climbers may benefit from a brief period of additional strength training (heavy pulldowns, some lock-offs, or a few sets on the campus board) afterward.

INDOOR BOULDERING

Bouldering on a home wall or at a commercial gym can be great fun and is arguably more effective for developing finger strength than bouldering outside. As discussed above, it's ideal to design or set indoor routes with a theme that trains a specific grip or arm position. Furthermore, you can vary the length and intensity of the indoor routes to train maximum strength and power (ten to twelve total hand movements) or anaerobic endurance (twenty to forty total movements). In doing so, it's best to set nontechnical routes so that the problem tests mainly your limitations of strength. Furthermore, select handholds that are void of razor edges or other features that might cause injury. Otherwise, apply the same training and rest guidelines outlined above.

System Training (B)

System Training may be the single best nonrock systemic exercise available to climbers. While not quite the best method of training absolute finger strength, it does provide a highly specific workout of the entire body—from the fingers to the toes—that will develop functional strength in the crucial muscles of the arms, upper body, and torso. The efficacy of System Training results from the ability to fatigue a specific combination of grip *and* arm position while performing actual climbing movements up a steep wall. For instance, you can lap a system wall using only the undercling arm position and the open-hand grip position, or you could climb the wall using identical gaston arm positions and half-crimp grip positions. On a well-built system wall, there are many other possibilities.

The base wall for System Training should be at least 6 feet wide, 8 to 10 feet in length, and at angle of between thirty and fifty degrees past vertical. Still, it's the type and arrangement of holds that make System Training work. You need to obtain (or make) a large number of identical holds that can be mounted symmetrically to enable training of all the different finger and arm positions (introduced earlier in this chapter). The best bet would be to purchase eight to twelve system holds that can be mounted in pairs side by side and at shoulder width going up the wall. You could also use matching modular holds or cut different-sized blocks of wood to create a variety of system routes up your wall. Regardless of the hold type, space the identical pairs of holds about 15 to 20 inches apart so you can move up them in a ladderlike sequence. Complete the wall with a variety of small footholds scattered about the wall—again, the ideal setup would possess perfect symmetry of both hand- and footholds.

There are many creative ways to train on a system wall, but the most fundamental is to climb the wall while isolating a specific combination of grip and arm positions. As shown in **Figure 6.3,** there are many possible permutations of grip and arm positions to train. One training strategy would be to do a single set (one up-and-down lap) using each grip–arm couplet. Another strategy would be to do several sets that train a specific grip–arm pair that's either a known weakness or common feature on some project you are working.

In System Training it's important to leverage the knowledge you gained in reading chapter 5. For instance, if you lack anaerobic endurance use larger hand- and footholds that will allow you to lap the system wall a few times (in other words, shoot for twenty to forty total hand movements). To train pure strength, however, you would want to climb on smaller holds and with more difficult arm positions that produce failure in ten to twenty hand moves (five to ten reps with each arm). Rest between sets for at least two to three minutes. Finally, keep a training log in which you detail the exact positions and holds used, the number of reps and sets, and the amount of rest between sets. This will help maintain motivation as well as quantify your strength gains.

Figure 6.3 **System Training Permutations**

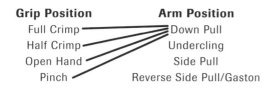

Work up to sixteen permutations of grip and arm positions.

Hypergravity Isolation Training (B/C)

In the mid-1990s I set out to develop the most targeted training method for developing maximum finger strength. Much experimentation with equipment designs and training protocol led to what I call Hypergravity Isolation Training (HIT). While similar to the System Training described above, HIT is more highly refined and better targets the forearm muscles. By removing the training of arm positions (as in System Training) and through the progressive addition of weight, HIT provides the maximum training of grip strength available to climbers.

Hypergravity Isolation Training (note weight belt).

The effectiveness of HIT is a result of its fulfillment of the four fundamental requisites for training maximum grip strength. While the other finger training exercises meet one, two, or three of these requirements, only HIT meets all four.

1. **The exercise must be high intensity throughout the entire set.** In climbing, higher intensity is created by increasing wall angle, decreasing hold size, or increasing hold spacing. Unfortunately, there's a definite limit to how far you can go with each of these. Beyond a certain point, it's more effective to increase intensity by adding weight to your body. Adding just ten pounds can make a huge difference in training intensity on overhanging walls and can yield a leap in finger strength in just a couple of weeks. Interestingly, very few climbers are aware of this fact!

2. **The exercise must produce rapid muscular failure, not failure due to technique.** In the weight-lifting world, muscular failure in five to ten reps is considered ideal (though various texts prescribe slightly different values). This is also valid for climbing, but translates to strenuous climbing with failure in ten to twenty total hand movements (five to ten moves per hand). In climbing, however, there's always the lingering question of whether failure resulted from muscle failure or failure of your technique—in other words, not being able to do a move. Thus, the best exercise for training grip strength would reduce the technical requirements as much as possible and eliminate training of footwork or arm positions (as in System Training).

3. **The exercise must be specific to climbing positions and movements.** The principle of specificity instructs us that strength gains resulting from a certain exercise will be specific to situations involving similar position and movement. The greater the difference between the exercise and sport use, the less the strength will transfer. Thus, the best strength-training exercise for climbing would involve actual climbing movements, whereas an exercise performed while standing or hanging would transfer less.

4. **The exercise must focus on a specific grip position for an entire set.** In climbing, the rock dictates a random use of varying grip positions. Since strength is specific to each grip position, such cycling of grips allows you to climb much longer than if you use the same grip repeated. That's great if you are climbing for performance; for purposes of training grip strength, however, it stinks. That's why a full season of climbing will build endurance but leave you with about the same maximum grip strength as last year. Effective grip-strength training must hammer a specific grip position until failure. Due to the limited transfer of strength from one grip to another, you'll need to train several different grip positions, including open hand, crimp, pinch, and the three two-finger pocket combinations or teams.

To set up a wall for this type of training, use an overhanging bouldering wall of ¾-inch plywood at an angle of forty to fifty degrees past vertical. I prefer fifty degrees past vertical, though HIT can be performed effectively on the common forty-five-degree home wall. Sitting at the base of the wall, mount the first of five HIT Strips at top-of-the-head height. Mount four more strips at 20-inch intervals. Two pinch holds are mounted at shoulder width above each HIT Strip. As an alternative to purchasing HIT strips, you could use ten identical crimper, bucket, pinch, and two-finger pocket holds (forty total holds), though use of HIT Strips may be more economical and effective.

MAXIMUM STRENGTH PROTOCOL (B+/C)

The HIT workout is best used as part of a training cycle or off-season program in which you can dedicate yourself to performing the exact protocols described below. It's vital that you be completely fresh (one to two days' rest since last climbing) before performing the workout; likewise, you must commit to taking a minimum of two days' rest after the workout for the neuromuscular system to recover. It's best to cycle on and off HIT workouts every couple of weeks. For instance, as part of an off-season (winter) program, you might do four HIT workouts over the course of two weeks, then spend two weeks training anaerobic endurance or climbing lots of routes at an indoor facility.

Start with a thirty-minute warm-up comprised of gentle stretching and bouldering of increasing difficulty. The HIT workout trains seven basic grip positions: full crimp, half crimp, pinch, open hand, and the three teams of two-finger grips. Perform one or two sets for each grip position—those new to the HIT workout should begin with one set—beginning with the most difficult grip position for you. Most people work through the grips in this order: pinch, two-finger third team (pinkie and ring fingers), two-finger second team (index and middle fingers), two-finger first team (middle and ring fingers), and full crimp, half crimp, open hand. The entire HIT workout is done with "open feet," meaning that you can place your feet on any holds on the wall.

Sitting below the first HIT Strip, begin by gripping the right-hand pinch hold, then pull up and grab the next higher left-hand pinch hold. Continue climbing with the next higher right-hand pinch hold and the next higher left-hand pinch hold until both hands are on the top two pinch holds. Begin descending immediately, alternating left and right pinch holds back down until you are holding the bottom two pinch holds—but keep going! Continue moving up and down the wall using alternating pinch holds until the grip fails. Upon stepping off the wall, use a stopwatch to time a rest of exactly two minutes before beginning the next set. Meanwhile, record the total number of reps or hand movements in your training notebook.

If you did more than twenty reps, you *must* add weight when training the pinch grip in the future. It's important to remember that doing more than twenty reps (ten hand movements per hand) will train anaerobic endurance, while training maximum grip strength requires adding weight to produce failure in ten or fewer reps per hand. Add five pounds around your waist if you failed at between twenty and twenty-five total reps.

Sample HIT Workouts

Grip to Work	Weight Added* —HIT Novice	Weight Added* —HIT Advanced	Reps**/ Rest Interval
Pinch	None	20 lbs.	20/3 mins.
2-F 3rd team	None	20 lbs.	20/3 mins.
2-F 2nd team	6 lbs.	40 lbs.	20/3 mins.
2-F 1st team	8 lbs.	40 lbs.	20/3 mins.
Full crimp	10 lbs.	40 lbs.	20/3 mins.
Half crimp	10 lbs.	40 lbs.	20/3 mins.
Open hand	14 lbs.	40 lbs.	20/3 mins.

* *Lower weight or stop training at the first sign of tendon or joint pain.*

** *End every set at twenty reps (twenty total hand movements) or failure—whichever comes first. If you reach twenty reps, add weight for the next set and/or next workout. Keep a training log with the details of each HIT workout.*

NOTE: Advanced climbers may want to perform two sets of training with each grip position. HIT Strips are available from Nicros (1–800–699–1975).

HIT Tips

- **Each set must be maximum intensity** and produce failure in twenty hand movements or less. Add weight if you achieve more than twenty reps.

- **No stopping or chalking** during a set. Climb briskly and without hesitation. Consider using a spotter so you can keep moving confidently up to the point of failure.

- **Try to climb through the reps** with normal foot movements and body turns. Smaller footholds are better, but too much thought on footwork will slow you down. Most important, keep the footwork simple—the goal is to train the fingers, not footwork and technique.

- **Rest breaks** between sets must be exactly two minutes. Use a stopwatch and stick to the planned order and schedule of exercises. This way you can quantify and track your finger strength! If you're sloppy on the length of rests, the numbers become meaningless.

- **Keep a training book** in which you log each set, weight added, and reps performed. This way you'll always know what weight you need for a given set and you can easily track your gains (weight and rep increases) from workout to workout.

- **Always do your HIT** in the same order and never increase the number of sets! There will be no added stimulus, and you'll only dig yourself a deeper hole to recover from.

- **Tape your fingers.** This is imperative as the added weight begins to exceed twenty pounds. It will also increase your skin comfort level, allowing you to push the envelope a bit farther. Sand down the HIT Strips or holds if the texture causes pain that prevents you from completing each set to muscular failure.

Otherwise, add ten pounds around your waist for the next set on the pinch grips. To add weight, buy a couple of five- and ten-pound weight belts at your local sports store or, alternatively, use a large fanny pack and add two-pound diver's weights (available at most scuba stores).

After your two-minute rest, proceed immediately with a second set of pinch grips. Climb up and down on the pinch holds in the same fashion as the first set. Upon failure, time another two-minute rest; then move on to the next grip position—probably the two-finger pocket third team.

Begin the next set by using the two-finger third team to grab the two pocket holds on the bottom HIT Strip. As with the pinch grip, climb the pocket holds up and down using exclusively this two-finger pocket team on alternating HIT Strips (or on identically sized and spaced two-finger pockets). Continue to failure, then rest for exactly two minutes before performing the second set with this grip. Record the total number of hand movements as well as the amount of weight added, if any.

After completing the second set of this two-finger team, move on to the next grip position. Continue executing the HIT workout through the remaining grip positions while taking just a two-minute rest between each set. It's vital that you limit the rest to exactly two minutes, and record the number of hand movements and the weight used (if any) for each grip and set. This information will guide your next HIT workout, and I guarantee the records will quantify gains in your grip strength in the sessions that follow!

This completes your HIT workout, though you

may wish to do a few sets of weighted pull-ups or some lock-off exercises to complete strength training of your upper body. As a cool-down, do ten minutes of light bouldering. You will likely need two or three days of quality rest and sound nutrition in order to supercompensate to a newfound level of maximum grip strength.

ANAEROBIC ENDURANCE (A-E) PROTOCOL (B)

HIT Strips are equally effective as part of your anaerobic endurance training (endurance of grip strength), though you will need to execute and track your workout according to a different protocol. This time, you heighten the training load not by adding weight but by increasing the number of reps (hand movements).

In doing an A-E HIT workout, the goal is to climb up and down the HIT Strips using a single grip position for a total of thirty to fifty hand movements. Once again, time a rest of exactly two minutes between sets. Begin with the weakest grip (usually pinch) and perform two sets of thirty to fifty reps for each of the seven grip positions discussed above. In A-E training the goal is not muscular failure, but instead to take the muscles in and out of the anaerobic energy mode in an interval-training fashion.

Again, it's fundamental that you track your A-E HIT workout on paper. Record in a notebook the number of reps (total hand movements) performed in each of the fourteen sets. Upon completion of all the grip positions, perform any supplemental training of the larger pull muscles (pull-up and lock-off exercises), then wrap up your workout with a good cool-down of light bouldering and stretching.

One-Arm Lunging and One-Arm Deadpoint Traversing (B)

In Chapter 5, I explained that plyometric training results in beneficial neural adaptations that don't result from normal static (isometric) finger training or climbing. Therefore, the inclusion of some form of plyometric training would be beneficial for intermediate and advanced climbers. The three best methods of

One-Arm Lunging

1. Pull inward and lunge upward.

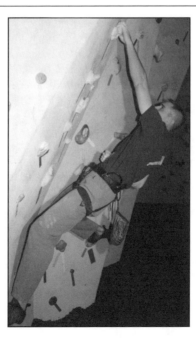

2. Catch the high hold.

3. Drop back down to starting hold, catching with elbow slightly bent.

Strength & Conditioning Exercises

plyometric exercise for climbers are one-arm lunging, one-arm deadpoint traversing, and campus training (to be discussed later).

Controlled one-arm lunging and deadpointing are ideal ice-breaker exercises for climbers wishing to add some plyometric training to their routines. Both exercises can be executed on a vertical to slightly overhanging (harder) modular wall, as found in all climbing gyms. In both cases one-arm movements end with a dynamic catch that "shocks" the forearm muscles. Unlike campus training, which is commonly done sans feet, this form of plyometric exercise is more controlled and less stressful. The strength gains you can achieve through this form of "plyometric light" training are limited, however—beyond a certain point you will need to graduate to campus training in order to stimulate further gains.

ONE-ARM "DEADPOINT" TRAVERSING (B)

This exercise requires a vertical indoor wall with enough room available to traverse up to 20 feet using medium- to large-sized holds. The goal here is to traverse the wall by lunging from hold to hold using only one hand. It's important that you perform controlled, low-stress lunges by using your arms and torso to initiate the dyno and then catching the next hold with a slight bend in your elbow. This drawing in of the body allows you to make a quick grab at the next hold while upward momentum briefly reduces your load—this is commonly called a deadpoint move. Attempt to traverse for a total of eight to twelve deadpoint movements, then take a three-minute rest. Perform two to four such traverses with each arm as a supplement to your other grip-strength training.

A word of warning: Shoulder and elbow injuries could result if you consistently catch the dynos with a straight arm. You can vastly reduce the risk of injury by making small lunges of about 1 foot, and by striving to catch each lunge with a slight bend in your elbow.

ONE-ARM LUNGING (B)

Once you are proficient at one-arm traverses on vertical walls, you can proceed to one-arm up-and-down lunges on a slightly overhanging wall. This exercise is also done feet-on, but the steeper angle creates greater dynamic force, especially on the downward catch. This extra stress is good if you are attempting to stimulate further neuromuscular adaptations. Still, this strategy clearly increases the stress on all components of the fingers and arms—proceed with caution.

Perform the one-arm lunges on a section of wall that overhangs between five and fifteen degrees past vertical. Arrange the modular holds so there are two small footholds to stand on (just 1 foot or so off the ground) and two nontweaky medium-sized holds, one in front of your face and the other about 2 feet above that. Execute the up-and-down lunges in a manner similar to the one-arm traversing discussed above. While standing on the two small footholds, draw your body upward and inward and lunge up to the top hold. Immediately drop back down to the starting hold and, without pause, explode back up to the top hold. Continue lunging one-armed and with fixed feet for a total of eight to twelve reps. Rest for three minutes, then proceed with the next set. Do just two to four sets per arm.

Keep in mind that this plyometric training will not result in the vicious forearm pump you are used to getting from bouldering, System Training, and such. Plyometric training stresses the nervous system and is fueled by the ATP-CP energy system. Therefore, the signs of fatigue are much less obvious. Don't make the mistake of doing more sets because "it didn't feel like the exercise was that fatiguing." The prescribed sets provide plenty of stimulation, so move on to the next portion of your workout.

Campus Board Training

Campus board training is fundamental for advanced climbers specializing in bouldering or sport climbing. No matter how naturally strong you are or how hard or often you climb, I speculate that you can quickly add another 10 percent (or more) to your contact strength and power with just a few weeks of campus training. Of course, such a gain is significant and may equate to a one-time, one- or two-letter or V-grade increase in climbing ability.

As explained in Chapter 5, the neurological adaptations of such plyometric training result from the explosive forces placed on the muscles. Unfortunately, the explosive forces are also placed on the joints and tendons, so too much campus training too soon can be disastrous. Therefore, it's important that you abide by the following guidelines.

- Engage in campus training only if you are an advanced climber (able to lead 5.12 or boulder V7) with at least two years of sport-specific training under your belt, and no recent history of finger or arm injuries.

- Warm up thoroughly; this should include about thirty minutes of progressively more difficult bouldering. Consider reinforcing the base of your fingers with a few tight turns of ½-inch athletic tape.

- Emphasize quality over quantity. Five quality sets on the campus board is better than ten sloppy, poorly executed sets. Remember, campus training is only a small portion of a good strength-training workout—don't treat it like it's the only method of training for climbing.

- Do not campus train while in a state of high fatigue—it's vital to maintain good technique and high-quality execution (for instance, not catching with completely straight arms).

- End the training session immediately upon any sign of joint or tendon pain.

- Rest a minimum of two days after a serious campus training workout. Limit yourself to two modest-length sessions per week, and cycle two weeks on and two weeks off.

You will need to build a campus board separate from your home climbing wall, or talk the owner of your local gym into building a campus board if there isn't one already. At home you'll likely be able to only build a modest-sized board if you have standard-height ceilings. Since the bottom of the board needs to be around 4 feet off the floor, you'll be limited as to the number of rungs you can mount. The plywood board onto which you mount the rungs should be angled at precisely fifteen degrees past vertical. Make or purchase rungs that range in depth from ¾ inch to 1½ inches. Mount small rungs about 6 to 8 inches apart; the largest rungs are best spaced about 8 to 12 inches apart. I'd advise you purchase campus rungs from one of the indoor training companies—these rungs are quite affordable, and most companies will provide you with detailed construction plans.

The three primary campus training exercises are laddering, lock-offs, and double dynos. Gradually introduce yourself to this new training method over the course of a few months. Begin with laddering during the initial session and progress to lock-offs and double dynos as your strength, confidence, and comfort allows.

LADDERING (AKA CAMPUSING) (B+)

Just as the name implies, this most basic exercise involves climbing no-feet up the board in a ladder climbing motion—on the rocks, this no-feet lunging from one hold to the next is often called campusing. If you are strong enough, you can also descend the board no-feet with controlled eccentric contractions.

The goal is to ladder up rungs spaced as far apart as possible. To help quantify your training, it helps to number the rungs from bottom to top. You might initially ladder up rungs 1-2-3-4-5, but progress to a more powerful 1-3-5-7 sequence. Most campus boards feature separate numbering of three different-sized rungs: small, medium, and large. As a rule, laddering on the smallest rungs tends to train contact (finger) strength more than upper-body power, whereas long lunges between the deepest rungs isolate more on developing upper-body power. Rest for three to five minutes before performing your next set on the board.

As emphasized above, quality of training is more important than quantity. A reasonable number of sets is anywhere from five to fifteen, according to your experience with campus training. As a final note, if you have a steep home wall but no campus board, you can campus up the home wall from hold to hold just as you would on a campus board. This method of campusing can be highly effective as long as you grab well-rounded, nonpainful holds.

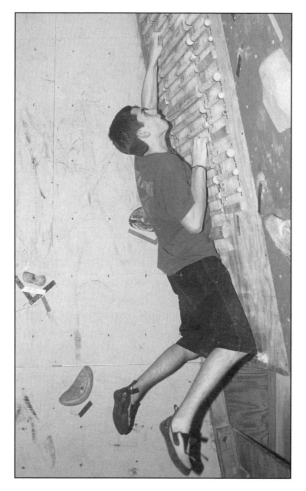

Laddering.

LOCK-OFFS (AKA TOUCHES) (B+)

This exercise combines the training stress of the lock-off arm position with a dynamic catch of the fingers. Begin by hanging on a lower rung of the board. Pull up with both hands to the lock-off position, then with one hand reach up as high as possible and touch (or grab) a rung. Hold the lock-off for a few seconds, then drop back down to the starting hold and return to a hanging position. Immediately pull back up to the lock-off position and reach up with your opposite hand. Again, hold the lock for a few seconds before dropping back down to the hang. Continue in this alternating fashion

for up to twelve total touches. Ideal form would be a solid static lock-off at the top positions but only an instant of pause at the bottom position before launching back up with the next touch. Rest for three to five minutes between sets.

As you become more advanced at campus training, progress to performing a few lock-off sets with just two fingers of each hand. Eventually you may even become strong enough to do this drill with one finger of each hand—as did Wolfgang Güllich in training for *Action Directe*. Regardless of the grip used, limit yourself to five to fifteen total sets.

DOUBLE DYNOS (C)

This exercise is the highly impressive dynamic-up, dynamic-down, double-hand campus training that's been featured in numerous videos. While not quite as difficult as it first appears, this explosive exercise is extremely stressful and best left to elite climbers.

Begin by hanging straight-armed from rung number 3 or 4. Let go with both hands simultaneously, dropping down to catch a lower rung and immediately explode back up to the starting rung. Without hesitation, drop down again, catch, and explode back up. Continue in this fashion until you fail to make one of the catches. Depending on the size of the rungs used, you may achieve anywhere from one to ten drop-down-and-explode-up reps (one full cycle). Rest for five minutes before considering another set.

As you become competent at this double-dyno campus training, you can move to the smaller rungs, or increase the distance of flight between the top and bottom rung used. As with the previous methods, it's useful to record in a notebook the number of reps and sets performed as well as the rung size and number used.

As a final note, the dynamic nature of this final exercise dictates use of the open-hand grip. Therefore, it would be best to do a few sets of lock-off campus training with different grips combined with a few sets of the double dynos. This will provide a more comprehensive upper-body workout.

Heavy Finger Rolls (B+)

Todd Skinner turned me on to this exercise back around

Double Dynos

1. Drop down from high rung. *2. Catch a lower rung.* *3. Explode back up to starting position.*

1990, and I've since become a true believer. Muscular gains from this exercise are reasonably quick and obvious, and they seem to translate fairly well to climbing despite the obvious lack of specificity to climbing. Todd credits these finger rolls for some of his most significant gains in finger strength since he first picked up on this exercise from a couple of Soviet climbers he met on the World Cup circuit in 1987. Interestingly, this exercise has been performed and advocated by Gunks hardman Dr. Mark Robinson since the early 1980s!

The Soviet climbers claimed that heavy finger rolls produce measurable gains in forearm circumference (a sign of muscle hypertrophy), whereas strength gains from fingerboard or campus training are prima-

rily the result of neurological adaptations. This statement seems reasonable, because the heavy finger rolls cause repeated, high-intensity eccentric and concentric contractions of the forearm muscles. Therefore, pairing up heavy finger rolls with plyometric training (campus training) could produce the synergistic gains that have been show to result from the complex training method discussed in Chapter 5.

Performing these heavy finger rolls is quite simple and requires twenty to thirty minutes. You will need access to a set of free weights and a bench-press bar with ball-bearing sleeves—maybe the only good reason for a climber to join a health club. A squat rack is also useful as a spotter.

Strength & Conditioning Exercises

93

The body position for this exercise is critical to reduce strain on the lower back, elbows, and wrists. Stand with good posture and hold the bar (palms away) in front of your thighs. Focus on keeping a slight bend at your knees, elbows, and waist. The motion of the finger curl is only the few inches from the open-hand position to the closed-hand position. Ideally you want to lower the bar as far as possible without it falling from your hand. I've found the squat rack quite handy in acting as a catcher in case I drop the bar; it's worth the effort to kick the muscleheads off the rack so you can work the full range of motion.

As far as weight is concerned, it must be *heavy!* Maximum strength training demands the use of an appropriately heavy weight that only allows you three to ten very intense repetitions. While finger rolls with a "light" weight (such as thirty- or forty-pound dumbbells) may pump you up, they are ineffective for developing maximum finger strength. After a warm-up set with the bar weighted to about 50 percent of your body weight, the goal is six heavy sets with a good rest of three to five minutes between sets. A weight about equal to your body weight is a good first guess for a working weight. Add more weight if you can do more than six reps, or remove weight if you can't do six sets of at least three repetitions. With practice, you should be able to build to 150 percent of body weight.

A few other suggestions: Never train the heavy finger rolls more than twice a week and, in accordance with the Principle of Variation, cycle on and off this exercise every few weeks. Also, tape the base of your fingers and consider placing a few turns of 1½-inch tape around your wrist when your working weight is greater than your body weight. Focus on keeping your wrists nearly straight throughout—you are *not* doing wrist curls. Finally, take a week or two off at the first sign of any pain in your finger tendons or wrist.

Pull-Up and Lock-Off Training

The standard pull-up has long been a staple exercise for climbers. Several sets of pull-ups performed a few days a week will provide most climbers with a base level of pull-muscle strength needed to learn all the basic climbing techniques. Beyond a certain interme-

diate level of difficulty, however, climbing requires more specific forms of strength such as the ability to lock off a handhold (to make a long reach) or make a quick, powerful upward movement. The standard pull-up falls far short of being able to build such specialized strength.

For example, we all know climbers who can knock off a decent number of pull-ups (say, greater than fifteen or twenty) but cannot regularly knock off 5.10s or 5.11s! Although poor technique may be part of the problem, many lack static strength in a variety of lock-off positions as well as the dynamic strength needed to power up hard moves on steep terrain. Consequently, if you can pass the "fifteen pull-up test" you will benefit little by drubbing yourself with more pull-ups. Instead, you need to engage in more targeted training of the pull muscles.

Before we dive into the details of the pull-muscle exercises, it important to reconsider what is, in fact, your weakest link on the rock. Surely pull-up power and lock-off strength are vital, but many climbers fail due to poor technique and mental control or even because their grip strength is below par. If any of this sounds familiar, then your training time will be better invested elsewhere.

Pull-Ups and Lat Pull-Downs (A/B)

As alluded to above, this most obvious exercise for climbers is very useful for beginners but next to worthless for enhancing the capabilities of an elite climber. If you are unable to do a single set of fifteen pull-ups, then you should continue training with them about three days per week. Still, there are a few strategies you can leverage to enhance the gains that result from this training. In fact, I believe most novice climbers can learn to do fifteen pull-ups in less than one year of training, given they use the following techniques.

- Perform your pull-up training on a pull-up bar or the bucket hold on a fingerboard. The initial goal is to train the pull muscles, not the fingers. Train only in the palms-away position (the way you usually grip the rock) and with your hands initially at shoulder width. Begin by doing five sets to failure, with a three-minute rest between sets. Three days per week is optimal. If you are climbing during the week, perform your pull-ups at the end of the climbing day, not on a rest day.

- If you are unable to do five consecutive pull-ups, employ one of these two powerful strategies. Place a chair below the pull-up bar and step up into a lock-off position with the bar just below your chin. Remove your feet from the chair and hold the lock-off for five seconds before lowering yourself down (eccentric training) to a slow five-second count. Immediately step back up on the chair to the top lock-off position and repeat the process exactly. Do five total repetitions, then rest for five minutes. Perform two to three total sets. The second strategy is to simply have a spotter hold you around the waist and lift a portion of your body weight so that you can do eight to ten repetitions. Do three sets in this manner with a five-minute rest in between. Dedicate to using these strategies three days per week, and you'll be shocked at how fast your pull-up ability improves.

Your long-term goal is to be able to crank out five sets of ten to fifteen repetitions with three to five minutes of rest in between. When you reach this goal, you will need to begin adding weight around your waist (begin with a ten-pound weight belt) or use a lat-pulldown machine at a health club. In using a pull-down machine, use a weight heavy enough to produce failure in between six and twelve reps. Do five total sets with three minutes' rest in between.

Eventually, you'll find that doing the same pull-up training becomes monotonous and provides little additional gain in climbing strength. At this point it's best to employ one of the following variations to the pull-up, or even cut back on pull-ups and replace the pull-muscle training with other exercises described on the pages that follow.

PULL-UP INTERVALS (A)

This exercise is designed to accustom the pull muscles to working during periods of high blood acidity (low pH). On long, sustained climbs, lactic acid buildup increases blood acidity, partially contributing to the burn and tightness you feel prior to complete muscu-

lar failure. Each pull-up interval is a minute long (use a stopwatch to time exactly) and consists of a number of pull-ups in a row to start the minute, followed by a rest and shakeout for the remainder of that minute.

Start with a set of four pull-ups (this will take about ten seconds), then jump down and rest for the next fifty seconds. When that minute is up, start the next set of four pull-ups, followed by a rest for the remainder. Continue in this fashion until you can no longer do the prescribed number of pull-ups. If you make it to twenty minutes—eighty total pull-ups—then increase the sets to five reps at your next workout.

THIRTY-SECOND PULL-UPS (A)

These are regular pull-ups performed in slow motion. Take ten seconds to go up, and come down to a slow count of twenty. Continue until you can't perform the exercise according to these guidelines. Do one to three sets.

POWER PULL-UPS (B)

Execute a normal pull-up motion, but explode on the up phase (pull up as fast as possible), then lower to a slow three-second count. You do not want to perform this exercise to failure. Instead, shoot for six to eight quality repetitions. Do one to three sets.

HEAVY PULL-DOWNS (A+)

Performing this exercise requires use of a standard health club pull-down machine. It will take a little experimentation at first, but the goal is to determine a weight that limits you to a maximum of six repetitions. If you are in really good shape, this may require loading approximately 150 percent of your body weight. Execute the pulldowns palms-away and crank out three to ten high-intensity reps. Rest for three minutes and do three to five total sets.

FRENCHIES (A+)

These babies are the single best anaerobic endurance pull-muscle exercise on the planet! Not only will they fry your muscles with a wicked lactic acid burn, but you will notice a marked improvement in your pull-up and lock-off ability after just a few weeks of doing them. The efficacy of this exercise results from the unique combination of isometric contractions superimposed over the pull-up motion.

Begin with a single pull-up (palms away, hands shoulder width apart) and lock off in the top position for a five-second count. Now lower to the bottom and pull up to the top again—but, this time immediately lower halfway down to an arm angle of ninety degrees. Hold a solid lock-off here for a five-count, then lower to the bottom. Immediately crank another pull-up, but this time lower to a lock-off with an arm angle of about 120 degrees. Again, hold for five seconds and lower to the bottom position. This sequence of three lock-offs constitutes a single cycle, but you should continue on with another cycle (or more) until you reach complete failure. Record the number of cycles (or partial cycles) in your training notebook as you take a five-minute rest. Do a total of two or three sets.

Use bungee cords or a spotter to remove some body weight if you cannot do at least two full cycles per set. Conversely, you should add a ten- or twenty-pound weight belt once you are able to do five full cycles in any given set.

Uneven-Grip Pull-Ups (B)

This is an excellent exercise for developing vicious one-arm strength and lock-off ability. Train with uneven-grip pull-ups long enough and you'll eventually develop a solid one-arm pull-up.

Execute the pull-up motion with one hand on the bar (or a fingerboard bucket hold) and the other holding on to a towel looped over the bar (or with two or three fingers through a loop of webbing) anywhere from 6 to 24 inches below your high hand. Of course, both hands pull, but the upper hand is emphasized— the greater the separation between hands, the more the upper hand is emphasized. Rest for two minutes after the first set, then switch hands to train the opposite side. Perform three sets on each side with the goal of four to eight reps per set. Increase the vertical distance between your hands if you can do more than ten reps; decrease the distance if you cannot do at least four repetitions. Do this exercise twice per week in place of other pull-up exercises.

Steep-Wall Lock-Off (B)

This exercise is highly functional in that the strength gains will transfer completely to the rock. Although you will perform this exercise on an overhanging bouldering wall, the goal is not to actually climb a problem. Instead, you will be performing repeated one-arm lock-offs while using the same hand- and footholds. This is very similar to the lock-off exercise described in the "Campus Board" section, except that you are doing it with your feet on the wall. This way, you can turn and tense your body as needed to facilitate a solid, efficient lock-off position. Such extreme specificity is what makes for the high level of transfer to the rock.

Execute this exercise on an overhanging wall that's between thirty and fifty degrees past vertical. Begin in a sitting position below the wall and grab on to two similar starting holds. A well-rounded incut edge or a deep two- or three-finger pocket will suffice, though the holds on HIT Strips or system holds are ideal. Place your feet on any two holds on the kickboard at the base of the wall. Pull up on the handholds and lock off on, say, your right hand. Allow your body to twist and tense as needed to make the lock-off most solid. Reach up with your opposite hand and touch the highest hold possible—do not grab the high hold, but instead allow your lock-off hand to hold the position alone for a five-second count. Lower down and grab back on with your left hand, but immediately pull back up and lock off again with the same hand for another five-count. Strive for four to eight complete repetitions before your muscles fail. If this is not possible, use larger hand- and footholds or a less steep wall.

Rest for one minute—just long enough to catch your breath and chalk up—then repeat this lock-off exercise with the other hand. Upon completing the second set, rest for five minutes before repeating the process with the first hand. The goal is three to five sets on both sides. This is a strenuous exercise that is best performed at the end of a bouldering session.

One-Arm Lock-Off (B+)

This is a popular advanced exercise that transfers quite well to hard bouldering and sport climbing (especially the static strength developed from one-arm lock-offs).

One-arm lock-off.

As a general rule, however, you should not train the one-arm lock-off exercise unless your one-set maximum number of pull-ups is at least twenty. These lock-offs can be performed on a pull-up bar, fingerboard (use a bucket hold), or free-hanging rings or Pump Rocks. The three variations described below are in order of difficulty. Cycle on and off these lock-off exercises every few weeks. In the long term these exercises enable many climbers to develop a solid one-arm pull-up.

PALMS INWARD (B+)

Begin with a regular chin-up (palms toward you). Lock off completely at the top on one arm, and let go with the other. Hold the lock-off with your chin above the bar as long as you can, all the while focusing on "pulling the bar to your armpit." The goal is to hold a solid lock position for twenty seconds. When you begin to lose the lock, either grab back on with your other hand or lower slowly (tougher, but worthwhile). Be

careful not to drop yourself rapidly into the straight-arm position! Dismount and gather yourself briefly, then do the other arm. Perform three to five sets for each side with about two minutes of rest in between.

If you can't hold the lock-off for at least five seconds, aid yourself by holding on with one finger of the other hand or by standing in a few loops of thick bungee cord. In a short time you will be holding a true one-arm lock-off for ten to fifteen seconds! Advanced climbers may find it necessary to add weight around the waist in order to produce failure in less than fifteen seconds.

PALMS AWAY (B+)

Perform these exactly as described above except with your palms facing away (pull-up position). You will find this to be harder, but it's more sport specific and useful when climbing. Perform three to five sets for each side with about two minutes of rest in between.

ARM ANGLES (B+)

This final variation involves performing the lock-offs below the bar at arm angles of about 45, 90, and 120 degrees. Pull up with two arms until you reach the desired angle. Let go with one hand and hold static as long as possible. These are very difficult and should be done only when you can perform a solid lock-off in the top position. Do two to three lock-offs in each of the three positions with a rest of two minutes between each lock-off. Conclude with two lock-offs in the top position (palms away).

Bachar Ladder and Rope Climbing (B+)

John Gill developed his awesome upper-body power largely through training on a 1½-inch gym climbing rope. Years later John Bachar developed an overhanging rope ladder that provided a similar workout, but its palms-away hand position provided greater specificity to climbing. For much of the 1970s and 1980s, the Bachar Ladder was a backbone exercise for high-end climbers. With the advent of the fingerboard and indoor climbing gyms, however, the ladder has fallen somewhat out of favor. Still, a well-conditioned climber can benefit from an occasional session on a Bachar Ladder or gym rope.

The author on his Bachar Ladder, late 1980s.

Both apparatuses are climbed feet-off, so a high level of fitness is needed to partake in these exercises. After a lengthy warm-up of pull-ups and upper-body stretching, the goal is to climb hand-over-hand up the ladder or climbing rope. Upon reaching the top, downclimb with slow, smooth eccentric contractions. The training goal is five to ten full laps with a rest of three to five minutes between each lap. As with all the training described on the previous pages, emphasize quality over quantity. Two good laps with solid lock-offs and slow eccentric contractions are better than four laps done sloppily and with dangerous dynamic drops during the down phase.

Only use Bachar Ladders constructed with static line rope. The springy nature of a ladder made with dynamic rope may lead to elbow tendonitis.

Training the Core Muscles

In climbing vertical to overhanging rock, the core mus-

cles of your torso play a key role in enabling your arms and legs to maximize leverage and transfer torque from hand to foot and vice versa. Many beginner and intermediate climbers making their initial forays on steep terrain find good-looking holds more difficult and pumpy to use and modest-length reaches feeling surprisingly long. The root of these difficulties is probably a complex blend of poor technique and insufficient strength in both the arms (obviously, they are the ones getting pumped up!) and, less noticeably, the torso.

As you might expect, one good way to strengthen these core stabilizer muscles is by climbing frequently on steep terrain. If your specialty is climbing overhanging routes or if you regularly boulder on steep cavelike routes, chances are you've already developed a high degree of strength in these muscles (though you could probably still benefit from additional conditioning). If you are new to climbing, however, or if you have previously climbed mainly vertical to less-than-vertical routes, you would likely benefit significantly from some targeted training of these core muscles.

Two "tricks" first popularized in climbing by John Gill are the gold standard of core-muscle strength. The front lever and straight-arm flag both require steely muscles of the torso. If you can do these two tricks, then your training time is better spent on areas other than the stabilizing muscles of the torso. Otherwise, employ a blend of bouldering and traversing on steep walls and executing the five isolation exercises described below.

To best target these muscles in bouldering, you want to force these stabilizers to work extra hard by purposefully eliminating certain body positions and holds. For instance, when climbing straight out a cavelike overhang, use a straight-on neutral position that disallows drop-knee and hip-turn moves. While this is clearly a bad strategy for style points, it does a better job of targeting the core muscles for the purpose of training. Upon reaching the top of the cave, downclimb the wall in the same style—downclimbing steep terrain is the single best method of bringing the core muscles into serious play. A final wall-training strategy is to traverse a slight overhanging wall with your hands high above your head while keeping your feet low. You will quick-

Side Hip Raise

1. Start in the straight-arm position.

2. Droop hip toward the floor.

Upper–Trunk Extension

1. Lie face-down on floor.

2. Raise chest and head.

ly feel the core muscles coming into play as you strain to prevent your body from sagging away from the wall.

In addition to these on-the-wall training methods, you can perform the following exercises twice per week at the conclusion of your climbing workout.

Side Hip Raise (A)

Lie on your side on the floor and press up into a straight-arm position until your body forms the hypotenuse of a triangle with the floor. Keeping your arm straight, droop your hip toward the floor until it touches, then immediately straighten your body out and return to the starting position. Repeat this process of lowering and raising the hips ten to fifteen times

(hard). Perform two sets on each side with a rest of a minute between sets.

Back Extension (A)

Some health clubs possess excellent back-extension machines that allow safe, effective training of the lower-back muscles. Otherwise, you can work all the important muscles of the lower back by performing two floor exercises known as the upper-trunk extension and aquaman.

UPPER-TRUNK EXTENSION (A)

Lie facedown on the floor with your legs spread about shoulder width apart and your arms by your sides.

1. Lie face-down on floor with arms extended overhead.

2. Raise one arm and opposite leg to provide tension.

Slowly raise your chest and head slightly off the floor, pull your shoulder blades back, and continue to raise your trunk up as far as possible without any spinal discomfort. Hold for a moment, then return to the starting position. Perform ten slow repetitions. Rest for a minute or two, then do a second set. Be sure to keep your neck relaxed and your pelvis pressed firmly against the floor throughout the range of motion.

AQUAMAN (A)

Lie facedown on the floor with your arms extended overhead. Begin with one arm and the opposite leg raised slightly off the ground to provide tension. Slowly raise the opposite arm and leg straight up while keeping your chest and pelvis in firm contact with the floor. Raise them upward as far as possible, hold for a moment, and then return to the starting position. Repeat with the other arm and leg, and continue for five to eight repetitions on each side. Avoid rotating or twisting your body throughout the range of motion.

Hanging Knee Lift (A)

This is a strenuous (but good!) exercise that works the lower abdominals, hip flexors, and serratus muscles on the side of your torso. Hang from a pull-up bar or the bucket holds of a fingerboard and lift your knees up to your chest. Lower them slowly until they return to a slightly bent position (not straight) and immediately begin the next upward repetition. It's important

to maintain some tension in your shoulders and concentrate on the feeling of a stiff upper body while your abs are contracting and lifting the knees to the chest. To work the serratus muscles, lift your knees on the right and left side every few reps. The goal is to build up to two sets of twenty repetitions.

Abdominal Crunch (A)

These are best done lying on the floor with your feet up on a chair and knees bent at ninety degrees. Cross your arms over your upper chest or place your hands on the sides of your head (harder). Now lift your shoulders off the ground and exhale as you "crunch" upward. The goal is to lift your upper back off the floor but not to ascend the whole way (as you would in an old-school sit-up). Continue for twenty-five to fifty repetitions, then rest for approximately two minutes. Ultimately, the goal is three sets of fifty repetitions; beyond this point it's debatable whether or not any additional crunches will benefit your climbing. As mentioned repeatedly throughout this book, you must constantly evaluate whether your training for climbing time could be better spent elsewhere.

Front Lever (B/C)

Gripping a pull-up bar or a set of free-floating rings (harder), simultaneously tense and raise your body to a position parallel to the floor; hold for three to five seconds. As you will see, this is an extremely difficult

Hanging Knee Lift

1. Hang from a pull-up bar or fingerboard.

2. Lift your knees up to your chest.

Abdominal Crunch

1. Lie on the floor with your feet on a chair and your arms crossed over your upper chest.

2. Lift your shoulders off the ground and crunch upward.

Front Lever

Begin training the front lever with bent leg (slightly easier). Graduate to levers with both legs held straight.

gymnastics move; you can make it somewhat easier, however, by bending one leg and drawing it in toward the center of your body. If you still can't hold the lever for three seconds, have a spotter help out by lifting at your heels. Perform a total of five levers with a rest of a minute between each.

Training the Antagonist Muscles

If you climb regularly, especially on the steep routes that are in vogue today, it's essential to engage in modest training of the antagonist muscles. Consider that the pull muscles—the prime movers when climbing—get a good workout every time you touch the rock, while the opposing push muscles perform much less work at only a fraction of the intensity. In the long term a growing muscular imbalance can lead to a variety of injuries, particularly in the elbows and shoulders.

As common as injuries are in this sport, it surprises me that so few climbers commit to regular training of the antagonist muscles of the shoulders, chest, and back of the forearm (finger/hand extensors). The time commitment is minimal, and the exer-

cises themselves are not that difficult. Bottom line: It takes only a little extra effort to maintain enough muscle balance to help stave off some of the common injuries that might otherwise be in your future.

There are some basic guidelines to follow in effectively training the push muscles for climbing, however. First, you only need to perform isolation exercises of these muscles for fifteen to twenty minutes, twice per week. Furthermore, you must avoid the tendency to go overboard with your antagonist-muscle training—the goal is to tone the muscles with moderate-intensity exercise, not to build large bulky muscles with a bodybuilder's "workout from hell."

Hand and Forearm Muscles

The musculature of the forearms is some of the most complex in the body. Climbing works these muscles in a very specific way that, over time, can result in tendonitis on either the inside or outside of your elbow (more on these injuries in Chapter 10). While chronic under-resting or even working the same type of move excessively may inevitably result in these

T R A I N I N G *for* C L I M B I N G

1. Rest forearm on your knee with palm down, wrist straight.

2. Curl wrist upward.

injuries, the two exercises below are a pretty good insurance policy.

REVERSE WRIST CURL

Using a five- to twenty-pound dumbbell, perform these wrist curls palms-down and with your forearm resting on your knee, a bench, or table. Do approximately twenty half repetitions; that is, beginning with your hand in the neutral position (wrist straight), curl the dumbbell upward to the top position, hold it there for two seconds, and lower it back down to the starting position (wrist straight). Do two to three sets of this exercise twice per week, preferably at the end of your climbing or training for climbing. Always per-

form the forearm stretches described earlier in the chapter before engaging in this exercise.

FOREARM ROTATION (AKA HAND PRONATOR)

There are numerous exercise machines and devices that work hand pronation, though they are hard to find. Do you belong to a gym or club that possesses such a machine? If not, don't fret—you can make a simple forearm trainer to leave lying around your home gym for use as part of your warm-up and cool-down. Cut a 12-inch piece of 1-inch-diameter dowel, or purchase a blank dumbbell bar. Mount a few one-pound weights on one end (two or three 1¼-pound York barbell weights are ideal), and you're in business.

1. Bend arm at a ninety-degree angle and prop elbow against your leg.

2. Turn hand back and forth from the thumb-in position to the thumb-out position.

Perform the exercise sitting down with your arm bent at a ninety-degree angle and your elbow propped against your leg. Hold the nonweighted end of the bar in this hand and turn your hand back and forth from the thumb-in position to the thumb-out position. Continue twisting your wrist back and forth for twenty to twenty-five repetitions. Perform two sets twice per workout; in fact, it may be best to perform two sets at the beginning and end of every climbing workout. Vary the resistance by either adding weight or moving your hand farther down the stick (away from the weighted end).

Training the Large Push Muscles

These exercises are equally vital for maintaining balance in the stabilizing muscles of the shoulders and upper torso. The three exercises described below will go a long way toward maintaining the necessary balance and, hopefully, the health of your shoulders through many years of rigorous climbing. If you have

an existing shoulder problem, these exercises may help mitigate the pain and prevent further injury. Still, it would be best to see a doctor or physical therapist for guidance specific to your affliction.

While the following exercises can all be performed on standard health equipment (Cybex, free weights, and so forth), I would not advise that you buy a club membership just to gain access to the necessary machinery. Instead, a one-time investment in a few dumbbells (less than $50) is all you need. Alternatively, you might ask the climbing gym you patronize to purchase a few dumbbells for the purpose of training the antagonist muscles of the forearms and upper torso.

SHOULDER PRESS

Using two dumbbells or a health club machine, perform two to three sets of twenty to twenty-five reps, twice per week. Total resistance should be limited to between 20 and 40 percent of your body weight. If you plan to purchase dumbbells, I'd suggest that

Shoulder press.

Push-ups. Move hands closer together to increase difficulty.

women purchase two ten- or fifteen-pounders and men purchase twenty- or thirty-pounders—there is no reason to go much heavier.

PUSH-UPS/BENCH PRESS

Perform two to three sets of standard push-ups, twice per week. The goal is twenty to twenty-five push-ups per set. If you can do more than twenty-five reps, increase the difficulty by moving your hands closer together. If you have access to a bench-press machine, follow the same guidelines as in doing the shoulder press. Keep the total weight below about 40 percent of your body weight—go much heavier and you risk

adding unnecessary muscle mass that will only weigh you down on the rocks.

DIPS/CHAIR DIPS/STAIR DIPS

Dips are an excellent exercise for strengthening the many muscles of the upper arm, shoulders, chest, and back. Of course, the motion is somewhat similar to that of pressing out a mantel on the rock, so you have

Chair Dips

1. Holding on to the seat of a chair, extend legs.

2. Bend elbows and dip your body down below the seat of the chair. Lower until upper arms are parallel with the floor.

double the reason to perform this exercise twice per week. Most health clubs have a parallel-bar setup ideal for performing dips. As a similar alternative, you may be able to position two heavy chairs or even use an incut ninety-degree corner of a kitchen counter to perform your dips. A final option is simply to use a chair or set of stairs positioned directly behind your hips to press out a behind-the-back dip.

As in the previous exercise, strive for two to three sets of about twenty repetitions, twice per week. This amount may seem improbable if you haven't done this exercise before. If you religiously train dips twice per week, however, you will experience rapid improvement. In the meantime, employ a spotter to help lift around your waist (reduce body weight) so you can achieve at least ten dips per set.

Aerobic Training

The most common forms of rock climbing require only ordinary aerobic fitness; big walls and mountaineering, however, clearly demand higher aerobic capacity. While detailing a complete training program for mountaineers is beyond the scope of this book, I will provide some basic guidelines for aerobic training.

Goals of Aerobic Training

As stated near the start of this chapter, optimizing body composition is a first-tier issue for rock climbers. Excessive body fat is a major liability for aspiring rock jocks, and a moderate amount of aerobic training along with improved dietary surveillance will produce noticeable improvements in this area. Also, a modest amount of aerobic training will enable you to climb longer at low to medium intensity and enhance your body's ability to remove lactic acid from the working muscles. The result is faster recovery while shaking out at a midclimb rest or between attempts.

Still, I do not advise a large volume of aerobic training for most climbers. Consider that simply climbing a lot produces some positive adaptations of the cardiovascular system; in fact, it has been shown that high-intensity anaerobic endurance exercise produces significant improvement in aerobic capacity.

Therefore, if you regularly climb to the point of being winded, you are training in a way that has the secondary effect of strengthening the heart-lung system.

Obviously, this method of training will not produce the level of adaptations needed to excel in alpine climbing. Chapter 1 introduced you to the SAID Principle that compels you to target your training on the type of climbing that is most important to you. If that's bouldering or sport climbing, excessive aerobic training will be counterproductive. If big walls or alpine climbing is your focus, though, regular high-volume aerobic activity is highly beneficial. The cardiovascular system clearly plays a more primary role when rock climbing at high altitude; thus, improving aerobic capacity should be a top training goal.

Strategies for Boulder, Sport, and Multipitch Climbers

Upon achieving optimal body composition, only limited aerobic exercise is suggested. The high levels of strength and power required for these climbing activities demand targeted training of the most common weakest link—the muscles of the forearms and upper body.

Fundamentally, high-volume aerobic training could be viewed as the enemy of strength and power training of the upper body. Not only would it divert time you could invest more effectively—say, in bouldering—but regular high-mileage aerobic activity results in systemic fatigue that may prevent you from training and climbing up to your potential. Furthermore, excessive aerobic training has a catabolic effect on the muscles of the upper body: that is, the body begins to metabolize muscle during long training sessions. For proof of this, you only need to look at the upper bodies of long-distance runners—they typically look like string beans (albeit string beans who could kick my butt in a marathon!).

Bottom line: If your ultimate training goal is to maximize upper-body strength and power, anything more than about three, fifteen- to thirty-minute runs (or other similar activity) per week would not be advantageous.

Strategies for Big-wall and Alpine Climbers

Obviously, these activities demand all-day or multiday endurance far more than they do fingers of steel. If this type of climbing is your cup of tea, your training should be specific to these demands. The two best training strategies here are high-volume climbing and high-volume aerobic exercise.

If you have the rock resources nearby, then no training could be more specific than chalking up many long days on the rock. You could do this in the form of climbing as many routes as possible from sunrise to sunset at a cragging area or by racing up a grade IV or V big-wall route in a day.

Otherwise, you'll need to persevere through sixty to ninety minutes of aerobic training, five days per week. Running, mountain biking, and trail running are the best activities, and you should strive for mileage over speed. As your conditioning improves, consider stepping up your workout to between forty-five minutes and an hour, twice a day. This is clearly an advanced aerobic training program, but it might be just the ticket in the weeks leading up to a long wall climb or high-altitude expedition.

Ian Spencer-Green* on Scarface *(5.11c),* *Indian Creek, Utah.

PHOTOGRAPH BY

STEWART GREEN

7

Personal Training Programs

Action without thought is a form of insanity; thought without action is a crime.

—*Albert Einstein*

For much of the twentieth century, the American climbing scene was dominated by eccentric, alternative types who, as a rule, rejected conventional styles of living and recreation. While this renegade bunch pushed the limits of difficulty and boldness on the rock, they were hardly of a mind-set that would consider doing any supplemental training (other than drinking!). In fact, the handful of individuals who did train, outside of climbing itself, were viewed with amusement and even called "cheaters" by a few traditionalists.

This all changed in the 1980s and 1990s as climbing went mainstream. Supplemental training just seemed natural to the large number of individuals entering climbing with backgrounds in other sports. At the same time, a growing number of elite climbers trained fervently while pushing the envelope of difficulty on the rocks. Suddenly the masses of climbers "got it"—there was indeed a causal connection between sport-specific training and climbing ability! Of course, John Gill exemplified this way back in the 1950s.

Today most serious climbers perform supplemental training, and tens of thousands of beginner and intermediate climbers are enamored of the idea of training to climb harder. Commercial climbing gyms

have opened in almost every major city, and home bouldering walls are the latest rage. Consequently, there is a greater need than ever for average climbers to follow a purposeful training program that will maximize their gains in ability while minimizing the chance of injury. This, of course, is the purpose of this chapter—to help you craft an effective training program given your current fitness level and climbing ability.

Keys to an Effective Training Program

The premise of this book is that a well-informed, motivated, and mature individual can grow to climb at an exceedingly high level in just a few years. The preceding chapters provided a comprehensive look at the fundamental elements of climbing performance—mental, technical, and physical—and you've also been armed with the knowledge of an introspective self-assessment test. You are now in a position to design and execute an uncommonly effective training program—one that will help you outperform the masses!

Premeditate Your Training

The mass of people who engage in some form of conditioning program do so in a haphazard, ad lib manner. There is little or no method to their madness other than to "climb a lot" and "get pumped." This unsystematic approach will produce mediocre results and can often end in injury.

Conversely, well-informed climbers are proactive in designing and modifying their training program for maximum effectiveness. Wisely, the program targets their weaknesses, is modified regularly to stave off

109

mental or physical stagnation, and is crafted in a way to produce a peaking effect for an upcoming road trip or competition.

TARGET YOUR WEAKNESSES

Several times throughout this book, I've highlighted the importance of training the weakest link. For many climbers this weakest link involves poor technique, tactics, and mental control. While the unintelligent climber trains only for more physical strength, you know that it's paramount to train your weaknesses in all aspects of the performance triad. The amount of time you dedicate to training technique, the mind, and physical strength depends on both the results of your self-assessment and your current ability level.

As a rough rule of thumb, beginner and intermediate climbers should focus about 70 percent of their training time on improving technique, tactics, and the mental game. For these climbers, only 30 percent of their training time should be invested in general and sport-specific conditioning. Conversely, elite climbers (who possess highly honed technical skills) would be wise to invest much more training time in the pursuit of maximum strength and power.

MANIPULATE THE WORKOUT TO "CONFUSE" THE BODY AND INCREASE MOTIVATION

Chapter 5 explained the importance of regularly modifying your training for climbing. Sadly, many individuals go through the same basic workout ritual week after week and get frustrated with their lack of progress. Furthermore, engaging the same weekday training or weekend at the crags will slowly quell your motivation to work hard and push beyond your current limits.

Clearly, an intelligently designed program must regularly vary the focus of your training and climbing. In the gym it's vital to vary the fundamental details of workout intensity, volume, length, and the amount of rest between sets (or climbs). On the rock motivation and achievement often come in proportion to your willingness to try new types of climbing, visit new areas, and test the limits of what is possible (given your current ability). Later in this chapter you will learn how to use a ten-week mesocycle and fifty-two-

week macrocycle to optimize the effectiveness of your training for climbing program.

PRODUCE A PEAKING EFFECT FOR A ROAD TRIP OR COMPETITION

Olympic and professional athletes design their training schedules to produce a peaking phase around the time of a major event or competition. No doubt some of the best competition climbers also use peaking strategies; I sense, however, that the vast majority of climbers do not deliberately plan their training in order to produce a peaking effect.

Really, it's not that difficult to structure your workout schedule to elevate yourself to peak form for a personal-best (hardest-ever) route or annual road trip. If you currently train and climb a few days per week, you're already doing the hardest part. All that's required now is to manipulate the intensity, volume, and rest frequency according to certain guidelines, and then track your progress in a training notebook. Details on all the above are forthcoming.

Structuring Your Workout Schedule

In this chapter you will learn to manipulate your workout schedule over the time frame of several days, a few weeks or months, and a full year in order to gain optimal results. In the lexicon of sport scientists, these crucial time frames are known as the microcycle, mesocycle, and macrocycle, respectively.

MICROCYCLE

The structure, content, and quality of your training over the course of a given week is the most important factor in determining the effectiveness of your program. Since it is in the microcycle where you choose what to train and how much to train (or rest), this is the most fundamentally important part of your workout schedule.

Many climbers' programs are flawed from the get-go, because they incorrectly prioritize their training during the course of a single workout or week. Maximizing effectiveness requires training the right things in the right way *and* in the right order. Hopefully, you gained a sense of the optimal workout hierarchy in reading the previous chapters. After a complete warm-up, the best order of training is:

1. Skill, strategy, and the mind

2. Maximum strength and power

3. Anaerobic endurance

4. Antagonist-muscle and general conditioning

5. Cardiovascular and general endurance

Certainly you can't effectively train all five of these areas every day. Instead, you must develop a list of short-term goals and an overall mission that narrows the focus of your actions in the microcycle. Whether you plan to train in two, three, or four of these areas, it's vital that you execute the training in accordance to this hierarchy. For instance, a beginner who plans to work on skill and strategy training as well as perform some general conditioning exercises would do so in that order. Similarly, an advanced climber might boulder to train skill and the mind, then proceed to training maximum strength and power via some targeted exercise. Working out in conflict with this hierarchy will severely compromise the quality of your training and results.

- **Planning Adequate Rest:** There are two crucial rest phases within the microcycle: rest between exercises (or climbs) and rest between workouts. For the enthusiastic climber, it's quite easy to fall into the trap of under-resting—between climbs *and* between workouts. Therefore, it would be prudent to rest more than you want or think you need.

  The length of rest taken between individual exercises and sets plays a primary role in the training stimulus. Rest periods of less than a minute or two (between climbs or exercises) result in high blood lactate concentrations and thus train anaerobic endurance (that is, endurance of strength). This mode is the hallmark of the highly effective interval-training strategy covered in Chapters 5 and 6. Conversely, resting longer than two minutes between sets allows for greater recovery and, therefore, higher quality and intensity of training. Longer rests are best used when training technique (new skills) or maximum strength.

The optimal amount of rest between workouts is more difficult to gauge. Depending on the intensity of training, it could take anywhere from twenty-four to seventy-two hours or more to fully recover and benefit from the training stimulus. Low-intensity general exercise or easy climbing that produces little muscle soreness can be done up to five or six days per week. The highest-intensity training (complex or hypergravity training), however, might require up to ninety-six hours for full supercompensation, limiting workouts to twice per week. Chances are, you will be training somewhere in between these extremes, so three or four days of training/climbing may be ideal for you.

MESOCYCLE

The Principle of Variation states that you must regularly vary your workouts in order to avoid long-term training plateaus, and it's in the mesocycle that you can best manipulate your schedule toward this end.

In terms of strength training, it's most effective to change focus every one to, at most, four weeks. The goal is to cycle the focus of your training from endurance, to maximum strength and power, to anaerobic endurance, every few weeks. The 4-3-2-1 training cycle is an ideal application of principle.

- **The 4-3-2-1 Training Cycle:** The 4-3-2-1 training cycle is what I advise for most non-novice and nonelite climbers. The phases of this cycle are: four weeks of climbing-endurance training, three weeks of maximum strength and power training, two weeks of anaerobic endurance training, and one week of rest (see **Figure 7.1**).

  The four-week climbing-endurance phase involves, well, climbing a lot! This climbing can be done indoors, outdoors, or as a combination of both. You must, however, faithfully obey a vital distinction of this phase—that is, not to climb maximally, but instead log lots of mileage on a wide variety of routes and at several different areas. The result of this four-week phase will be improved technique and tactics, acquisition of new schemas (climbing skills), and the development of local endurance in

Figure 7.1 The 4-3-2-1 Training Cycle

4 weeks of
endurance
climbing

3 weeks of
maximum power
and strength

2 weeks of
anaerobic
endurance

1 week
of rest

the arms, upper body, and torso. Climbing four days a week is ideal as long as you are not climbing at your limit or to extreme levels of fatigue.

Three weeks of maximum strength and power training is the next stop in the cycle, and Chapters 5 and 6 detail numerous methods you can employ. Of course, hard bouldering, hypergravity training, campus training, and complex training are excellent choices during this period, with maximum intensity, maximum speed, and maximum effort being the hallmark of this phase. Consequently, you will want to take more rest between boulder problems, exercises, and workout days. It would also be best to not train on consecutive days. One day on, one day off, or one day on, two days off, is optimal during this training phase. Therefore, your total commitment to training and climbing will be just two or three days per week.

The two-week anaerobic endurance phase is the most fatiguing and painful portion of the cycle. Training at moderately high intensity and with reduced rest between exercises or climbing sets will result in a vicious pump and lactic acid burn that tests the mettle of your mind and body. Interval training is the cornerstone method of developing anaerobic endurance (A-E). The common practice of climbing as many hard routes as possible in, say, a ninety-minute gym workout (essentially, ninety-minutes of interval training!) is, in fact, pure A-E training. Unfortunately, many climbers overuse this method and end up injured or on a training

plateau. The A-E training stimulus during this two-week phase should be applied in a one-day-on, two-days-off (accomplished climbers) or two-days-on, two-days-off (elite climbers) stratagem.

The final phase of the ten-week cycle is simply seven days away from climbing or climbing-specific training. Begin with a day or two of complete rest, then add in some active-rest activities (see page 143) for the rest of the week, if you like. This week off is as important as any other week in the cycle, because it allows both your physical strength and motivation to rebuild to new heights. It also allows your technical climbing ability to reach a new peak thanks to the proven phenomenon of reminiscence.

The Reminiscence Effect relates to the common experience of skill sport athletes when their intuitive feel and technical execution peak after a period away from training or competition. A week or two off every few months is all it takes to benefit from this "less is more" effect. Upon returning to the rock, you will feel more relaxed, automatic, and natural as your body remembers (reminisces) the well-learned motor skills. Of course, you will also be more physically and mentally fresh after a week off from training—this makes for the perfect time to begin a road trip or launch into a new training cycle.

- **The 3-2-1 Training Cycle:** Since the elite climber possesses highly refined technical skills and a voluminous library of schemas, there is much less to be gained during the four-week volume-climbing phase of the 4-3-2-1 cycle. For these 5.12-and-above climbers, gaining the next higher level of maximum strength, power, and anaerobic endurance is key to unlocking the higher grades. Of course, at these lofty levels tiny technical flaws or even invisible cracks in mental focus can bring you down in a nanosecond—no climber should ever take on the closed-minded attitude that more strength is the end-all answer to climbing harder. Pursue your weakness (physical, mental, or technical) vigilantly.

With that said, the very best climbers need to spend a disproportionate amount of time training maximum strength and power over technique or endurance. In using the 3-2-1 training cycle, you simply follow the second, third, and fourth phases of the 4-3-2-1 cycle: Train maximum strength for three weeks, anaerobic endurance for two weeks, followed by a week of rest (see **Figure 7.2**).

MACROCYCLE (LARGE FIFTY-TWO-WEEK TABLE)

The macrocycle relates to your annual game plan of off-season training, on-season training and climbing, and off-season breaks away from climbing. In traditional sports the macrocycle is planned around the competitive calendar, with the goal of peaking for a major competition. In our sport, however, the idea is to plan your training to produce a peaking effect for a major road trip or the best climbing season (weather-wise) in your region.

You can loosely map the macrocycle on a calendar by identifying the months of your on-season road trips or competitions, the months you expect to perform off-season training, and any downtime you plan to take during the year. Note that downtime is vital for recharging your motivation and healing any known

Figure 7.2 The 3-2-1 Training Cycle

1 week of rest → 3 weeks of maximum power and strength → 2 weeks of anaerobic exercise

(or unknown) injuries that have likely developed during the course of a long climbing season. For many climbers, taking the month of December off makes the most sense and offers the nice reward of holiday parties after a year of dedicated training and tight dietary surveillance.

Figure 7.3 depicts a typical macrocycle. Note that a few 4-3-2-1 training cycles are fit into the off-season training period, along with a couple more during the

Figure 7.3 Sample Macrocycle

Name/Year	Training Objectives and Seasonal Climbing Goals			
Gordon Sumner 2002	Build strength and power for PR ascents this season.	Peak for road trip in late June.	Perform quality training cycle to prepare for fall season.	Finish season with more PR redpoints. Climb a 5.12c.

Month	Jan	Feb	Mar	Apr	May	Jun	Jul	Aug	Sep	Oct	Nov	Dec

Week: 1 2 3 4 5 6 7 8 9 10 11 12 13 14 15 16 17 18 19 20 21 22 23 24 25 26 27 28 29 30 31 32 33 34 35 36 37 38 39 40 41 42 43 44 45 46 47 48 49 50 51 52

Training Focus:
- Climbing/endurance: XXXX · · · XX · · · · · · XXX XXXX · · · XXXXXX XXX
- Max. strength and power: XXX · XXX XX · · XXX · XX
- Anaerobic endurance: XX · XX XX · XX
- Rest: X · X · X XX · X · X · XXXX

Total number of days per week of finger training or climbing (scale 1–7)

Benchmark achievements and notes:
- Record # of pull-ups—25!
- Redpointed 5.12a in gym.
- Awesome HIT workouts! up to 20 lbs....
- Feel good on weekend trips to New River.
- Killer road trip sent hardest route ever!
- Begin a new 4-3-2-1 cycle.
- Climbed 5 straight.
- Weekends, too many sends to list!
- Still climbing, but weather is getting cold....
- Month off! Relax!!!

midseason. The fall months are targeted as the peaking period, followed by a month off to conclude the year. A blank fifty-two-week macrocycle is contained in Appendix A for your use.

Targeting Training on Your Preferred Subdiscipline

In Chapter 1 you learned the importance of obeying the SAID Principle (specific adaptation to imposed demands) in optimizing your training for your favorite subdiscipline of climbing. **Figure 1.7** on page 11 depicts how the demands of these subdisciplines vary over a continuum from bouldering to alpine climbing. Maximizing the effectiveness of your training requires targeting your workouts accordingly.

The vast majority of climbers reading this book participate in the three subdisciplines of bouldering, sport climbing, and multipitch climbing, and this text is obviously focused on helping these climbers improve their performance. Still, big-wall and alpine climbers should be able to glean plenty of useful information. For instance, in accordance with the SAID Principle, a serious alpine climber would benefit much more from high-volume endurance StairMaster training and trail running than from bouldering on a home wall or hanging on a fingerboard. Of course, the most specific and effective training for big-wall and alpine climbers is simply doing *lots* of submaximum climbing.

Conversely, building a home wall or joining an indoor gym is the single biggest advantage that boulder, sport, or multipitch climbers could give themselves. Beyond this investment, the time these climbers spend training or on the rock should mimic the performance demands of their preferred focus. Boulderers should dedicate more of their mesocycle to maximum strength and power training, while multi-pitch climbers would want to spend many more weeks of the mesocycle on training anaerobic endurance and local endurance (as in the 4-3-2-1 training cycle). Sport climbers possessing a high degree of technical skill, however, would do best to cycle their focus back and forth between maximum strength/power and anaerobic endurance. As they become more advanced, the 3-2-1 training cycle described above would be ideal.

Clearly, the best training program for you will change over time as your technical ability and your physical strengths and weaknesses change. For this reason, active self-coaching, with regular self-assessments and goal setting, is critical in maintaining a successful training program. The time invested in plotting your program intelligently (copy the blank macrocycle chart in Appendix A) and striving to stay on course over the long term will pay huge dividends in how far and how fast you progress in this sport. Furthermore, if you sense you lack the self-analysis skills and intuition needed to effectively modify your program over time, I strongly suggest you employ a personal climbing coach to help guide your training.

IMPORTANCE OF A HOME WALL OR GYM MEMBERSHIP

Regardless of your ability, nothing beats indoor climbing for year-round and time-efficient sport-specific training. Therefore, having access to an indoor climbing wall is paramount for rock climbers serious about improving their ability.

Hopefully, there is a good commercial facility within a reasonable distance of your home or workplace. If so, join the gym and use it at least twice per week—this is the number one thing you can do to improve your climbing ability and climbing-specific fitness. Many of us, however, are not so fortunate (the nearest good climbing gym to my home is almost an hour away), so it's vital to invest in a home wall in place of that gym membership.

If your space is tight, simply build an 8-foot by 8-foot forty-five-degree overhanging wall. While this setup has obvious limitations (physical and mental), it will enable you to get an excellent upper-body workout as well as help improve your sense of climbing movement and body position. If a larger space is available, it would be wise to construct a roof section and a slightly overhanging (ten to twenty-five degrees past vertical) traverse wall in addition to the forty-five-degree wall. A garage with a high ceiling is ideal, especially if there is a way to control the climate in the summer and winter.

Another excellent strategy is organizing a com-

Steep home walls rule for time-efficient, sport-specific training.

munity wall. Recruit five or ten energetic climbers to pitch in a couple hundred dollars each. Rent a garage or some similar structure that has room to build several hundred square feet of climbing surface with a variety of angles, and then complete your facility with a campus board and fingerboard. Put your creative mind to work and get proactive at pulling the resources together—no doubt you can build one wickedly fun and highly effective training facility, and you will emerge a much better climber next season.

Crafting an Effective Personal Training Program

Obviously, there is a limit to how precisely I can pre-scribe an optimal training program for you via the static format of a book. On the pages that follow, how-ever, I lay out the basic, fundamentally important guidelines that you should follow in developing your training program. Do so, and you will be far better off than the typical climber who trains in a haphazard, trial-and-error manner.

Most important, you must adopt the appropriate training outline for your current ability level. Over time you can tweak this program according to the results you experience and in line with the good train-ing sense you've developed from reading this book. As long as you act in ways consistent with the principles and concepts described throughout this text, you will remain on course toward your goals.

One of the most basic and powerful concepts in this book states that you must train in the manner best suited to you and *not* do as others do. Remember, to outperform the masses, you must do things they aren't doing! Toward this end, you will find training guidelines for three basic groups of climbers—begin-ners, accomplished, and elite—described below. These categories are defined in **Figure 7.4**.

Beginner-Level Workout

PRIMARY MISSION

Maximize learning of climbing skills and optimize body composition and general conditioning. Engage in mental training to improve thought and emotional control before, during, and after a climb or workout.

WORKOUT GUIDELINES

Climb up to four days per week (ideally climbing out-doors two of the days) and visit at least one new climb-ing area per month. Reduce body fat with improved dietary surveillance and up to four days of aerobic train-ing per week. Train the antagonist muscles twice per week using the exercises described in Chapter 6. If you cannot climb during the workweek, you should instead engage in some pull-muscle training (use only the A exercises in Chapter 6). Time spent training and climb-ing should break down according to **Figure 7.5**.

SAMPLE MICROCYCLES

Two slightly different microcycles are shown in **Figure 7.6**—one for those able to climb during the workweek (home or commercial gym, or outdoors) and the other for those unable to climb except on weekends.

SAMPLE MESOCYCLE

I do not advise the use of a formal strength-training mesocycle (such as the 4-3-2-1 cycle); nor do I suggest you attempt to climb at maximum difficulty or push excessively hard on the rock. Instead, your medium-term goals should be to increase your volume of climbing as well as the diversity of techniques used. For beginners it's prudent to regularly take a week off from climbing to allow for systemic consolidation of skills and supercompensation. I propose roughly a 4-1 cycle in which you perform the above microcycles for

Figure 7.4 Climber Classifications for Training Programs

Beginner	Accomplished	Elite
• < 1 year climbing	• actively climbing > 1 year	• minimum 3 years of active climbing
• toprope ability < 5.9	• toprope ≥ 5.9	• on-sight lead ability at 5.11 trad and/or 5.12 sport
• little/no lead climbing experience	• lead climbing up to 5.10 trad or 5.11 sport	• boulder > V6
• boulder < V3	• boulder V3 to V6	

Figure 7.5 **Workout Time—Beginner**

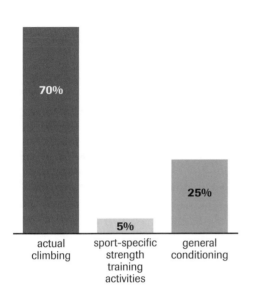

Beginners should invest the majority of the training time in actual climbing. Any fitness training should mostly focus on general conditioning.

four weeks, then take a week off from climbing and training (except for general conditioning and dietary surveillance).

Executing a "perfect" macrocycle is less important for beginners than it is for accomplished and elite climbers, though you can still benefit from some long-term planning relating to possible road trips and when you might take your annual month off. You might simply repeat the 4-1 cycle throughout the year, except for when on an extended climbing trip or during your month off. Use the blank macrocycle in Appendix A to plot your training.

SUMMARY OF TRAINING FOR A BEGINNING CLIMBER

- Climb up to four days per week and at as many areas as possible. Climb for volume over difficulty—maximum learning of a wide range of skills and tactics is far more important than the grade of routes ascended.

- Engage in conditioning exercises that focus on optimizing body composition, improving flexibility, and toning the antagonist muscles. Improved dietary surveillance is crucial for improving body composition.

- Sport-specific strength training should be limited to the A exercises, and actual climbing should be given preference over doing these exercises.

- Strive for awareness of your thoughts and emotions throughout the day and while climbing. Mental training is vital for all climbers, even beginners!

Figure 7.6 **Beginner Sample Microcycles**

(weekday climbing available)

Mon	Tue	Wed	Thur	Fri	Sat	Sun
GC	CL/A	GC	CL/A	R	CL	GC or CL

(no weekday climbing possible)

Mon	Tue	Wed	Thur	Fri	Sat	Sun
GC	SS/A	GC	SS/A	R	CL	CL

CL—climb

GC—general conditioning (aerobics, stretching, and so on)

A—antagonist-muscle training

SS—sport-specific strength training

R—rest

Accomplished Climber Workout

PRIMARY MISSION

Maximize economy of climbing movement with constant focus on refining mental and technical skills. Expand motor skill schemas and experience by avoiding specialization as long as possible. Minimize time spent on general conditioning and increase the volume of sport-specific strength training that targets improving maximum grip strength, lock-off ability, pulling power, and anaerobic endurance.

WORKOUT GUIDELINES

Climb three to four days per week (indoors and/or outdoors). Strive to climb at as many areas as possible and with a diverse range of techniques and styles. Serious strength training should be executed according to the 4-3-2-1 cycle with a strong focus on B-level exercises. Any climbing should be done before your strength training, and never climb or work out more than a total of four days per week. Train the antagonist and core muscles twice per week. Maintain close dietary surveillance during the latter portion of off-season training and during on-season training/climbing. Err on the side of over-resting, not overtraining! Breakdown of time spent training should be roughly as shown in **Figure 7.7**.

SAMPLE MICROCYCLES

Detailed here are four possible microcycles—two for those who are able to climb during the workweek and two for those who cannot (see **Figure 7.8**). Use these microcycles when you are not using the 4-3-2-1 mesocycle. Otherwise, train according to the 4-3-2-1 mesocycle described in **Figure 7.1**.

SAMPLE MESOCYCLE

Dedicated periods of serious strength training for gains (not on-season maintenance training) are best scheduled according to the 4-3-2-1 cycle. **Figure 7.1** shows a highly effective ten-week program that allows for adequate rest and thus produces maximum strength gains without the risk of overtraining or injury. High-end accomplished climbers may ben-

efit more by using the 3-2-1 mesocycle as shown in **Figure 7.2**.

SAMPLE MACROCYCLE

The average accomplished climber gets outdoors twenty or more weekends per year and may go on as many as two to four extended road trips per year. Therefore, careful macrocycle planning is vital to maximize conditioning for these trips and to help produce peaking for an extreme project or personal-best ascent. Use the blank macrocycle in Appendix A to structure an effective long-term training plan that accounts for your travel plans, the best outdoor climbing season, and when you choose to take your month off from climbing.

Figure 7.7 Workout Time—Accomplished

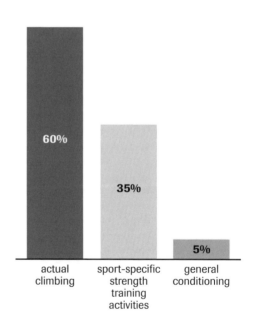

Accomplished climbers need to spend about one-third of total training time on sport-specific strength training activities.

Figure 7.8 **Accomplished Climber Sample Microcycles**

(weekday climbing available)

Mon	Tue	Wed	Thur	Fri	Sat	Sun
R	CL/SS/A	R	CL/SS/A	R	CL	CL or GC

or

Mon	Tue	Wed	Thur	Fri	Sat	Sun
R	CL/SS/A	CL/SS	A	R	CL	CL or GC

(no weekday climbing possible)

Mon	Tue	Wed	Thur	Fri	Sat	Sun
R	SS/A	GC	SS/A	R	CL	CL or GC

or

Mon	Tue	Wed	Thur	Fri	Sat	Sun
R	SS/A	SS	A/GC	R	CL	CL or GC

CL—climb

GC—general conditioning (aerobics, stretching, and so on)

A—antagonist-muscle training

SS—sport-specific strength training

R—rest

SUMMARY OF TRAINING FOR AN ACCOMPLISHED CLIMBER

- Climb up to four days per week and gain exposure to as many different types and styles of climbing as possible. Refine mental and technical skills to maximize economy of movement—the fastest way to becoming a stronger climber.

- Engage in regular, scheduled sport-specific strength training to increase maximum grip strength, upper-body power, and anaerobic endurance. Focus primarily on the B exercises, and always perform any planned climbing before doing the strength training.

- Commit to training the antagonist muscles twice per week. These are critical for maintaining muscle balance and preventing injury.

- Work on becoming a more mental climber. Practice mental-training strategies throughout the week, and strive to leverage all your mental tools when you step onto the rock.

Elite Climber Workout

PRIMARY MISSION

Identify and correct any technical weak spots or energy leaks (no matter how small) that compromise climbing performance. Constantly evaluate and refine mental skills—eliminate subtle forms of self-sabotage with renewed focus on the process, not outcome, of climbing. Perform the optimal amount of targeted strength training to increase maximum strength and power in the fingers, arms, and upper body.

WORKOUT GUIDELINES

Unlike the mass of climbers, the elite performer needs to spend a disproportionate amount of training time on sport-specific strength training (see **Figure 7.9**).

Figure 7.9 **Workout Time—Elite**

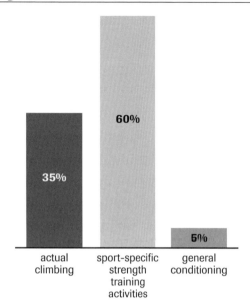

	60%	
35%		5%
actual climbing	sport-specific strength training activities	general conditioning

Only elite climbers need to focus extensively on sport-specific strength training activities—up to sixty percent. Design workouts to target a preferred subdiscipline or "project route."

Several weeks or even a month or two at a time may be dedicated to strength training and hard bouldering with little or no actual roped climbing. Access to an indoor climbing wall is absolutely necessary for this highly targeted training. Use of the 3-2-1 cycle and a heavy focus on B and C exercises and complex training is required to squeeze out additional gains in strength, power, and anaerobic endurance. Sound performance nutrition is critical for accelerating recovery from severe workouts and to ensure maximum supercompensation. Brief bouts of antagonist-muscle training and copious rest are vital to help stave off injury and overtraining.

SAMPLE MICROCYCLES

There are numerous possible microcycles, though intensity of training and your personal recovery ability are fundamental to determining the appropriate amount of training stimulus. Several possible microcy-

cles are depicted in **Figure 7.10,** though you can also employ the schedule shown in the 3-2-1 mesocycle.

SAMPLE MESOCYCLE

Many elite-level climbers train intuitively using their acute physical self-awareness as the training guide. Some of these high-end climbers also get injured, sick, and experience long-term plateaus in performance. While it's possible that you can avoid these pitfalls, following a predetermined training schedule is the best safeguard against overtraining. Toward this end, it may be advantageous to adopt a schedule along the lines of the 3-2-1 mesocycle (see **Figure 7.2**).

SAMPLE MACROCYCLE

Elite climbers tend to be very goal oriented and compulsive long-term planners. It's in the macrocycle that you need to book road trips, competitions, and the month off from climbing, so you can plan the most effective training schedule to produce a physical peaking for key events. You can plot your own macrocycle using the blank chart found in Appendix A.

SUMMARY OF TRAINING FOR AN ELITE CLIMBER

- Plan and execute an optimal—not maximum—strength-training program that targets your personal weakest link. The goal is to maximize grip strength, upper-body power, and anaerobic endurance.

- Keep a vigilant watch out for any chinks in your technical and mental armor. Economy of effort while climbing is paramount, and it's your mental, technical, and tactical skills that determine your fuel efficiency. Use your Mental Wings 24/7; only then will you be absolutely sure they are helping elevate you toward your life goals.

- Err on the side of over-resting instead of overtraining. Use performance nutrition and generous amounts of sleep and rest to enhance recovery and maximize gains from training.

- Be a compulsive planner of training, travel, and rest. Try to leave nothing to chance, and avoid

Figure 7.10 Elite Climber Sample Microcycles

Mon	Tue	Wed	Thur	Fri	Sat	Sun
R	A/GC	CL/SS	A	R	CL	CL

or

Mon	Tue	Wed	Thur	Fri	Sat	Sun
R	CL/SS/A	R	CL/SS/A	R	CL	CL

or

Mon	Tue	Wed	Thur	Fri	Sat	Sun
R	CL/SS/A	CL/SS	A/GC	R	CL	CL

CL—climb

GC—general conditioning (aerobics, stretching, and so on)

A—antagonist-muscle training

SS—sport-specific strength training

R—rest

trial-and-error training or getting drawn into some else's (flawed) training routine.

Training Considerations for Females and "Juniors"

This final section takes a look at special considerations for female or junior climbers. I've intentionally keep this section brief, because I feel that female and junior climbers are particularly gifted for climbing; there are only a few things they need to consider or do differently compared to the typical male climber.

Unique Issues for Female Climbers

Female climbers differ from males both physiologically and psychologically. While the psychological differences are more difficult to measure, there are clear physiological differences that may be an asset or liability in terms of climbing performance. The average female is about 5 inches shorter, thirty-five pounds lighter in total body mass, and forty-five pounds lighter in lean body mass (due to a higher percentage of body fat) than the average male. This large difference in lean body mass (muscle) is largely attributed to greater levels of the hormone testosterone in males (Broomfield 1994).

Consequently, the average female possesses approximately 40 percent of the upper-body strength and 70 percent of the lower-body strength when compared to men. In terms of strength-to-lean-body-mass, however, the ratio is notably less—females possess about 55 percent of the upper-body strength and about the same in lower-body strength as men (Wilmore 1974). Thus, it's clear that the greater level of adipose tissue in females has a negative effective on physical performance, especially in sports requiring a high strength-to-weight ratio. The female climber, therefore, will benefit much more from regular aerobic training (to lower her percentage of body fat) than her male counterpart—running for twenty to forty minutes several days per week will effectively increase strength-to-weight ratio in many females (due to changes in body composition).

Though females are naturally weaker than males (less testosterone and lean mass), they do respond to strength training in the same ways as men. Consequently, the serious female climber should not hesitate to engage in sport-specific strength-training exercises described in Chapter 6. In particular, the focus should be on increasing maximum strength in the pull muscles and the general condition of the core and antagonist push muscles.

The first few weeks or months of training will produce marked improvement thanks to neural adaptations. Beyond that, strength gains will come more slowly as hypertrophy (muscle growth) becomes a more significant player in producing strength gains. For this reason it's vital that strength training for the female climber be just as focused as for the male climber. The typical health club workout is no more appropriate for female climbers than for males, and in the long run could have a negative effect on climbing performance.

Technically and mentally, the beginning female climber is often a better performer than the male climber, and this is something that every female climber should recognize and leverage to the greatest possible extent. More flexibility, a lower center of gravity, less body weight, shorter fingers, and a more measured approach to climbing can all help a female climber outperform her male counterpart despite possessing less strength. So while sport-specific strength training is a must for any serious female climber, she should not overlook her gifts of style, strategy, creativity, and finesse.

As a final note, the belief that physical performance tends to be worse during menstruation is not absolute. While the menstrual cycle's affect on performance varies widely among individuals and from sport to sport, at least one study has shown that grip strength was greater during the actual menstrual phase (Davies 1991). Ultimately, you need to develop an awareness of just when is your best performance time of the month. You can then plan your training and climbing to exploit this period, whether it's for a few high-intensity workouts or making a personal-best ascent!

Training for Junior Climbers

Kids can unquestionably learn complex sports skills more rapidly than adults, and in recent years we've seen numerous "wonder kids" take the sport-climbing world by storm. Clearly, these young, generally prepubescent climbers possess the slight physique ideal for difficult climbing. There are numerous other physiological traits that work in their favor to enhance func-

tion and rate of recovery. Unfortunately, these young climbers often lack the maturity, self-awareness, and life experience to transfer their sport-climbing prowess to a wide range of climbing pursuits. They are also not prepared for the rigors of serious sport-specific training as outlined in this text. Therefore, I do not advocate any sport-specific training for climbers under the age of thirteen, and only limited strength training for teenagers between the ages of thirteen and seventeen.

TRAINING FOR PRETEENAGE YOUTHS (UNDER AGE THIRTEEN)

Preteens are much better off simply climbing for fun over performance. Climbing indoors or outdoors up to four days per week will allow their natural ability and strength to surface. The coaching emphasis should be on skill training and the fundamental aspects of the mental game. No strength training is advised other than basic body weight exercises such as pull-ups, push-ups, dips, abdominal crunches, and the like. With this approach most preteens will progress rapidly in bouldering, indoor climbing, and sport climbing, developing the foundation for becoming successful all-around climbers in the future if they choose to do so. Some preteens—most likely those with the best coaching or natural ability—will experience a meteoric rise in ability and apparent strength, all without any training outside of climbing.

The thirteen-year-old phenom Tori Allen is a classic example. She began climbing at age ten and has progressed to redpointing 5.13 sport routes in just over three years. Her "training program" is simply climbing indoors a few days per week and getting out on real rock during the weekend. Otherwise, Tori is a normal teenage girl who excels in school and a number of other pursuits outside of climbing. She is a perfect model whom I feel all young climbers should follow.

TRAINING FOR TEENAGE CLIMBERS (AGES THIRTEEN THROUGH SEVENTEEN)

The greatest gains in strength and power come during the period of the adolescent growth spurt—around thirteen for girls and fourteen for boys (Bloomfield 1994). Still, anthropometric changes may have a positive or negative impact on performance. Teenagers lacking strength and power can begin some sport-specific strength training, including A- and B-level pull-muscle, antagonist-muscle, and core-muscle exercises. They should not engage in the most stressful forms of training (campus training, hypergravity, HIT), however, until age sixteen or seventeen, at the earliest.

Still, the training emphasis should remain focused on developing good technical and mental skills. Teenage climbers would benefit tremendously from exposure to an expanding range of climbing activities such as traditional climbing and limited alpine and ice climbing. Some individuals may naturally gravitate toward competition climbing, though this should be the youth's choice, not the choice of an overbearing parent.

As teenage climbers transition into young adulthood (age seventeen or eighteen), they can begin a more serious and formal training program for climbing. Many of these late-teen climbers will already be accomplished or elite, and they can now engage in the appropriate training program as outlined earlier in the chapter.

Twelve-year old Laura Griffiths, a top juniors climber, training at Rockreation in Costa Mesa, California.

Lisa Ann Hörst on
Double Jeopardy *(5.11b),*
Susquehanna River Crags,
Lancaster, Pennsylvania.

PHOTOGRAPH BY
ERIC J. HÖRST

8

Performance Nutrition

*Judge your success by what you had
to give up in order to get it.*

— *The Dalai Lama*

The foods and beverages you consume play a primary role in determining your mental acuity, physical performance output, and recovery ability from vigorous training or climbing. Therefore, a thoughtfully designed diet will provide a noticeable edge in performance, whereas engaging in a "see-food diet"—you see food and you eat it!—will continue to hamper your performance in a covert way that you may never recognize.

Clearly, it's impossible to say exactly how big a part diet plays in climbing performance, but I estimate that average climbers can realize a 10 to 20 percent improvement in their training, recovery, concentration, energy, and overall climbing performance if they dedicate themselves to improved dietary surveillance

As a serious athlete and performance coach, I follow the changing trends in nutrition with great interest. In the late 1980s high-carbohydrate diets were the rage; in the early 1990s high-protein diets were in vogue; and most recently the high-fat, low-carbohydrate diets are what seem to sell the most books. Interestingly, all these diets are backed by scientific studies that show they work (in producing weight loss) to some degree given that you execute them exactly and presuming you are faced with one or more of the health issues common to obese Americans. For a reasonably fit athlete, however, there is no need to engage

in one of the fad diet regimens—nor any benefit. Proper performance nutrition is not that complex a subject; in the pages that follow, I will provide you with basic guidelines that will make eating right easy.

I was fortunate to realize the causal connection between nutrition and performance many years ago. Though I occasionally fall from the wagon, I credit sound nutrition—about forty-eight weeks per year—for my ability to train exceedingly hard, avoid injury, recover quickly, and still climb at a high level after twenty-five years and despite my aging and abused joints, tendons, and muscles. I hope I can help you do the same, too!

Macronutrients

There is no single perfect diet for climbers, just as there is no single perfect training program. To some extent, the amount and best type of foods for you depend on your climbing preference. For instance, alpine climbers have significantly different nutritional needs and energy requirements than those of folks who partake in cragging or bouldering.

Our study of performance nutrition begins with a look at the three macronutrients: protein, fat, and carbohydrate. As in the prior chapters, the focus will remain on the best strategies for rock climbers, with only general information for alpine climbers.

Protein

Protein has many functions in the body, including building and repairing of tissue, acting as a major component of the immune system, and making up enzymes, which facilitate every reaction that goes on in the body.

According to Registered Dietitian and Nutritionist Barb Branda Turner, growing individuals need more protein than adults do simply because they are actually laying down large amounts of new tissue. Healthy adults have a fairly extensive protein pool to draw on; that is, the proteins we consume are recycled several times for different functions in the body. For this reason daily protein requirements for adults are modest, even if they are training to increase muscle mass. Successful training is much less a factor of consuming a lot of protein than of using the appropriate training strategy and eating enough carbohydrates to fuel your training.

DAILY REQUIREMENTS

Between 1.2 and 1.5 grams of protein per kilogram of body weight per day is adequate for most climbers. For a 72-kilogram (160-pound) individual, this translates to 86 to 108 grams per day. This is higher than the 0.8 to 1.0 gram per kilogram recommended for sedentary individuals by the FDA. Some studies have shown a slightly higher need in athletes, not just to increase muscle mass, but also to facilitate recovery from exercise and compensate for the catabolic (tissue-consuming) effects of long, intense exercise. Still, I (and most scientific nutritionists) do not buy in to the massive protein-intake guidelines (as much as 1.7 to 3.0 grams per kilogram per day) prescribed in some fitness magazines.

BEST PROTEIN SOURCES

Low-fat dairy products such as skim milk and yogurt, plus lean chicken, fish, or lean red meats, provide you with the best protein value for your calorie. For example, a three-ounce piece of lean red meat such as tenderloin contains only 180 calories and twenty-five grams of high-quality, complete protein. A glass of skim milk contains about ten grams of complete protein and almost zero fat. If you prefer not to eat much meat (like me) or dairy products, whey protein powder mixed into skim milk, 100 percent pure fruit juice, or water is an excellent source of high-quality protein.

Incomplete proteins—these sources that do not contain all twenty amino acids—are also useful when eaten in combination. This is of particular importance to vegetarian athletes, who, by the way, are more likely to be protein deficient.

Fat

It's true that most Americans eat far too much fat, which contributes to our high incidence of heart disease, cancer, hypertension, and obesity. Still, getting too little fat has serious implications as well. Dietary fat is necessary as a source of essential fatty acids, which are involved in critical physiological processes such as the functions of the immune system and hormone production. Furthermore, our cell membranes consist largely of phospholipids (fatty acid derivatives), without which we would not be able to make healthy new cells, including muscle cells. A dietary fat deficiency in female athletes has been shown to cause amenorrhea (menstrual cycle irregularities), which may affect the development and maintenance of bone tissue.

DAILY REQUIREMENTS

On average the body's minimum fat requirement is fifteen to twenty-five grams per day. Usually fat-intake recommendations are expressed in terms of percentage of total calories consumed daily. For climbers, 15 to 30 percent of total calories should come from fat, depending on your climbing preference.

For cragging and bouldering, where a low percentage of body fat is desirable and the energy demands are largely anaerobic, fat intake should be restricted to 15 to 20 percent of total calories consumed. Alpine climbers, however, may be better off consuming up to 30 percent of daily calories from fat. These endurance climbers place great demands on the larger muscles of the body (especially the legs) and expend much more energy per day than, say, sport climbers. Fat is more calorie dense than carbohydrate and protein (see **Figure 8.1**), and it's a good fuel for long, slow aerobic activities. Both these attributes make foods with a higher fat content more advantageous for alpine climbers than for crag climbers.

Figure 8.1 Caloric Content of Macronutrients

Macronutrient	Calories/gram
Carbohydrate	4
Protein	4
Fat	9

FOUR TYPES OF FATS

In consuming your daily requirement of fat, it's important to know which of the four types of fat—saturated, monounsaturated, polyunsaturated, and trans fatty acids—are "good" and "bad." Although each contains the same nine calories per gram consumed, they are not all created equal in terms of their role in performance nutrition. Consequently, it's important not only to eat the optimal amount of fat but also to have the best ratio of the different types of fatty acids.

- **Saturated fats** are most common in animal products such as milk and dairy products, meats, and poultry. They are also present in significant amounts in some nuts, including Brazil and macadamia. Although excessive saturated fat intake does increase serum cholesterol, in particular the LDL or "bad" cholesterol, a certain amount is needed by our bodies to be made into fatty-acid-containing compounds such as hormones and phospholipids.

- **Monounsaturated fatty acids** are found in vegetables and oils including canola, olive, peanut, and avocado. These "monos" are thought to be the most beneficial in protecting against heart disease because of their ability to lower LDL without reducing HDL (the "good" cholesterol).

- **Polyunsaturated fatty acids** are common in fish, especially tuna, mackerel, salmon, and trout, and in corn, sunflower, and soybean oils. The omega-3 "polys" found mainly in fish and flaxseeds are currently being investigated for their roles in fighting inflammatory diseases such as arthritis and

other illnesses, including migraine headaches and heart disease.

- **Trans fatty acids** are found in trace amounts in almost all sources of natural fats, but most of those in our diet come from hydrogenated oils. During the process of hydrogenation, liquid vegetable oils are converted into solids by bombardment with hydrogen atoms (as in the making of margarine and shortening). Hydrogenation in effect converts unsaturated fatty acids into saturated fatty acids largely through the formation of trans bonds. Recent studies have raised concerns about these bonds, because they produce effects similar to those of saturated fats and may, in fact, be cancer causing.

While most well-trained athletes have a very healthy cholesterol profile (unless they smoke or have a genetic predisposition to problems), it would be very wise to limit your intake of trans fatty acids. Unfortunately, hydrogenated oils and partially hydrogenated oils are found in such a wide range of foods that they are hard to avoid. For instance, almost all the breads, cookies, and snack foods you buy off the shelf at the grocery store contain high amounts of these harmful oils. (Read the labels—you'll be surprised how many foods you eat daily contain them!) Most commercial fried foods are cooked in oils that contain trans fatty acids. Even some health foods like MET-Rx bars contain partially hydrogenated oils. Clearly, you can't avoid them completely, but it's worth the effort to minimize your exposure to them.

Because of their diverse functions, it might be best to consume about equal amounts of saturated, monounsaturated, and polyunsaturated fatty acids and minimize intake of trans fatty acids. It's a good strategy to try to eliminate hydrogenated oils from your diet, and in doing so you will reduce your consumption of these unhealthy fats to acceptable levels. (Unfortunately, you just can't escape them completely in this world of processed and fast foods.)

Examine the labels of the foods you eat most regularly and determine which items are doing you the most nutritional damage. Chances are you can make huge strides by eliminating just a handful of killer items like french fries, fried meats, snack cakes and muffins, salty snacks (buy baked chips and crackers instead), and any highly processed food designed for maximum shelf life (no doubt, high in hydrogenated oils).

Carbohydrates

Although fat and protein can also be used to provide energy, carbohydrates are the most efficient and effective source of energy for the muscles and brain. A high-carbohydrate diet is also important for athletes due to its protein-sparing effect. If you do not consume enough carbohydrates to meet your energy needs, muscle protein will be broken down for energy—the last thing any strength or power athlete would ever want! Consequently, the popular low-carbohydrate diets (Atkins, Zone, Ketogenic, and so forth) are inappropriate for most active climbers.

Carbohydrates come in two forms: sugars and starches. The sugar foods include fruit, sugar, soda pop, jam, honey, and molasses, while common starches are breads, rice, cereals, and pasta. Because these are the best sources of energy for high-intensity training and climbing, I'm sure you are already consuming plentiful amounts of these foods. Not all carbohydrates are created equal, however: Different carbohydrates release sugar into the bloodstream at different rates. The very best athletes know how to leverage this information to maintain stable energy throughout the day and to significantly increase the rate of recovery after a hard workout or day of climbing. If you are serious about climbing better, this subject should be of great interest to you. Enter the glycemic index.

GLYCEMIC INDEX

Until recently, nutritionists classified carbohydrates only into the two basic groups of simple carbohydrates (sugars) and complex carbohydrates (starches). Simple sugars were said to produce a rapid rise in blood sugar and quick energy, while complex carbohydrates were said to provide slow, steady energy. Although this concept holds true in general, recent studies have found that there is a large variability in the rise in blood sugar following the ingestion of various foods from both the sugar and starch groups.

To investigate and more accurately classify the metabolism of carbohydrates, researchers developed the glycemic index (GI). This index determines how the ingestion of a particular food affects blood sugar levels in comparison to the ingestion of straight glucose. Consumption of high-GI foods causes a rapid increase in blood sugar and a large insulin response. Low-GI foods produce more subtle changes. Climbers can use knowledge of the glycemic index to control energy levels and to speed recovery after a workout. Here's how.

Stable insulin levels are optimal for long-duration stop-and-go activities such as all-day climbing and long training sessions. Experts also agree that a steady insulin curve promotes muscle growth and discourages fat storage. This makes low- to medium-GI foods preferable for climbers in most situations.

High-GI foods produce large swings in blood sugar and an insulin spike. One minute you are jonesing to crank another hard route and the next you're in the tank and ready to call it a day.

Figuring the glycemic index of certain foods is more difficult than it might seem at first. For instance, most foods classified as simple carbohydrates (cereal, candy, some fruit juices) are high-GI foods. However, so are potatoes, white rice, bread, and bagels—all considered complex carbohydrates. Low-GI foods include vegetables, whole grains, brown rice, and milk (see **Figure 8.2**).

As a general rule, the more processed and easily digestible a food, the higher its glycemic index (for instance, liquids have higher index than similar food solids). High-fiber foods tend to elicit a slow insulin response and have a relatively low GI. Finally, foods containing some protein and fat along with carbohydrates come in lower on the scale.

This last piece of information is useful if you don't have the gumption to memorize and use this index. Consuming some protein and fat during each of your carbohydrate feedings serves to moderate the overall glycemic response of the meal. So for a long day at the crags, pack energy bars that contain several grams of protein and fat in addition to the carbohydrates.

The one good time to consume high-GI foods

Figure 8.2 Glycemic Index of Common Foods

High (≥70)		Medium (50–69)		Low (<50)	
bagel	72	banana	55	bulgur	48
carrots	71	bran muffin	60	spaghetti	41
corn chips	73	oatmeal	61	whole wheat	37
corn flakes	77	raisins	64	All Bran	42
doughnut	76	rice	56	orange	43
honey	73	sweet potato	54	pear	36
jelly beans	80	wheat crackers	67	apple	38
potatoes	83	cookies	60	peas	48
rice (instant)	91	sucrose	65	baked beans	48
rice cakes	82	soft drinks	68	lentils	28
Rice Krispies	82	orange juice	57	milk (skim)	32
Grape Nut Flakes	80	granola bars	61	fructose	23
cracker (soda/water)	76	macaroni	64	grapefruit	23
glucose	100	Shredded Wheat	58	yogurt (w/fruit)	30
Gatorade	78	ice cream	60	peanuts	14

such as candy, juice, soda pop, and most sports drinks (like Gatorade) is at the end of your workout or day of climbing. Intense exercise primes the muscles to immediately reload energy reserves in the form of glycogen. High blood sugar and the insulin spike help drive this repletion process. The optimal window for these high-GI foods is the first two hours following exercise. After that, favor low- to medium-index foods for slow, steady refueling.

DAILY REQUIREMENTS

Carbohydrates should account for nearly two-thirds of your daily caloric intake. This means that roughly two-thirds of your plate should be covered with pasta, rice, potatoes, and vegetables, with the other third comprised of lean, protein-rich foods. Be sure to apply the same rules when snacking. Try to pair up carbos such as a bagel or fruit with some protein like skim milk or yogurt. The protein helps slow down the digestion of carbohydrates and results in longer-lasting energy.

You can also calculate your approximate need for carbohydrates according to your body weight. Training for two hours per day, you would need roughly seven grams of carbohydrate per kilogram of body weight. For example, if you weigh seventy-two kilograms (160 pounds), the requirement would be for approximately 500 grams of carbohydrates; at four calories per gram of carbohydrate, this would equal 2,000 calories. Engaging in a full day of climbing, however—compared to two hours of training—may demand as much as ten to fourteen grams per kilogram of body weight.

Water

Water may be the most important nutrient to get right when you are climbing, yet I sense that many climbers are chronically dehydrated. Dr. Kristine Clark, director of sports nutrition at Penn State's Center for Sports Medicine, says that "even a 1 to 2 percent drop in water will cause problems in performance." The earliest symptoms of mild dehydration are a loss of concentration and enhanced fatigue. Clark adds that "a 3 percent drop in water level can create headaches, cramping, dizziness." Furthermore, a recent study has shown that dehydration leading to just a 1.5 percent drop in body weight resulted in a statistically significant drop in maximum strength (Schoffstall 2001).

In a sport as stressful as climbing, dehydration also increases your chance of a joint or tendon injury. Consider that proper hydration facilitates transport of nutrients to the cells, helps protect tissues from injury, and maintains joint lubrication. Therefore, for the purpose of injury prevention, maintaining proper hydration as you train or climb is as important as a proper warm-up.

RECOMMENDATIONS FOR PREVENTING DEHYDRATION

As a rule of thumb, it's a good idea to prehydrate before you go to the gym or head out climbing by drinking two tall glasses of water. Follow this with a minimum of an eight-ounce glass every hour throughout the day. This would total two quarts of water consumed over an eight-hour period on the rocks. This is a bare minimum amount—what you might drink, say, on a cold day when you perspire very little. Climbing on a humid, eighty-degree day, however, would roughly double this requirement. That means carrying four quarts of water with you for an eight-hour day of climbing. Of course, I doubt you

know of very many, if any, climbers who carry four quarts of liquid to the crags—thus, the mass of climbers are unknowingly detracting from their ability due to mild dehydration.

Optimal Macronutrient Ratio

As you may have gleaned from the previous sections, the optimal macronutrient ratio for a climber depends on the type of climbing activity. High-intensity, stop-and-go climbing like bouldering or cragging is best fueled with a 65/15/20 ratio of carbohydrates, protein, and fat, respectively. The long, slow distance training and climbing of an alpine climber would demand a higher total calorie count per day than the typical rock climber, and this need would be more easily met with a higher-fat diet (though adequate carbohydrates are still necessary). Consequently, a macronutrient ratio of 55/15/30 would be more suitable. See **Figure 8.3** for sample calorie counts for a typical male and female rock climber, though you personally could have significantly different requirements.

Micronutrients and Sports Supplements

The subject of micronutrients and sports supplements is so broad that it's impossible to discuss in a comprehensive manner in an instructional text like this. Still, the use of vitamin supplements and functional foods is so common in sports that the subject is worthy of at least a primer.

Sales of vitamin and sports supplements is a multibillion-dollar industry that bombards us with multilateral, never-ending advertising. Some of the weight-loss and strength-gain claims are remarkable, but very few of these claims are backed by reliable scientific studies. Many products are promoted with strong anecdotal claims and well-paid pitchmen, but very few actually do what the advertisers claim.

It's my belief that up to 90 percent of the sports supplements on the market are nothing other than modern-day snake oil, yet a serious athlete looking to maximize performance must be careful not to throw the baby out with the bathwater. On the pages that follow, we'll sort out the handful of products that

Figure 8.3 Estimated Nutrient and Calorie Needs

Climber	Macronutrient	Grams Needed	Calories	Total
Male	Carbohydrate	520g	2,080	
Active Day	Protein	115g	460	3,170
(160 lb/72kg)	Fat	70g	630	
Male	Carbohydrate	360g	1,140	
Rest Day	Protein	85g	340	2,230
(160 lb/72kg)	Fat	50g	450	
Female	Carbohydrate	350g	1,400	
Active Day	Protein	80g	320	2,170
(110 lb/50kg)	Fat	50g	450	
Female	Carbohydrate	250g	1,000	
Rest Day	Protein	60g	240	1,582
(110 lb/50kg)	Fat	38g	342	

Estimated nutrient and calorie needs for rock climbers (active versus rest day).

could potentially enhance your training response and climbing performance.

Micronutrients

Vitamins and minerals are the essential dietary micronutrients. Although the body needs only very small amounts of these nutrients (compared to protein, fat, or carbohydrate), they do play a vital role in almost every bodily function—from muscular growth and energy metabolism to neural conduction and memory. Consequently, your health and athletic performance can suffer in a number of ways if you are not consuming enough of these micronutrients.

Studies have shown that as much as two-thirds of self-selected diets contain less than the recommended daily allowances (RDA) of certain vital vitamins and minerals. Furthermore, despite being updated in recent years, RDAs are still believed by many experts to rep-

resent low-end requirements for a serious athlete.

VITAL VITAMINS

High-intensity and high-volume exercise (as in bouldering and alpine climbing, respectively) both place great metabolic demands on the body and generate elevated levels of free radicals, which may slow recovery and increase your chance of illness. The antioxidants that combat these free radicals, like vitamin C and vitamin E, are crucial micronutrients you would be wise to consume in greater than the RDA-suggested amounts.

One study showed that supplementing with 1,200 IU of vitamin E modulated free-radical production and reduced the amount of muscle damage following heavy weight training, in comparison to a placebo group (McBride 1998). Vitamin C has also been shown to help reduce muscle damage, in addition to being necessary for the formation of collagen (the substance that forms connective tissue in the skin and muscles) and supporting the immune system. Therefore, it would be wise to consume extra vitamin C and vitamin E, above and beyond what you can acquire through your diet or from a daily multivitamin. Consider taking one to two grams of vitamin C and 400 to 800 IU of vitamin E daily, split into two doses (morning and evening).

Certainly, there are a host of other vitamins that you might benefit from consuming in amounts higher than the RDA guidelines. Still, eating a decent well-rounded diet and taking a generic daily multivitamin supplement should adequately meet your needs for these other vitamins.

PRECIOUS MINERALS

Magnesium and zinc are two minerals shown to be consumed in less than recommended amounts by a majority of the population. For athletes, a deficiency in these minerals could mean you're getting short-changed on training response. Several recent studies have shown a statistically significant increase in muscular strength in a group of athletes taking supplemental magnesium and zinc (in the form of a patented supplement known as ZMA) versus a control group of athletes taking a placebo (Brilla 1998). Clearly, any climber engaging in serious strength training could benefit from taking this ZMA supplement (available from several different companies).

Another important mineral is selenium, known primarily for its function as an antioxidant. If you are consuming extra vitamin C and vitamin E, you might want to add 100 to 200 micrograms of selenium (taken in split doses with meals) to your supplement regimen.

Calcium and iron are two other minerals that some climbers may be lacking. Vegetarians often fall short on iron consumption, and some women may not get enough iron and calcium in their diets. A multivitamin is the best way to obtain extra iron, especially since its absorption is enhanced in the presence of vitamin C (also in a multivitamin). Females wanting to get extra calcium in their diets could take a calcium supplement (Tums are cheap and taste good!) or simply drink a few glasses of skim milk each day.

Sports Supplements

The most effective way to increase climbing performance is through a long-term, dedicated effort to improve your technique, mental control, and upper-body strength. Unless you are working to dial in on each of these areas, the few sports supplements that do work are probably a waste of money. If you are actively honing your technical skills and training to increase your physical and mental fitness, however, you may be able to further improve your performance through use of a handful of ergogenic (performance-enhancing) supplements.

PROTEIN POWDERS

As discussed earlier, athletes have a greater daily protein requirement than sedentary people, since strenuous exercise results in a higher protein turnover.

While mega amounts are not necessary (as some supplement companies and fitness magazines suggest), a 160-pound climber does need to consume between 86 and 108 grams of protein per day. This modest amount can be met through a well-rounded diet; it may be tough to consume adequate protein, however, if you do not eat meat such as chicken, fish, and lean red meats. There is also the limiting factor relating to the biological value of the protein source consumed. Not all protein sources are equal when it comes to providing your body with the necessary building blocks.

Consequently, scientists have developed a number of ways to measure the quality of protein sources. The biological value (BV) is one of the most commonly used; it's based on how much of the protein consumed is actually absorbed and utilized by the body. The higher the BV, the greater the amount of protein that is actually available to be used by the body to strengthen muscles and connective tissues, and to support enzyme formation, among other things.

When the BV scale was originally developed, the egg was considered the perfect protein source (remember Rocky?) and sat alone atop the chart with a value of one hundred. Since then, new technologies have enabled the creation of superproteins that are equally valuable to the body but without the fat found in many high-protein foods. Whey is the current superstar of proteins with a BV of one hundred (though for some reason a few companies inflate this number). Therefore, whey protein could be viewed as superior to the lower-BV foods such as fish, beef, chicken, or soy in helping meet the protein needs of an athlete.

While whey protein costs approximately $0.50 to $1.00 per twenty-gram serving, the investment is a good one considering its ease of use and high BV. Many brands are available from health food stores, supplement catalogs, and online merchants, so shop around for the best deal. Designer Whey Protein by Next Proteins is one excellent brand with several good flavors that mix easily in milk, juice, or water. Such liquid protein is ideal first thing in the morning, and it can increase your rate of recovery when consumed immediately following your workout or a day of climbing (more on this in the next chapter).

One of the highest-quality and most affordable protein sources is milk (see **Figure 8.4**). Since each glass contains ten grams of protein, consuming a quart or two of milk per day would provide forty to eighty grams toward your total protein requirement. As someone who only occasionally eats meat, I have relied on skim milk as my primary source of protein for the last twenty-five years (since I first read that John Gill slammed back milk protein after climbing). At 2½ gallons of milk per week for twenty-five years, I've somehow consumed about 3,250 gallons of skim milk since I started climbing. All I can say is, "Got milk?"

Even those who are lactose intolerant can consume milk without any nasty side effects by purchasing acidophilus milk. Regardless, be sure to always select 1 percent or skim milk, since whole milk contains a significant amount of saturated fat.

Figure 8.4 Biological Values of Protein Sources

Food	BV
Whey	100
Whole egg	100
Milk	91
Egg white	88
Fish	83
Beef	80
Chicken	79
Soy	74
Beans	49
Peanuts	43

Not all protein sources are equal when it comes to providing your body with the necessary building blocks. Select mostly high-BV foods from the top half of the list.

SPORTS DRINKS

Since the invention of Gatorade in the early 1970s, sports drinks have grown into a massive industry. It's now hard to find a serious athlete who does not consume sports drinks to help replenish energy. Dozens of different sports drinks are available in bottled form, including Gatorade and All Sport, the two most popular drinks on the market right now. Many others are sold in a bulk powdered form ideal for mixing up at home before a workout or day at the crags.

As you might expect, not all sports drinks are the same. Some are merely glorified sugar water, while others include electrolytes or any number of vitamins, minerals, herbs, or other nutrients said to increase athletic performance. Clearly, many of the claims are unsubstantiated—and at two bucks a bottle some are just a big rip-off.

The active ingredients in these products fall into two main categories: electrolytes and fuel replacements. A simple understanding of both will help you understand how these drinks might be of benefit to you.

- **Electrolytes** such as potassium, magnesium, calcium, sodium, and chloride are critical for concentration, energy production, nerve transmission, and muscle contraction. Fortunately, electrolyte loss during exercise is quite slow, so even a full day of climbing won't cause significant depletion. A reasonable diet and multivitamin provide you with all the electrolytes you need for ordinary training or a day of climbing. Still, a sports drink with electrolytes may be beneficial if your food supply will be limited for a few days, as in big-wall or alpine climbing.

- **Fuel sources** in the sports drinks are mainly carbohydrates, including glucose, sucrose, fructose, maltodextrin, and lactates. Glucose and sucrose (table sugar) are the fuel sources in the original sports drink Gatorade and have since been adopted by many other companies. Ironically, some athletes now shun drinks with large amounts of glucose and sucrose to avoid a blood sugar spike. Unless you are engaged in an activity that continues steadily for a couple of hours (such as long-distance biking, running, or hiking), this quick increase in blood sugar may be followed by an energy crash as insulin kicks in to reduce the elevated blood sugar level. In a stop-and-go sport like climbing, this pull-back on blood sugar can leave you feeling more fatigued and tired than before you consumed the drink!

Consequently, you should avoid any drink whose the first ingredient (after water) is glucose or high-fructose corn syrup—both are signs the drink has a high glycemic index and will release sugar rapidly into the blood. Instead, shop around for powdered sports drink mixes that list fructose (not the same as high-fructose corn syrup) as the first or second ingredient. These have a lower glycemic index and hence provide a slower, more sustained release of carbohydrate ideal for climbers.

Carbohydrate (glycogen) depletion in the muscles and liver is a primary cause of fatigue when performing long-duration activities of more than ninety minutes. The traditional use of sports drinks is for situations when additional fuel is needed for prolonged activity lasting more than ninety minutes. Therefore, consuming a fructose-based sports drink during the course of a day at the crags will help maintain energy levels throughout the day, though consuming some food would be beneficial as well. Conversely, an hour or two of bouldering or a short gym workout will not benefit from the added fuel of a sports drink.

While a slow-release, fructose-based sports drink is ideal for when you are climbing, it might be better to consume a high-GI drink upon completion of your workout or day of climbing. Numerous studies have shown that elevating blood sugar as soon as possible after exercise provides the substrate for synthesis of muscle glycogen (Robergs 1991). This is especially important if you plan to climb the very next day—replenishing glycogen stores takes up to twenty-four hours, so you need to get the process started immediately and at high speed (see Chapter 9 for more recovery tips).

ENERGY BARS

Energy bars have been a dietary mainstay of many climbers since PowerBar hit the scene back in the late 1980s. Originally intended for endurance athletes like bikers and runners, many of the energy bars are designed to deliver a rapid release of sugar into the bloodstream. Therefore, many energy bars possess a moderately high glycemic index (greater than sixty); these are easily identified by their first ingredient, high-fructose corn syrup. While a food with a glycemic index in the sixties is better in comparison to a bagel (seventy-two) or Gatorade (seventy-eight), climbers in search of sustained energy are better off sticking to foods with a GI of less than sixty.

The numerous balanced-style bars that have entered the market in recent years typically possess a glycemic index in the forty to sixty range. The higher amount of protein and fat contained in these bars helps slow the release of sugar into the bloodstream. The balanced 40/30/30 macronutrient ratio also helps conserve glycogen and may even help spare muscle protein from being used for energy during a long day of climbing. Consequently, consuming a couple of Balance Bars (Fig Newtons are also good) and drinking lots of water may be the single best combination to maintain energy, spare muscle protein, and prevent dehydration.

MUSCLE AND STRENGTH BUILDERS

There are dozens of sports supplements that claim to help build muscle and increase strength. While most are, in fact, worthless, both creatine and HMB have been shown to produce increases in muscular strength. If so, then both are surely must-use supplements for climbers, right? Not so fast, my friend—let's look at both of these a little closer before we jump to any conclusions.

- **Creatine** is by far the most effective sports supplement on the market. Not only has it been shown to enhance explosive strength in numerous well-controlled studies (Toler 1997; Kreider 1998), but when it's consumed in large doses, users actually see their muscles get larger and harder, and they gain lean muscle mass (that is, weight). Consequently, creatine has become the biggest-selling sports supplement in the country, and it's widely used by football and baseball players, weight lifters, bodybuilders, and millions of fitness buffs. But is it a good supplement for climbers? Let's take a look at how creatine works.

Creatine is a compound that's natural to our body, and it's used in the muscles to help create ATP (the energy source for brief, explosive movements). Creatine is also present in animal foods such as red meat, but the amount consumed in a normal diet is quite small (a couple of grams per day). Studies have shown that taking twenty grams per day of supplemental creatine for five or six days will enhance performance in short-duration, high-intensity exercise such as sprinting or weight lifting. This creatine-loading protocol is the method used by most athletes—but it's the wrong protocol for climbers!

Two side effects of creatine loading are weight gain and what's known as cell volumizing. Both these effects occur because creatine associates with water as it is stored in the muscles. Over the six-day loading phase, more and more creatine is stored and an increasing amount of water is drawn into the muscle cell. This gives muscles a fuller, "pumped" feel and look—just what bodybuilders and fitness buffs want. This loading process, therefore, results in a water weight gain of several pounds or more in most individuals. This is a good thing for athletes in sports where increased weight and speed (inertia) can be used to your advantage (football, swinging a bat, or swinging your fist). In a sport that requires a high strength-to-weight ratio, however, it can have a negative impact on performance.

Some climbers have argued that stronger muscles (due to creatine loading) can easily lift the extra weight gained in the growing process. The problem, however, is that creatine loads in all muscles of the body, not just the climbing muscles, and will load proportionately more in the largest muscles of the body—the legs! Of course, increasing leg

strength and weight is a bad thing for climbers, since they are never the limiting factor. There's just no way around it: Creatine loading is not a good thing for climbers.

If you are still not convinced, let's consider the cell-volumizing effect of creatine loading. Bodybuilders love the fact that their muscles pump up more easily when they are loaded with creatine. I quickly noticed this same effect when I experimented with creatine after it first appeared on the market in 1993. It seemed strange at the time, but I pumped out faster when I was on creatine—this despite the fact that I felt like I had a little more zip in my muscles. What I quickly concluded was that the cell volumizing partially occluded capillaries that intervene in muscle, thus slowing blood flow and causing the rapid pump. In climbing, the goal is obviously to avoid the dreaded full-on pump as long as possible.

That said, I do believe that well-timed, small doses of creatine can help climbers recover more quickly and without the nasty side effects of loading. The protocol I've developed and used for several years now is to add just five grams of creatine to a quart of sports drink that I sip throughout the day when climbing. This provides a slow trickle of creatine into the blood and muscles to aid recovery between routes. For training, I wait until the end of the workout; then I initiate the recovery cycle by consuming five grams of creatine mixed into a sports drink.

Bottom line: Use creatine in small doses and it may enhance your recovery with no noticeable weight gain or other negative side effects. If you decide to supplement with creatine, follow the above guidelines closely and never consume more than five grams per day.

- **Beta hydroxy-beta-methylbutyrate (HMB)** is a metabolite of the essential amino acid leucine. As with other amino acids, HMB appears to play a role in the synthesis of protein that builds new muscle tissue, and it may help slow muscle protein breakdown that results from long, intense training or exercise. Research has shown that taking three grams of HMB per day for several weeks in conjunction with a strength-training program increases lean body mass (Nissen, Panton 1996) and strength (Nissen, Sharp 1996) more than in a placebo group. Another study found that two weeks of HMB supplementation in cyclists helped increase both VO_2 max and lactate threshold (Vukovich 1997).

Manufacturers suggest taking one gram of HMB, three times per day. Considering the proposed protein-sparing effect of HMB, however, it may be more effective to take one gram in the morning and two grams just before training or midway through a day of climbing. Furthermore, since HMB is a relatively expensive supplement, you might want to limit its use to the most high-intensity weeks of your training schedule and when you are climbing on consecutive days or on a long road trip (in other words, experiencing a higher volume of climbing than usual).

SPORTS SUPPLEMENTS THAT DON'T WORK

The list of sports supplements that don't work is too long to completely cover in this text. I can, however, list a few of the most popular, most hyped supplements that have little or no reliable research to back up the big claims.

First and foremost is androstenedione (aka andro) and other testosterone boosters. The research on these substances is largely contradictory and somewhat scary. One study showed that andro increased testosterone in women, while another showed it increased estrogen in men! Several other studies showed absolutely no effect to taking these supplements. Stay away from this stuff.

Without getting long-winded, here's a list of other supplements that will only piss your money away (no proven ergogenic effect): vanadyl sulfate, pyruvate, OKG, gamma oryzanol, inosine, chitosan (and other "fat whackers"), algae (of all colors), GHB, MCTs, shark cartilage, and many homeopathic supplements.

9

Accelerating Recovery

*Knowing is not enough;
we must apply. Willing is not
enough; we must do.*

— *Johann Wolfgang von Goethe*

If you are serious about climbing performance, then you must be serious about accelerating recovery. Knowing how to limit fatigue and speed recovery is as important as knowing how to perform a drop-knee, lock a finger jam, or float a deadpoint. Bottom line: If you are not playing a proactive role in the recovery process, you are definitely not training optimally or climbing up to your capability.

We all know, firsthand, that physical fatigue is a primary limiting factor whether pulling down at the crags or training in the gym. Therefore, it stands to reason that being able to accelerate recovery means you will get more back during a midclimb shakeout and while resting between climbs and days of climbing. As a result, you will perform better on the rocks today, tomorrow, and on all your future outings. Similarly, more rapid recovery between training sessions can translate into more long-term strength gains, since you can work out more often while still getting adequate rest and without risk of overtraining.

While many of today's enthusiastic climbers are keen on staying current on the latest climbing and training techniques, surprisingly few individuals are aware of the numerous strategies for accelerating recovery. Recovery from exercise has been the subject of dozens of recent research studies, and any serious climber would be wise to heed the findings of these sports scientists. On the pages that follow, I will present the leading-edge recovery strategies used in these studies, as well as provide instruction on specific techniques that will help you slow fatigue and speed recovery while on the rock.

Clearly, recovery ability is a function of several factors, including age, sex, and level of conditioning. Regardless of these factors, however, I guarantee that you can recover more quickly by playing a proactive role in the recovery process—instead of just letting it happen, as many climbers do. By placing the same importance on optimal recovery as you do on training optimally, you will enhance your training response as well as your overall climbing performance!

The Basics of Fatigue and Recovery

Proactively managing fatigue and taking the steps to accelerate recovery require an understanding of the basic physiology processes involved in energy production, fatigue, and recovery. We'll begin our primer on this subject with a look at what causes fatigue, and then look at three recovery time frames.

Causes of Fatigue

Several factors contribute to the fatigue you experience while training or climbing. These factors include the depletion of muscle fuels, the accumulation of metabolic by-products, low blood glucose, muscular cramps and microtraumas, and finally, central fatigue.

Russ Raffa on Yellow Wall *(5.11c),*
Trapps, Shawangunks, New York.

PHOTOGRAPH BY **TYLER STABLEFORD**

DEPLETION OF ATP-CP

Adenosine triphosphate (ATP) and creatine phosphate (CP) are energy-rich phosphate compounds stored within the muscle cells in small amounts. Brief, maximum-intensity activities (such as a short, vicious boulder problem, a one-arm pull-up, or a 100-meter sprint) are fueled by ATP and CP; the supply of these fuels, however, limits this action to between five and fifteen seconds.

This limitation on maximum energy output explains why it's next to impossible to perform no-feet campus boarding for more than fifteen seconds, or why you have less than fifteen seconds to pull a maximum move (for you) on a route before your muscles give out. Continued exercise beyond this threshold is only possible by lowering the intensity of the activity, so that the lactic acid energy system can contribute to energy production.

Fortunately, ATP is continually synthesized within the muscles (by little ATP factories called mitochondria), and ATP stores become fully replenished in just three to five minutes of complete rest (Bloomfield 1994).

ACCUMULATION OF METABOLIC BY-PRODUCTS

Constant, moderately high-intensity activity that lasts between fifteen seconds and three minutes is fueled primary by anaerobic metabolism of glycogen fuel (see **Figure 5.4,** page 58). Unfortunately, metabolic by-products of this energy production—chiefly, lactic acid—result in muscular discomfort and, eventually, muscular failure. How long you can exercise during periods of rising lactic acid concentration depends on your lactate threshold—that is, how high in intensity can you exercise before blood lactate levels grow greater than your body's ability to metabolize it.

Anaerobic endurance training will increase your tolerance to lactic acid as well as elevate your anaerobic threshold. Furthermore, anything you do to enhance blood flow through the working muscles will help disperse lactic acid to your liver and nonworking muscles, where it's converted back to glucose. Continued high-intensity exercise (with no rest), however, will cause lactic acid levels to skyrocket and muscular failure to occur in less than three minutes. This explains why the "pump clock" runs out in less than three minutes on long, near-maximum (for you) crux sequences. You must get to a rest in less than three minutes or you'll end up taking a lactic acid bath!

During rest periods, the clearance time of lactic acid can be anywhere from ten to thirty minutes, depending on the initial level of the lactic acid accumulation and whether the rest is active or passive (more on this later).

DEPLETION OF GLYCOGEN

Steady, long-term exercise typically depletes glycogen stores in ninety minutes to two hours. Running out of glycogen causes the infamous hitting-the-wall phenomenon in marathon running, and is a contributing factor to your inability to climb hard toward the end of a long day on the rock.

Fortunately, climbing is a stop-and-go activity, so a full two-hour supply of glycogen can be stretched out to last nearly all day. You can also spare your glycogen supplies through regular consumption of additional fuel (sports drinks and foodstuffs) throughout the day. Research implies that carbohydrate feeding during exercise can help extend your glycogen supply by 25 to 50 percent (Coyle 1984).

Your starting level of glycogen is also a crucial factor in determining how long and hard you will be able to climb. If you are climbing for a second or third straight day, you will certainly have less than the full ninety-minute to two-hour supply of glycogen. This is because complete replenishment of glycogen stores takes twenty-four hours—a good dinner and a full night's sleep is not enough to restock the supply completely. When climbing on successive days, it's therefore vital to consume more calories throughout the day (to spare glycogen)—though you will still likely hit the wall sooner on day two than you did on day one.

LOW BLOOD GLUCOSE

Blood glucose (sugar) is but one of the possible fuel sources for working muscles, but it's the only fuel source available to the brain and nervous system. As glycogen supplies dwindle during long-duration activity, the working muscles become increasingly reliant on blood glucose for fuel. As a result, blood glucose levels drop and increasing levels of exhaustion and mental fatigue set in.

As mentioned above, ingestion of carbohydrates will help delay this fatigue by helping to maintain an adequate level of blood glucose.

MUSCLE CRAMPS AND MICROTRAUMAS

Muscle cramps and microtraumas can contribute to the sense of muscular fatigue, though in somewhat different time frames. Muscle cramps typically occur near the end of an exhausting period of muscle action—for instance, when some of the muscles in your back or arms lock up after a long, strenuous section of jamming or upon reaching complete exhaustion in the midst of a long sport climb. In such an instance, twenty to thirty minutes of rest, gentle stretching and massage, as well as consuming some fluids will help alleviate the cramping and restore normal muscular function.

Microtraumas are a primary cause of the all-too-common delayed-onset muscle soreness (DOMS). This muscle soreness, which becomes evident from twenty-four to forty-eight hours after strenuous exercise, is a result of microscopic muscle tissue tears and the accompanying tightness and swelling (edema). Strength will be diminished for as long as pain persists, possibly as long as two to five days.

CENTRAL FATIGUE

In addition to muscular fatigue, strenuous exercise can have adverse affects on the central nervous system (CNS). This so-called central fatigue can impair coordination, concentration, and your ability to perform difficult motor skills. Repeated high-intensity movements such as lunging and campus training are the hardest on the CNS. However, excessive amounts of any specific training stimulus—pull-ups, fingerboard, HIT—or performing the same type of bouldering movement over and over can also produce central fatigue.

Unfortunately, severe central fatigue can take longer to recover from than any of the other causes of fatigue. Consider that recovery of a nerve cell takes up to seven times longer than a muscle cell (Bompa 1983). Of course, this level of fatigue may never be experienced by the typical recreational climber; still, elite climbers who push the envelope both in the gym and on the rock are likely to experience central fatigue. If you still feel "off" after a few successive rest days, you may be experiencing central fatigue. It may take another five to ten days away from training and climbing to recuperate completely, but you will find yourself performing better than ever after this break away from climbing (per the Reminiscence Effect described in Chapter 7).

Three Recovery Periods

Recovery is not linear, but instead exponential (see **Figure 9.1**). For example, recovery from an exhaustive crux sequence, climb, workout, or day of climbing will initially be rapid, with about 70 percent of complete recovery taking place in the first one-third of the recovery period (Bompa 1983). Recovery improves to 90 percent after two-thirds of the time needed for complete recovery.

Figure 9.1 **Recovery Curve**

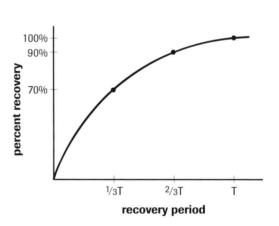

Recovery to 90 percent of baseline levels occurs in about two-thirds of the time needed for complete recovery.

Knowing that recovery is an exponential process is powerful information that can be applied to the three crucial recovery periods that I've defined as recharge, refuel, and rebuild.

RECHARGE (SHORT-TERM RECOVERY)

This first recovery period takes place from ten seconds to thirty minutes following the completion of muscular action. For example, this recharge period includes the ten-second shakeout you take in the midst of a crux sequence as well as the midclimb rest you milk for five, ten, or even thirty minutes, if possible.

The two metabolic processes at work during this recovery period are resynthesis of ATP and the removal of lactic acid from the working muscles. As stated earlier, ATP resynthesis takes less than five minutes, and complete lactic acid removal occurs in less than thirty minutes. As depicted in **Figure 9.1,** however, recovery to 90 percent of baseline levels occurs in about two-thirds of the time needed for complete recovery. Therefore, you can assume that the majority of ATP resynthesis has occurred in just over three minutes and about 90 percent of the lactic acid has been removed in about twenty minutes. Strategies to further hasten recovery during the recharge period will be detailed later in this chapter.

It should be noted that nothing you consume during this initial recovery period has any impact on exercise resumed immediately after this brief rest. Water takes at least fifteen minutes to empty from the stomach, and sports drinks or foodstuffs take even longer. If you have concluded your climbing or training for the day, however, this initial thirty-minute period is vital for enhancing long-term recovery (more on this in a bit).

REFUEL (MEDIUM-TERM RECOVERY)

The refuel recovery period occurs from thirty minutes to twenty-four hours following cessation of exercise. Therefore, this phase of recovery takes place during the two-hour break between climbs that you might take during the hottest part of the day and, of course, during the overnight period following a training or climbing day.

With ATP resynthesis and lactic acid removal completed in the first thirty minutes, the refuel stage is defined by the replenishment of blood glucose and glycogen stores (in muscles and the liver), and some minor repair of tissue microtraumas. Since refueling is the hallmark of this period, consuming a large amount of the right type of carbohydrates is necessary to facilitate the process.

Numerous strategies for enhancing this replenishment process will be described later in the chapter, but—as mentioned earlier—you can assume that about 90 percent of this refueling has taken place in about sixteen hours (two-thirds of the total recovery period). Thus, the typical twelve-hour break between consecutive days of climbing will result only in approximately 80 percent replenishment of glycogen stores (assuming you begin refueling immediately upon finishing up the first day on the rocks).

REBUILD (LONG-TERM RECOVERY)

Muscle growth and neuromuscular adaptation typically take place from one to four days following strenuous exercise. The degree of delayed-onset muscle soreness experienced is proportionate to the amount of microscopic damage inflicted on muscle fibers during exercise. Minor DOMS may subside in forty-eight hours, while severe soreness signals a greater degree of damage that may take four or more days to rebuild.

You can now see that a single rest day is enough to allow the muscles to recharge and refuel, yet complete supercompensation—that is, rebuilding the muscle to a stronger level than before the exercise stimulus—requires additional rest for the neuromuscular system to recuperate. Therefore, while you may be able to perform at a reasonably high level after just one day of rest, truncating the rebuilding process negates the supercompensation period (per Chapter 5) and will inhibit gains in strength. In the long term, chronic underresting can result in decreased performance, injury, and even risk of illness.

Whether you are training indoors or climbing a personal-best route outside, the ability to accelerate recovery is tantamount to elevating your absolute level of performance. In the gym faster recovery between exercises or climbs translates to higher-intensity stimuli or faster learning, respectively. On the rock hastened recovery at a marginal rest may make the difference between a brilliant on-sight or hardest-ever flash and dangling on the rope in frustration.

On the pages that follow, you will learn thirteen powerful techniques for accelerating recovery and, thus, improving the quality of your training and climbing. But knowing is not enough—you must apply these strategies with the same dedication and resolve as when pursuing your endeavors in the gym or at the crag.

Accelerating Short-Term or Intraclimb Recovery

Your capacity to perform difficult moves or exercises repeatedly, with only short rest breaks, is directly proportionate to your recovery ability in the short term. Described as the recharge period above, only certain recovery mechanisms come into play during the first ten seconds to thirty minutes following strenuous activity. The goal during this time is to help expedite the recharge process. This is done by minimizing the magnitude of fatigue (in the first place), enhancing forearm recovery with the G-Tox and active rest, and proper prehydration and consumption of lactic acid buffers.

Limiting Fatigue by Climbing More Efficiently

Let's start off with the most simple, yet powerful method to enhance short-term recovery—limit the magnitude of fatigue, as much as possible, through economy of movement and optimal climbing technique. Obviously, you will use less ATP and CP, as well as producing less lactic acid, if you can lower the intensity of muscular contraction and the total time under load. In this way you immediately reduce the magnitude of the fatigue you must recover from, and you will return to baseline strength more quickly.

It's in this area that the average climber can realize a windfall of unknown capability. The fact is, most climbers move too slowly, possess less-than-ideal technique, and hesitate (or stop) to place gear or think when they should really push on to the next rest.

Clearly, experience and technical ability are the limiting factors, but your slow climbing and hesitation will lead you to believe that a lack of strength is the primary problem.

Chapter 4 contains numerous drills for improving climbing technique and strategy. Through regular practice of these drills, you will naturally climb more efficiently, and you will be surprised to find yourself blowing through hard terrain more quickly and with less total fatigue. And, of course, you'll recover from this lower level of fatigue more rapidly and ultimately discover a whole new level of ability!

Enhance Forearm Recovery with the G-Tox

The dangling-arm shakeout is the technique universally used to aid recovery in commonly fatigued forearm muscles. A few seconds or, hopefully, a few minutes of shaking out provides some recovery, but often not enough. The effects of a full-on pump can take frustratingly long to subside, and when hanging out at a marginal rest, it's possible to expend as much energy in one arm as is being recouped in the other. Such a zero-net gain in recovery does nothing to enhance performance—in such a situation you would likely have fared better by blowing off the so-called rest and climbing onward.

Luckily, there is a more effective method of refreshing your forearms that the majority of climbers ignore or are not aware of. For more than a decade, I have been promoting the benefits of alternating the position of your resting arm between the normal dangling position and an above-your-head raised-hand position. This simple practice provides a marked increase in recovery rate. I call this accelerated recovery technique the G-Tox, because it uses gravity (as an ally, for once) to help detoxify the fatigued muscle and speed recovery.

The discomfort and pump that develop in the forearms while climbing are largely the result of accumulating lactic acid (LA) and restricted blood flow. As described in Chapter 5, LA is a by-product of the anaerobic metabolism of glycogen, an energy pathway that comes into use during extended contractions of greater than about 50 percent of maximum intensity.

Worse yet, contractions of as little as 20 percent of maximum intensity begins to hamper capillary blood flow, and at 50 percent contraction blood flow may be completely occluded (closed off). As a result, LA concentrations skyrocket until blood flow can resume during periods of low-intensity contraction or complete rest.

What's more, when dangling your arm in the shakeout technique, it's common to experience an initial *increase* in the sensation of being pumped. This is because, as the muscle relaxes, blood flow resumes into the muscle—but the venous return of the "old blood" out of the muscle is more sluggish. This traffic jam perpetuates the pump and slows recovery, yet many climbers continue to dangle their arms and complain about how sickening a pump they have.

The G-Tox technique puts gravity to work by aiding venous return of blood toward the heart. By helping get blood out of the arm more quickly, this practice enhances the removal of lactic acid and, therefore, returns you to a baseline level of blood lactate more quickly. The effects of this technique are unmistakable—you will literally see your pump drained as you elevate your arm due to the interesting fact that arterial flow into the arm is less affected by gravity than is venous return flow.

So why not just use the raised-arm position for the full duration of the rest instead of using the alternating technique as described above? Since the raised-arm position requires some muscular contraction in the upper arm, shoulder, and chest, these muscles would fatigue and possibly hamper climbing performance if you held the raised-arm position for a long time. Consequently, the best protocol for recovery is alternating between the two arm positions every five to ten seconds. Do so, and you will definitely feel the difference the G-Tox makes!

Engage in Active Rest

Along with the G-Tox, active rest is another underused yet highly effective strategy for accelerating recovery. While the G-Tox shines in its effectiveness to enhance recovery at a midclimb rest, use of active rest *between* climbs is an equally effective strategy for increasing the rate of lactic acid removal from the working muscles and bloodstream.

Several recent studies, including one excellent study on climbers (Watts 2000), have shown that active rest significantly reduces blood lactate compared to the more common practice of passive rest. In the Watts study fifteen expert climbers attempt to redpoint a 20-meter, 5.12b gym route, with eight of them engaging in active rest (recumbent cycling) and the others assigned to passive rest immediately following completion of the route. Periodic measurements of blood lactate revealed that the active-rest group returned to preclimb levels within twenty minutes, while the passive group took thirty minutes to return to baseline levels. Therefore, low-intensity active rest accelerated the clearing of lactic acid from the blood by almost 35 percent.

Applying this research finding at the crag is simple. Upon completing a pumpy route or redpoint attempt, instead of sitting down and having a smoke, grab your water bottle and go for a casual twenty-minute hike. This will help clear lactic acid more quickly as well as provide a mental break from the action. Both these factors will enhance your performance on the next route!

Another recent study compared the recovery after maximum exercise in four groups: passive rest, active rest, massage, and combined massage and active rest (Monedero 2000). After fifteen minutes of rest, blood lactate removal was greatest in the group performing combined active rest and massage. Therefore, you may be able to further improve the Watts strategy of active rest by performing some self-massage on the muscles of your forearm and upper arm.

Prehydration and Lactic Acid Buffers

While consuming food before or during exercise will have little or no effect on short-term recharge recovery, being fully hydrated and taking lactic acid buffering supplements may enhance the process.

Muscle is comprised of more than 70 percent water, and it plays a vital role in cellular function and the transport of nutrients and metabolic waste. If you are dehydrated, you may be hurting your performance and slowing recovery. Therefore, it's prudent to prehydrate by consuming two or three eight-ounce glasses of water in the two hours preceding a workout or climbing. Continue sipping water throughout the duration of activity at a minimum rate of an eight-ounce glass every hour (twice this, if it's hot).

Since the 1950s sports scientists have known that they might be able to enhance performance through ingestion of certain bicarbonate and phosphate compounds. Many studies have since shown that sodium bicarbonate has an alkalinizing effect on the blood that helps blunt the lactic acid response during intense exercise (Rupp 1983). Similarly, sodium phosphate has been shown to be performance enhancing; in fact, one study found that it increased the anaerobic threshold (Kreider 1992).

The protocol used in most of the studies involves a loading of the bicarbonate and phosphate compounds at a total of four grams per day for three days leading up to a performance. This amount, though not large or dangerous, can cause some gastrointestinal discomfort. The best supplement on the market may be Twinlab's Phos Fuel, which advises taking four capsules per day during the days leading up to performance. I would suggest beginning with two capsules per day, then increasing the dosage as long as you don't experience stomach upset.

In summary, lactic acid buffers do work, and they may provide as much as a 5 to 10 percent edge in performance. Whether you want to spend the money and risk an upset stomach is another matter.

Accelerating Medium-Term or Intraday Recovery

Intraday recovery is the medium-term recuperation that occurs throughout the day and up to twenty-four hours following exercise. What you do (or don't do) during this recovery period plays a direct role in how much energy you will have during the latter part of a long day of climbing; it's also the primary factor in how much recovery you acquire in a single night of rest. Of course, this is of big-time importance if you are in the midst of a long, all-day route or when you plan to climb two days in a row.

Earlier I referred to this medium-term recovery phase as the refuel period, since restoring a normal blood glucose level and replenishing glycogen is the basis for most recovery gained from thirty minutes to twenty-four hours following exercise. Consequently, consuming the right carbohydrates at the right time is the single most vital action to accelerate recovery. Still, stretching, massage, and the use of relaxation exercises will also increase your rate of recuperation. Let's delve deeper into each of these areas.

Refuel Early and Often

The single biggest error in recovery strategy by most climbers is delayed consumption of calories during and after a day of climbing. The natural tendency is to become so engaged in the activity of climbing that you forget to eat and drink. This is compounded by the fact that strenuous exercise naturally suppresses hunger.

REFUELING WHILE YOU CLIMB

Earlier it was explained that consuming calories throughout the day would help maintain blood glucose and, thus, help slow the use of your limited supply of glycogen. Toward this end, you should consume your first dose of calories between one to two hours after beginning your climb. If you are cragging, this might mean eating a piece of fruit, a Balance Bar, or a cup of sports drink after completing the first strenuous climb of the day. Continue eating a small serving of food every two hours throughout the day; in the case of all-day climbing, this means eating two pieces of fruit, two energy bars, and a few quarts of water (or something equivalent).

This may seem like an awful lot of food, and it is if you are only climbing for half a day or going bouldering (halve these amounts in these situations). To keep climbing hard throughout the day *and* to speed recovery for a second day of climbing, however, you should consume a minimum of 600 to 800 calories during the course of the day.

Selecting the right kinds of food at the right time is a matter of the glycemic index (GI). As introduced in Chapter 8, high-GI foods elicit a rapid rise (then drop) in blood sugar, while medium- and low-GI foods release fuel into the bloodstream more slowly. In a stop-and-go sport like climbing, steady blood sugar is vital for maintaining steady concentration and steady energy. Therefore, consume only low- and medium-GI foods while you are still engaged in physical activity (see the GI list of foods in Chapter 8). However, upon completing your day on the rocks or reaching the end of your workout, it's best to consume higher-GI foods and beverages. This latter distinction is powerful—there is a growing body of research indicating that what you eat in the first thirty minutes after exercise is the single largest determining factor in how fast you recover.

KICK-STARTING GLYCOGEN REPLENISHMENT AFTER CLIMBING OR TRAINING

As incredible as it may seem, recent research has shown that waiting two hours after exercise to consume carbohydrates will reduce your glycogen replenishment by 50 percent compared to eating immediately upon cessation of the activity (Burke 1999). Therefore, when planning to climb a second day, you significantly handicap your next day's performance by delaying refueling. Similarly, delayed refueling after training slows the recovery and rebuilding processes and, possibly, delays complete recovery by as much as a full day.

Let's take a closer look at the best refueling strategies in the hours following climbing or a vigorous workout.

- **First thirty minutes after climbing:** Ingestion of high-GI foods immediately after exercise substantially increases the rate of muscle glycogen replacement (Richter 1984). More recent studies have shown that glycogen synthesis may take place another 40 percent faster if protein and carbohydrate are consumed together, due to a greater insulin response (Niles 1997). Consequently, the best protocol for accelerating glycogen replenishment appears to be a four-to-one ratio of carbohydrate and protein consumption (Burke 1999).

  Since solid foods enter the bloodstream more slowly than liquids, it's best to drink this carbohydrate–protein blend as soon after exercises as pos-

sible. For example, a 160-pound climber would want to consume approximately one hundred grams of carbohydrate and twenty-five grams of protein. Drinking a quart of Gatorade, All Sport, or another glucose- or high-fructose-corn-syrup-based sports drink would provide nearly a hundred grams of high-GI carbohydrate. Two glasses of skim milk, a high-protein energy bar, or a whey protein shake would provide roughly twenty-five grams of protein. Take these actions immediately after your workout or climbing and you will jump-start recovery, big time!

- **Two hours after climbing:** Assuming you consumed the initial feeding of carbohydrates and protein within the thirty-minute time frame, you can wait until about two hours postactivity to eat a complete meal. Ideally, the meal should be comprised of foods providing a macronutrient ratio of about 65/15/20 (carbohydrate/protein/fat), as explained in Chapter 8. Such a meal might include a large serving of pasta, a chicken breast, and a salad or some vegetables. Whereas high-GI foods are best eaten immediately after exercise, medium- and low-GI foods are more advantageous in the two to twenty-four hours after exercise. They will provide a slower, longer-lasting trickle of glucose into the bloodstream that will support steady glycogen resynthesis.

- **Before going to sleep:** A small meal of carbohydrate and protein within thirty minutes of going to sleep will further support glycogen resynthesis and tissue rebuilding overnight. Skim milk may be the perfect before-bedtime food—it possesses low-GI carbohydrate, high-quality protein, and the amino acid tryptophan, a precursor to serotonin, which slows down brain activity. Drink a tall glass of skim milk or have some milk on a small bowl of whole-grain cereal before bedtime. It'll do your body good!

Stretch and Massage the Working Muscles

Earlier, you learned about an impressive research study showing that combining active rest and massage accelerated recovery by enhancing the removal of lactic acid from the blood. Sports massage is also an effective practice to enhance medium- and long-term recovery as well as an excellent complement to pre-climbing warm-up activities.

The guy who literally wrote the book on the subject is Jack Meagher. In his text *Sports Massage*, he explains how the use of a specific form of sports massage can provide up to a 20 percent increase in performance, in addition to reducing the risk of injury and accelerating recovery.

HOW IT WORKS

Traditional massage has long been used to increase blood flow and oxygen transport in the muscles. The benefits of this superficial "rubbing" are brief, however, and have little residual effect on performance.

Sports massage utilizes a deep-fiber-spreading technique that produces hyperemia (a dilation of the blood vessels) through the full depth of the muscle. Furthermore, the state of hyperemia lasts long after the procedure has ended, so the enhanced blood flow can benefit muscular activity and performance.

Sports massage also helps reduce the number of small and generally unfelt spasms that regularly occur in the muscle. These spasms may go unchallenged by conventional stretching and warm-up exercises and, left unchecked, may rob you of coordination and induce mechanical resistance and premature fatigue.

HOW TO DO IT

There are several strokes you may want to learn, but the most effective is called cross-fiber friction. This stroke is best executed with a braced finger. The motion is a simple push in followed by a short push

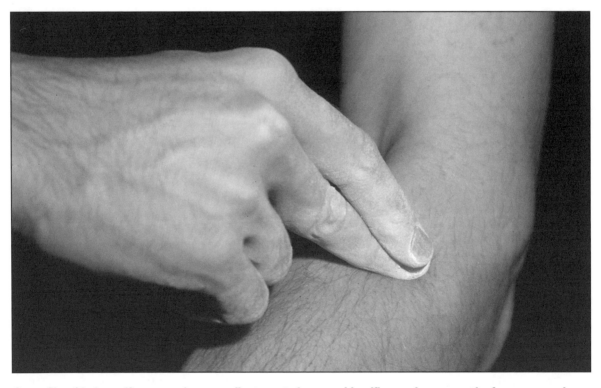

Cross-fiber friction self-massage is an excellent way to increase bloodflow and warm-up the forearm muscles prior to training.

TRAINING *for* CLIMBING

back and forth across the muscle fiber. Keep the stroke short and rhythmic; only gradually increase the pressure to penetrate deeper into the muscle.

Although sports massage can be used on all muscles, focus your efforts on the upper body and, in particular, the finger flexors and extensors (the forearm muscles) and the biceps and triceps (muscles of the upper arm). Incorporate five to ten minutes of massage into your regular warm-up routine. This, along with the stretches detailed in Chapter 6, will better prepare you for an excellent workout or day on the rocks.

SPORTS MASSAGE TO ACCELERATE RECOVERY

Your body has inherent mechanical weaknesses where sport-specific movements can trigger stress overload. In climbing, these overload areas are the forearms, upper arms, and back. These muscles are the first to tire, and they are typically the slowest to recover. Fortunately, you can modulate fatigue and hasten recovery through application of sport massage to the specific stress points inherent to climbing movements.

To become familiar with these stress points, it's best to have some understanding of how a muscle works. First, voluntary muscles have two ends, each of which is attached to a bone via a tendon. One end is a fixed attachment called the origin, and the other is a movable attachment called the insertion. For example, the origin of the bicep muscle is at the shoulder, and the insertion is just below the elbow. The motor nerve enters the muscle in the thick muscle belly between the origin and insertion. It is here that all contractions begin, and they spread toward the ends of the muscle as more forceful contractions are needed. Consequently, only a maximum effort will recruit the high-threshold fibers situated near the ends of the muscle.

For this reason a proper (submaximum) warm-up does not work the whole muscle. The end fibers (near the origin and insertion) largely miss out on the warm-up process, and thus they are more likely to underperform when called into action for high-intensity movements. These locations are also more likely to harbor stress and become cramped. Fortunately, sports massage applied to these points before a workout or climb helps warm even the least used fibers, and enables maximum efforts with minimal resistance and risk of injury.

Address these pressure points with what is called the direct-pressure stroke. Simply push straight in with a braced finger and hold for fifteen to sixty seconds. Direct pressure is especially useful when applied to the pressure points near the base of the muscles. This will not only relieve any unknown tiny spasms, but also help warm up those hard-to-recruit end fibers. Be sure never to apply sports massage tactics to tendons, joints, or injured tissues, however.

Use Relaxation Techniques

The "Mental Training" chapter described an excellent relaxation technique called the Progressive Relaxation Sequence. Though commonly used before going to sleep, progressive relaxation is also highly effective for relaxing the muscles and quieting the mind during a midday break from climbing. When resting between climbs or taking a break before returning to work on a project, find a quiet spot, lie down, and spend ten to twenty minutes performing progressive relaxation. Upon completing this process, sit up for a few minutes and enjoy the day before proceeding to the next climb.

Make a midday relaxation break a regular part of your climbing ritual and you'll find yourself climbing better, and with less fatigue, late into the day.

Accelerating Long-Term or Interday Recovery

The interday recovery period involves the long-term recuperation from a severe workout or a couple of hard days of climbing. Depending on the intensity and volume of the activity, full recovery could take anywhere from one to four days.

When you wake up in the morning with sore muscles (delayed-onset muscle soreness), it's a sign that you incurred microtraumas and that a recovery period of at least another twenty-four hours is needed. Of course, you have two choices in this situation. The first is to go climbing (or workout) for a second straight day, despite the soreness, realizing that your performance will be less than ideal and your risk of injury is increased. Or you could take a day or two off and allow your neuromuscular system to recuperate to a level of capability higher than before the workout (supercompensation).

Certainly, there are times when you will select the first option of climbing a second day straight, but there should be an equal number of instances when you decide that "less will be more." Weekend climbing trips are the classic situation in which you'd want to climb two days in a row, regardless of sore muscles. Given proper nutrition, a good warm-up, and a prudent approach to pushing yourself on the second day, you will usually get away with climbing sore.

Choosing to take a day or two of rest, however, is clearly the intelligent decision when climbing indoors or during an off-season training cycle. Hopefully, you gleaned from Chapter 5 that proper rest is as important as training stimulus in becoming a stronger climber, and that under-resting is a primary cause of injury. Enthusiastic indoor and sport climbers are most commonly guilty of under-resting, but regardless of your preference, it's important that you distinguish yourself from the mass of climbers who overtrain. If you find yourself drawn to overtrain with the crowd, remember that in order to outperform the masses, you cannot do what they are doing!

Eat Frequent, Small Meals

Instead of eating the typical three meals per day, you can accelerate recovery by consuming six smaller meals or snacks spaced evenly throughout the day. Avoid high-GI foods; they are less effective for recovery after the first two hours postexercise. Instead, select low- and medium-GI foods for all your meals and drink at least ten glasses of water throughout the day.

At least three of your meals should contain a significant portion of protein. For instance, breakfast could include a couple of eggs, skim milk, or whey protein; lunch might include some yogurt, skim milk, or a can of tuna; and for dinner it might be good to eat a piece of lean red meat, chicken, or fish. Each of these meals should also include some carbohydrate, and at all costs avoid fat-laden fried foods and any snack foods containing hydrogenated oils. Strive for a macronutrient profile of roughly 65/15/20 (carbohydrate/protein/fat) for each major meal.

While the other three feedings need be only a couple hundred calories, they are vital for maintaining steady blood glucose and continuing the recovery processes throughout the day. Low- and medium-GI foods are the best choice, with a piece of fruit, a balanced-type energy bar, and a glass of skim milk being ideal selections.

Take a Multivitamin and Antioxidants

In today's world of highly processed foods, it's often difficult to consume enough of the vitamins and minerals that athletes need by simply eating a well-rounded diet. Chapter 8 set forth a basic supplement program that I feel all serious climbers should abide by. It's most important to consume extra vitamin C, vitamin E, and selenium; taking a daily multivitamin would also be wise.

Stretch and Massage Sore Muscles

Gentle stretching and sports massage are widely accepted as effective means to enhance recovery from strenuous exercise. Professional athletes have full-time trainers who help with stretching and postexercise and off-day massage (must be nice!). Though I won't pay for you to add a masseur to your climbing-support staff, I do suggest that you stretch for five to fifteen minutes per day and partake in some sports massage of sore muscles. Follow the stretching procedures outlined in Chapter 6 and, of course, the primer on sports massage provided earlier in this chapter.

Get Plenty of Sleep

Here's an important recovery technique that this full-time working, two-day-a-week-training, weekend-climbing, book-writing, twenty-five-year veteran of the rocks wishes he could get more of! Although most neuromuscular regeneration occurs during sleep, I always fall back on the fact that nothing is produced and no action taken during sleep.

Seriously, sleep is vital for any climber serious about training and passionate about maximizing ability. The bare minimum amount of sleep per night is seven to eight hours, though nine to ten hours is ideal following strenuous training or a long day of climbing. No doubt, it's a busy world—and sleep often seems like the only activity that's expendable. If you discipline yourself never to give up sleep for low-importance tasks like watching TV or surfing the Net, however, it will pay big dividends in the long run.

Engage in Light Activities

Earlier you learned of a couple of great research studies that showed the value of active rest in accelerating recovery from strenuous exercise (by enhancing removal of lactic acid). In the context of long-term recovery, active rest is also beneficial because it enhances circulation to the damaged muscles and produces a general loosening effect on stiff muscles.

The best active-rest activities for climbers are hiking, jogging, light mountain biking, and even some limited less-than-vertical climbing. Still, it's crucial that each of these activities be performed at a low enough intensity that you never get winded and only break a light sweat. Limit yourself to thirty to sixty minutes of active rest, and be sure to exercise discipline in not letting yourself escalate the activity into anything more than active rest.

Possess a Positive, Calm Personality 24/7

This last recovery tip is subtle, yet very powerful. Possessing a positive, relaxed, and easygoing attitude not only puts you in a better performance state, but has been proven to increase recovery and maybe even encourage muscular growth.

Strenuous exercise and stressful situations cause a drugstore's worth of chemicals and hormones to be released into the bloodstream. Some of these hormones have long-term positive effects, such as growth hormone, which is anabolic. The "fight-or-flight" hormones like epinephrine and cortisol, however, can have a long-term negative effect when released chronically. In particular, cortisol has been shown to be catabolic, meaning it results in breakdown of muscle.

In light of the above factors, elite athletes have long been interested in enhancing the release of growth hormone and preventing high levels of cortisol. This is the very reason some athletes take anabolic steroids.

Fortunately, you can modulate levels of growth hormone and cortisol with proper training and adequate rest as well as through adjustments in your lifestyle. For instance, individuals with Type A, aggressive behavior naturally exhibit higher levels of cortisol (Williams 1982) and reduced levels of growth hormone. It's also been shown, however, that behavior modification and reduction of the stressors in life can reverse this effect and provide more beneficial training (Dinan 1994). Therefore, possessing a relaxed approach to climbing and a humorous attitude about life in general will play an underlying but very positive role in enhancing the quality of your training adaptations and climbing performance.

Conclusion

It's important to recognize that training (climbing) and recovery are opposite sides of the same coin. You must place equal importance on doing both optimally and to the best of your ability. Clearly, it requires a shift in perspective to actually plan and engage in the process of recovery in the same way you plan and engage in the process of training. But in doing so, you will distinguish yourself from the masses by producing uncommonly good results, and by avoiding downtime due to injury and illness.

Thirteen-year-old Tori Allen "climbing her age," Omaha Beach, the Motherlode, *Red River Gorge, Kentucky.*

PHOTOGRAPH BY **MICHAEL LANDKROON**

Injury Treatment & Prevention

Our greatest glory is not in never failing, but in rising up every time we fail.

— Ralph Waldo Emerson

This last chapter might not be necessary if this was a book on training for curling or training for badminton. Despite what we tell our parents, however, climbing is a sport with an unusually high incidence of injury. Several studies report that up to three-quarters of all recreational and elite climbers have suffered a climbing injury. Fortunately, only a small number of injuries are acute traumas produced by falls—the rest are overuse injuries that most commonly occur in the fingers, elbows, and shoulders. These insidious overuse injuries, while far from life threatening, can become chronic and debilitating, and they are extremely frustrating for an otherwise healthy individual passionate about climbing.

The goal of this chapter is to increase your awareness of the causes and symptoms of the most common overuse injuries. Early identification is the best way to mitigate an overuse injury, whereas ignoring the early pangs and hoping that it will go away is almost always a recipe for a chronic injury that could sideline you for months. Ultimately, learning to recognize at-risk situations both when training and climbing, and embracing a prudent approach to these activities that errs on the side of caution, is the best medicine for preventing injury.

Over the last decade numerous relevant studies have been presented by British, French, German, and American researchers, and several excellent articles were published in climbing magazines by physicians experienced in treating injured climbers. Based on this growing body of knowledge, I will present what seems to be the current treatment protocol for the most prevalent injuries; still, I urge you to seek professional treatment from a physician familiar with climbing injuries (call around and ask this question straight out). Countless climbers have fallen into the trap of self-treatment and trying to climb through an injury—these approaches often make matters worse and can lead to unnecessarily long-term downtime. Bottom line: Read this chapter as an injury primer that encourages proactive, professional treatment of all injuries, and not as an absolute guide to the subject.

Overview of Climbing Injuries

A wide variety of injuries can result from climbing and sport-specific training activities, and a survey of available literature yields a broad range of pathologies from tendonitis to broken bones. While acute trauma resulting from falls is a very real issue, this overview of climbing injuries focuses on the chronic overuse injuries that typically result from the process of climbing and training, instead of falling.

Types of Injuries

Injury surveillance data from several recent studies confirms that the majority of climbing injuries are not the result of falls. A well-designed British study revealed that three-quarters of climbing injuries were of the chronic overuse variety (Doran 1999). In this study 111 active climbers of all ages and abilities were questioned with regard to injuries incurred over the two previous years. One hundred forty overuse injuries from forty-nine climbers were reported— obviously some climbers in this sample experienced multiple or recurrent injuries during the twenty-four months of the study.

A breakdown of these overuse injuries confirms what experienced climbers have known anecdotally for years—the fingers, shoulders, and elbows are the three most common sites of nonfall injuries (see **Figure 10.1**). Of all the injuries revealed in the British study, 40 percent occurred in the fingers, 16 percent in the shoulders, and 12 percent in the elbows. Other common sites for injury, though much less prevalent, were the knees (5 percent), back (5 percent), and wrists (4 percent). These findings agree surprisingly well with a German study (Stelzle 2000) of 314 climbers of both sexes and all degrees of climbing ability, which identified the most common injuries as finger tendon (39 percent), elbow (11 percent), and knee (about 5 percent).

Contributing Factors

An almost unanimous conclusion of the many injury studies is that occurrence of overuse injuries is directly proportionate to climbing ability and the perceived importance of climbing to the individual. Other cofactors contributing to increased risk of overuse injury include use of indoor climbing walls and use of campus boards and fingerboards in training for climbing.

The British study depicts a dramatic increase in injury rate in 5.11 climbers versus 5.10 climbers (see **Figure 10.2**). At the 5.12 level, nearly 88 percent of climbers surveyed had experienced overuse injuries in the prior two years. By comparison, only 20 percent of individuals climbing at levels below 5.9 incurred overuse injuries, the lowest relative frequency of all categories (Doran 1999).

At least two studies show a statistically significant relationship between perceived importance of climbing and incidence of injury. Doran (1999) says, "The

Figure 10.1 Sites of Nonfall Injuries

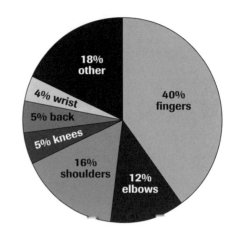

Figure 10.2 Overuse Injuries

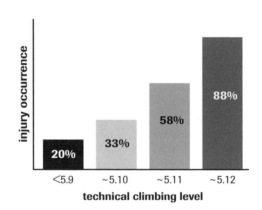

Occurrence of overuse injuries is directly proportional to climbing ability.

frequency of injury occurrence was significantly higher in those who perceived climbing to be very important to those who rated it as not so important." An important corollary to this relationship is that enthusiastic climbers are more likely to return to climbing before full rehabilitation has occurred, thus leading to a pattern of recurrence.

Another British study of 295 climbers at a recent World Cup event found that those most at risk for overuse injuries were climbers with "the most ability and dedication to climbing." The analysis showed a linear relation between lead climbing grade and overuse injuries (Wright 2001).

A number of other variables have been identified as cofactors in contributing to overuse injuries, including climbing preference and training practices.

Consensus among experts in the field is that incidence of overuse injuries has increased since the advent of indoor walls and sport-climbing tactics. An article in *Sports Medicine* proposes that the preponderance of overhanging terrain at indoor climbing facilities is a contributing factor to the increase in upper-body injuries (Rooks 1997). At the least, indoor walls do enable year-round climbing and make it oh so easy to test your absolute limit, thanks to toprope belays or well-bolted leads. Clearly, this is an environment that can lend itself to overtraining and a general lack of rest time away from the stresses and strains of climbing. I know of a few individuals who climbed indoors five or six days per week—and all, sooner or later, suffered significant finger, elbow, or shoulder injuries.

Training practices have also been implicated as a contributing factor in overuse injuries of climbers at all ability levels. One study found that 37 percent of individuals engaging in sport-specific training used a fingerboard or some other similar setup to perform one- and two-finger pull-ups. Of this group of low- and high-end climbers, 72 percent reported at least one injury of the hands or arms (Bannister 1986).

Doran (1996) reports that most of the climbers in his study performed some form of supplementary training; in particular, fingerboards and dynamic up-and-down campus training were popular among the injured climbers. The obvious implication is that these high-stress, ultraspecific forms of training may be injurious or at least exacerbate low-grade preexisting injuries. These conclusions all make good sense and, therefore, underscore the importance of a prudent, mature approach to sport-specific training that knows when to say enough and errs on the side of over-resting rather than overtraining.

One puzzling part of the Doran (1996) study is the finding that climbers who conducted a regular warm-up had an increased frequency of injury in comparison to those who did not warm up. Not only is this idea counterintuitive, but it is contradictory to a large body of literature claiming that a proper warm-up is vital for preventing injury. Toward this end, another British researcher had previously found that increased frequency of injury was partially attributable to an absence of (or too brief) a warm-up regimen (Bollen 1988).

It's my sense that it would be best to not abandon your warm-up activities based on a single study. There are several possible explanations for the unlikely findings of the Doran study. First, one of the hallmark findings of this study was that ability level was proportionate to frequency of overuse injury. Therefore, high-end climbers were far more likely to experience overuse injuries than low-end climbers. I wonder, however, if high-end climbers are more likely to engage in warm-up activities (since they take climbing and training so seriously), while low-end climbers are more likely to "just go climbing" and skip the warm-up regimen. Could this explain the unusual findings that warm-up activities increase the risk of injury?

Another possible explanation of this finding could be that climbers who regularly warm up before training and climbing do so too quickly, severely, or excessively. For instance, it's widely accepted that stretching cold can injure connective tissues and muscles. Furthermore, excessive amounts of stretching can lead to loose joints and aggravate existing injuries. In the final analysis, I suspect that we will find that a slow, incremental warm-up does not increase the risk of overuse injuries and is, in fact, a worthwhile and beneficial activity prior to training or performance climbing.

Common Injuries and Treatment

Based on the research outlined above, we know that about 75 percent of all climbers have had or will experience an overuse injury. Furthermore, it's well documented that the four most common sites of injury are the fingers, elbows, shoulders, and knees. In this

Figure 10.3 Finger Anatomy

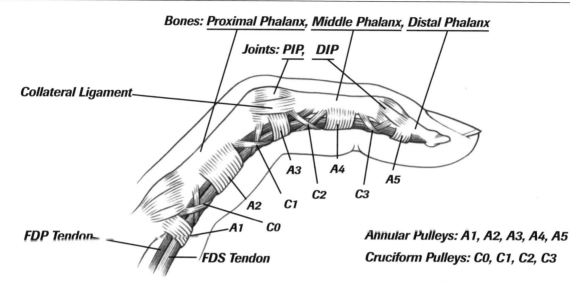

Bones: Proximal Phalanx, Middle Phalanx, Distal Phalanx

Joints: PIP, DIP

Collateral Ligament

A3 **A4**

A5

C2 **C3**

A2 **C1**

A1 **C0**

FDP Tendon

FDS Tendon

Annular Pulleys: A1, A2, A3, A4, A5

Cruciform Pulleys: C0, C1, C2, C3

section we'll take a closer look at each of these problem spots. Hopefully, this information will empower you to recognize symptoms early on and thus modify your activity or seek medical attention before the injury becomes more severe or chronic. One caveat that all climbers should recognize straight up is that you *must* seek medical attention for any condition that gets *worse* after withdrawal from climbing and training. This could indicate a tumor, infection, or other disease that needs immediate medical attention.

Finger Injuries

Considering the incredible mechanical loading we place on our fingers when climbing, it's no surprise that they are the most common site of injury. Unfortunately, these pesky finger injuries are often hard to diagnose precisely and, worse yet, in the early stages tend to be ignored. Many climbers rationalize that they can climb through one injured finger, since they have nine healthy fingers and can still manage to crank at a near-maximum level. Continued climbing on an injured finger may increase the severity of the injury, however, and thus double or triple (or more)

the downtime needed to recover.

Understanding the most common injuries requires some knowledge of hand anatomy (see **Figure 10.3**). To begin with, there are no muscles in the fingers. Flexion of the fingers and wrist is produced by the muscles of the forearm that originate from the medial (inside) elbow and terminate via long tendons that attach to the middle phalanx (MP) and distal phalanx (DP) of each finger. The flexor digitorum superficialis (FDS) muscle inserts into the palm side of the MP and produces flexion of the proximal interphalangeal (PIP) joint. The long tendon of the flexor digitorum profundus (FDP) muscle passes through a split in the FDS and then inserts on the palm side of the DP. The FDP controls flexion of the distal interphalangeal joint (DIP).

Both flexor tendons (FDS and FDP) pass through a tunnel-like, synovia-lined tendon sheath that provides nourishment and lubrication. The flexor tendon and sheath are held close to the bone by five annular pulleys (A1, A2, and so forth) and three (sometimes four) cruciform pulleys that prevent tendon "bowstringing" during flexion. Biomechanical studies have shown that the A2 and A4 pulleys are the most important (Lin

Figure 10.4 Annular Pulley Injuries

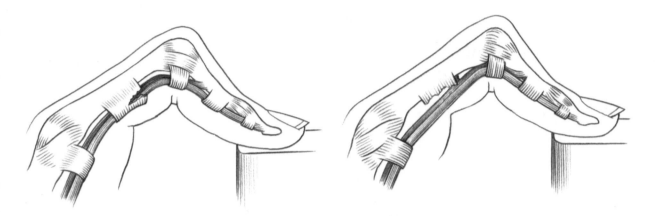

A2 pulley injury—partial tear (left) versus complete tear (right).

1989). As a conceptual model, visualize the whole system of the flexor tendon, sheath, and annular pulley as functioning like a brake cable on a bike.

TENDON PULLEY INJURIES

The most common finger injuries experienced by climbers involve partial tears or complete ruptures of one or more of the flexor tendon annular pulleys. In many cases only a partial tear of a single pulley occurs; in more serious incidences, however, one or more pulleys may rupture entirely, resulting in palpable or visible bowstringing, respectively. The exact nature and extent of the injury is difficult to diagnose without use of magnetic resonance imaging (Gabl 1996), though a recent Austrian study has shown Dynamic Ultrasonography to be highly effective at depicting finger pulley injuries in rock climbers as well (Klauswer 2002).

The A2 pulley is the most commonly injured of the five annular pulleys, and you can blame the common crimp grip as the main culprit. In using the crimp grip, near ninety-degree flexion of the PIP joint produces tremendous force load on the A2 pulley, in addition to forceful hyperextension of the DIP joint. Injuries to the A2 pulley can range from microscopic to partial tears and, in the worst case, a complete rupture (see **Figure 10.4**). Small partial tears are generally insidious, because they develop over the course of a few climbs, a few days of climbing, or even gradually during the course of seasons of climbing. Less frequent are acute ruptures that result during a maximum move on a tiny crimp hold or one-finger pocket. Some climbers report feeling or hearing a "pop"—a likely sign of a significant partial tear or complete rupture—though other injuries could also produce this effect.

Depending on the severity of an A2 pulley injury, pain and swelling at the base of the finger can range from slight to so debilitating that you can't perform everyday tasks like picking up a jug of milk. Swelling may limit the range of motion during flexion, and bowstringing may be felt or seen (Marco 1998) if one or two additional pulleys (usually A3 and A4) are ruptured, respectively. Slight tears may be asymptomatic when the finger is at rest, but become painful during isometric contraction (as in gripping a hold) or when pressing on the base of the finger near the top of the palm.

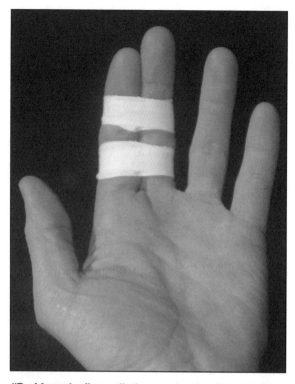

"Buddy taping" or splinting can be beneficial during the first week or two after injury, especially if you find it hard to limit your use of the injured finger.

Treatment of an A2 pulley injury must begin with completed cessation of climbing and discontinuation of any other activity that requires forceful flexion of the injured finger. Doing anything that causes pain will slow or prevent healing of the injured tissue and, more likely than not, make the injury worse. Therefore, the intelligent climber will cease climbing on the very day of the injury so that the healing process may begin and the time frame for healing be most brief. By contrast, the immature climber may try to climb through the injury, which all but guarantees a worse tear and an even longer, eventually forced, exit from climbing.

The goal during the first few days following injury is to control inflammation with ice (several times a day) and anti-inflammatory medicines like ibuprofen or Naprosyn. Cease these treatments after five days—

long-term use of ice and anti-inflammatory medicines can interfere with the healing process. "Buddy taping" or splinting of the injured finger can be beneficial during the first week or two after injury, especially if you find it hard to limit use of your injured finger.

Depending on the severity of the tear, pain typically subsides in two to ten weeks. Becoming pain-free, however is not the go-ahead to resume climbing! This is where many climbers go wrong—they return to climbing too soon and reinjure the partially healed tissue. As a general rule, wait an additional two weeks beyond becoming pain-free, then slowly return to climbing. In the case of a modest A2 pulley injury, this may mean a total of about forty-five days of downtime.

A French study of twelve elite climbers with A2 pulley injuries found that eight subjects were able to successfully return to climbing after forty-five days of rest (Moutet 1993). More severe pulley tears, however, may require as much as two or three months of rest before progressively returning to climbing. The bottom line on these frustrating pulley injuries is to nip them in the bud by immediately initiating a rest and healing period away from climbing. Each successive day you continue to climb on the injured finger may effectively multiply the length of the healing process (and your eventual time away from climbing).

In the case of a complete or multiple annular pulley rupture, surgical reconstruction is possible. Hand surgeons have long performed reconstruction of annular pulleys in nonclimbing cases where a deep laceration had damaged the flexor tendon and tendon pulleys. Free tendon grafts are the most common method of pulley reconstruction (Seiler 2000). The grafts can be harvested from the flexor digitorum longus of the second toe, the dorsal wrist retinaculum, or a resected portion of an injured FDS tendon (Seiler 1995; Lister 1979), and loops of the tendon are sewn in place of the damaged pulley. It has been shown that reconstruction with three loops can withstand as much force load to failure as a normal annular pulley (Lin 1989).

An Austrian study reveals that annular pulley reconstruction has produced good functional and subjective results in climbers after eighteen to forty-three months of recovery time (Gabl 1998). Still, American physician Joel Rohrbough has examined numerous climbers who exhibit chronic bowstringing and continue to climb hard without disability. Based on this, he recommends against surgery, though he does encourage individuals to make an educated choice after discussion with a qualified surgeon (Rohrbough 2000).

So how can one protect injured fingers from further damage? Reinforcing flexor tendon pulleys with cloth athletic tape is a popular method—but is this practice really effective? Several physicians are on record stating that firm circumferential taping is beneficial. Rohrbough (2000) notes that "tape is a tremendous help, giving support to a weak or healing pulley, helping to hold the tendon against the bone." Robinson (1988) says, "Use of tape around the fingers between joints is helpful," because it acts to reinforce the flexor tendon pulleys, protect the joint from extreme positions by limiting range of motion, and helps protect the skin.

Prophylactic Taping Methods

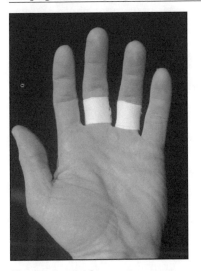 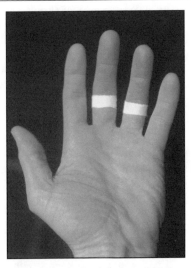 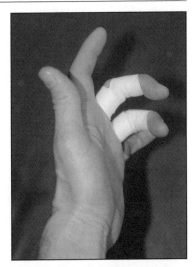

*The **A2 ring** is the most common method of prophylactic finger taping. Use the widest piece of tape possible without interfering with PIP flexion (anywhere from ½ to a full 1 inch, depending on the length of your fingers) and wrap three firm turns of tape around the base of the finger, directly supporting the A2 pulley. Apply the tape as tightly as possible without restricting blood flow. This may take a bit of experimentation, but remember that loose taping serves no function other than protecting the skin.*

*The **Swiss method** (as used in the Swiss study mentioned above) involves firm circumferential taping at the distal end of the proximal phalanx—that is, just above the A2 pulley and immediately below the PIP joint. Use a narrower strip of tape, approximately ⅜ inch in width, and wrap as tightly and as close to the PIP joint as possible without restricting blood flow or flexion.*

*The **X method** may provide additional tendon support to the A3, A4, and cruciform pulleys, and it's very effective at preventing skin wear (and pain) when climbing on sharp pockets or rough indoor holds. Tear a long strip of tape, approximately 16 inches in length by ¾ inch in width. With a slight bend in the finger, begin with two turns of tape over the proximal phalanx (on top of the A2 pulley), then cross under the PIP joint and take two turns around the middle phalanx. Cross back under the PIP joint and conclude with another turn or two around the base of the finger.*

Jebson (1997) advises using protective taping for two to three months, upon returning to climbing after an A2 pulley injury.

Despite these endorsements of prophylactic taping, a recent article in *Rock & Ice* states that taping "doesn't make the tendon any stronger—in fact, it may restrict blood flow to the repairing tendon and weaken it" (Crouch 1998). Furthermore, a study done in Texas found "no statistically significant difference in load to A2 pulley failure between taped and untaped fingers" and concluded that "we do not support taping the base of fingers as a prophylactic measure" (Warme 2000). Let's sort things out.

Based on an objective analysis of all available studies, it seems that the above statements about the ineffectiveness or even harmful effects of taping are flawed. First, the statement about taping "restricting blood and weakening the tendon" might be true if tape was worn all day and night. It's hard to imagine that taping for a few hours while training or climbing could have such a negative effect, however; after all, athletes in a wide range of sports tape everything from feet and ankles to wrists and fingers while in training or competing. Why would climbers' intermittent use of supportive taping be uniquely dangerous?

What about the recent study that found no difference in A2 pulley strength between taped and untaped fingers? Well, that study was done using fresh-frozen cadaveric hands that were rigidly mounted in a specialized jig to maintain a crimp grip position. One has to wonder if the warm hands of a living climber might exhibit different properties with regard to tendon strength and might even use a subtly different grip than our "climbing cadaver."

Interestingly, a Swiss researcher has apparently answered this question for us (Schweizer 2000). He built a device to measure tendon and tendon pulley forces in vivo—that is, live climbers' hands—and determined the force of bowstringing as well as the force applied to the pulley tape. Two slightly different taping methods were used—over the A2 pulley at the base of the finger and over the distal end of proximal phalanx near the PIP joint—as he tested sixteen fingers in the typical crimp grip position. This study

revealed that taping over the A2 pulley decreased bowstringing by 2.8 percent and absorbed 11 percent of the force, while taping just below the PIP joint (just beyond the A2 pulley) decreased bowstringing by 22 percent and absorbed 12 percent of total force. The obvious conclusion is that circular taping does provide a small reduction in total force on the tendon pulley system, though the author does not feel it would be enough to prevent a pulley rupture.

Therefore, it seems that taping should have a small positive effect in reinforcing the A2 pulley, and you should consider this practice for providing some protection of a previously injured tendon. Three different taping techniques are shown on page 157.

FLEXOR TENDONITIS, AND TENDON RUPTURE AND AVULSION

Several other injuries can produce pain and diminished function in ways similar to an injured annular pulley. (As stated earlier, diagnosis can be difficult—see a physician to be completely sure what you are dealing with.) Tendonitis can develop in the FDS or FDP tendon as a result of repetitive stress. In this case pain may be limited to the palm side of the finger or extend into the palm or forearm (Jebson 1997). Extended rest is the primary treatment, followed by a gradual return to climbing a few weeks after cessation of pain (as described for tendon pulley injuries).

In rare cases a flexor tendon may rupture or avulse (pull out at the point of insertion). Jebson (1997) states that an FDS tendon rupture may occur with the crimp grip, while an FDP tendon rupture is more likely with a pocket grip. Either rupture or avulsion would occur acutely with immediate onset of pain. Jebson states that symptoms include pain at the FDS or FDP tendon insertion, finger swelling, and an absence of active flexion of the PIP joint (FDS rupture) or DIP joint (FDP rupture). Surgical reattachment may be required.

You may be surprised to learn that flexor tendon ruptures, avulsions, and to a lesser extent annular pulley injuries occur occasionally among football players. These acute injuries, commonly called "jersey finger," occur when a tackler with an outstretched arm catches a finger on the jersey of the ball carrier sprinting past him. It is interesting to observe that many linemen and linebackers use prophylactic taping to support the flexor tendon and the A2 and A4 pulleys—it would seem that professional football players have also concluded that prophylactic taping works!

COLLATERAL LIGAMENT INJURIES

Ligaments connect bone to bone across a joint, providing stability (see **Figure 10.3**). Collateral ligament sprains and avulsions at the PIP joint are known to occur in climbers, particularly as a result of a powerful lunge or awkward torque off a "fixed" finger (as in a jam or tight pocket). A sprain manifests with mild to moderate pain and swelling around the PIP joint, but with no loss of stability (Jebson 1997). A rupture or avulsion will produce significant pain and swelling as well as loss of stability, medially or laterally.

Treatment of incomplete collateral ligament injuries typically involves splinting of the PIP joint for ten to fourteen days, after which buddy taping can be used and range-of-motion exercises started (Bach 1999). Climbing can gradually be reintroduced despite persistent low-grade pain and swelling, which may take months to resolve (Jebson 1997).

Complete collateral ligament injuries at the PIP joint are usually treated operatively. If the collateral ligament is completely avulsed from the bone, nonoperative treatment may result in chronic swelling and long-term instability (Bach 1999). Surgical repair can improve this, and full function is often restored in approximately three months.

Other Finger and Hand Injuries

A wide variety of other finger and hand injuries are possible in a sport that requires fingers to crimp, pinch, and jam under high passive and dynamic force loads. No doubt, you will experience your share of household injuries like torn tips or back-of-hand gobies. There are a few more subtle injuries that can affect climbers, however, including carpal tunnel syndrome and swollen or arthritic PIP and DIP joints.

CARPAL TUNNEL SYNDROME

Carpal tunnel syndrome (CTS) is a condition in which a nerve passing through the wrist, with the flexor tendons, is exposed chronically to too much pressure. This syndrome affects a small number of climbers, but its occurrence does not appear to be disproportionately common in climbers (Robinson 1993). Therefore, it's difficult to conclude whether a climber with this syndrome incurred it from the repetitive gripping of rock holds or from some other source. Regardless, the symptoms include numbness, burning, and tingling of the fingers; these symptoms may become worse at night or during activity or elevation (Lewis 1993). Treatment involves cessation or lowering intensity of climbing, anti-inflammatory medicines, and splinting of the wrist in a neutral position at night for three to six weeks. Surgical decompression of the carpal tunnel may be required if this conservative treatment fails and symptoms are severe enough to be disabling.

ARTHRITIS

For years I have heard speculation that active "rock climbers will someday become severe arthritis sufferers." Fortunately, anecdotal evidence of many twenty- and thirty-year veterans, as well as a recent study of sixty-five longtime climbers, indicates that these predictions are not quite panning out. In this study, radiographs of the hands of veteran elite climbers were compared to an age-matched control group. An increased rate of osteoarthritis for several joints was found in the climber group, though no significant difference in the overall prevalence of osteoarthritis was found between the two groups (Rohrbough 1998). This study is really good news for those of us entering middle age with many years of climbing under our belts!

Still, it's likely that individuals who predominantly use the crimp grip may experience some mild swelling and arthritis in the PIP and DIP joints. As shown in **Figure 10.4,** use of the crimp grip produces hyperextension of the DIP joint under large passive force, while the PIP joint is sharply flexed under great force. Therefore, both the DIP and PIP joints are possible sites of mild swelling and arthritis (Robinson 1993).

If you are an aging climber who experiences some swelling, pain, or stiffness of the DIP and PIP joints, you will find some relief through use of nonsteroidal anti-inflammatory medications. A growing body of research also points to a supplement called glucosamine sulfate as an effective treatment for mild osteoarthritis. Daily supplementation of 1,500 milligrams of glucosamine sulfate has been shown to reduce pain and stiffness, and—more important—to slow the degradation of affected joints (Reginster 2001). Acquiring these benefits requires a long-term commitment to taking glucosamine sulfate, because the effects are cumulative, not immediate as in taking anti-inflammatory medicines. But the promise of slowing or halting joint degradation is a huge benefit for individuals—climbers and nonclimbers—over forty years of age who take glucosamine sulfate daily.

Some supplement manufacturers are now adding a compound known as chondroitin to their glucosamine sulfate supplements. Chondroitin is believed to produce benefits similar to glucosamine sulfate's, and one study showed positive results in patients with joint problems from four to eight weeks of taking both supplements together. The study proposes a five-to-four ratio of glucosamine sulfate to chondroitin with a total daily dose of 1,500 and 1,200 milligrams, respectively (McAlindon 2000). All of the studies showed these compounds to be safe, and with almost no side effects.

Elbow Injuries

Tendonitis around the elbow joint is another common ailment among climbers. This overuse injury can develop near the bony inside (medial) area of the elbow or on the outside (lateral), top portion of the elbow. Let's take a closer look at the pathology and treatment of each.

MEDIAL EPICONDYLITIS

Tendonitis near the medial epicondyle is commonly called golfer's elbow or climber's elbow, since it occurs most frequently among participants in these sports. Inflammation occurs in the tendon connecting the many forearm flexor muscles (responsible for finger flexion and forearm pronation) to the knobby, medial epicondyle of the inside elbow.

This overuse injury usually reveals itself gradually through increasing incidence of painful twinges or soreness during or after climbing. A small number of cases seem to occur acutely, however, when sharp pain develops in the midst of a single hard move, like cranking a powerful boulder problem or a one-arm pull-up. Even in these cases cumulative microtrauma may be involved in making the tissue vulnerable to the single-event trauma.

In most cases medial epicondylitis is caused by muscular imbalances of the forearm that result from climbing too often, too hard, and, most important, with too little rest. Consider that all the muscles that produce finger flexion are anchored to the medial epicondyle. Furthermore, the muscles that produce hand pronation (turning of the palm down and outward) originate from the medial epicondyle. This subtle fact plays a vital role in causing this injury: Biceps contraction produces supination (turning of the palm upward), but in gripping the rock you generally need to maintain a pronated, palms-out position. This battle, between the supinating action of the biceps pulling and the necessity to maintain a pronated hand position (to maintain grip with the rock), strains the typically undertrained forearm pronator muscles and their attachment at the medial epicondyle.

Given the above factors, it's easy to see why the tendons attaching to the medial epicondyle are subjected to repeated high stress loads and, inevitably, microtraumas. Just as muscular microtraumas are repaired to new level of capability, the tendons increase in strength and can withstand higher stress loads given adequate rest. Unfortunately, the repair and strengthening process occurs more slowly in tendons than in muscles. Eventually, the muscles are able to create more force and accumulated stress than the tendons can adapt to—the result is tendonitis.

As in treating other injuries, you can more easily manage epicondylitis and speed your return to climbing by recognizing and proactively treating the injury in its earliest stages. Treating the problem early versus climbing through it could mean the difference between six weeks and six months of downtime.

Treatment of epicondylitis has two phases. Phase I is pain relief; Phase II, rehabilitation and prevention of recurrence. Phase I demands withdrawal from climbing (and all sport-specific training) and commencement of anti-inflammatory measures. Icing the elbow for ten to fifteen minutes, two times a day, and use of anti-inflammatory medication will gradually decrease inflammation and pain. A cortisone injection may be helpful in chronic or severe cases, though this practice is somewhat controversial among physicians and, in fact, may be detrimental to the healing process (Nirschl 1996). Depending on the severity of the epicondylitis, successful completion of Phase I could require anywhere from two weeks to several months.

The goal of Phase II is to retrain and rehabilitate the injured tissues through use of stretching and strength-training exercises. Since forearm-muscle imbalance plays a primary role in this injury, it's vital to perform exercises that strengthen the weaker aspects of the forearm—hand pronation and hand/wrist extension.

Always perform some general warm-up activity or, ideally, warm the elbow directly with a heating pad before beginning the stretching and strengthening exercises. Initially, stretch the muscles of the forearm as shown in the photos on page 72, twice daily. Introduce strength training with the dumbbell exercises shown in the photos on pages 103 and 104 only when stretching exercises have successfully restored normal range of motion and produced no pain. It's important to progress slowly on the weight-training exercises, and to cut back at the first sign of pain. Begin with just a couple of pounds of resistance and gradually increase the weight over the course of a few weeks. Use the stretching exercises daily, but do the weight-training exercises only three days per week.

After three to four weeks of pain-free training, begin a gradual return to climbing. Start with low-angle and easy vertical routes, and take a month or two to return to your original level of climbing. Continue with the stretching and strength-training exercises indefinitely—as long as you are a climber, you must engage in these preventive measures. Failed rehabilitation may signal a need for surgical intervention.

Finally, let's take a look at the use of counterforce bracing, or circumferential taping of the upper forearm, as a curative (or preventive) measure for elbow tendonitis. A counterforce brace designed specifically for medial or lateral epicondylitis can provide some comfort by dispersing forces away from the underlying tissues (Nirschl 1996). These braces are not a substitute for proper rehabilitation, however; they instead act only to help prevent recurrence after full rehabilitation. There is little evidence that supportive taping of the forearm provides the same benefit as use of a counterforce brace.

LATERAL EPICONDYLITIS

Lateral epicondylitis, commonly called tennis elbow, is an inflammation of the tendon that attaches the forearm extensor and hand supinator muscles to the lateral epicondyle on the outside of the elbow. The forearm extensor muscles are antagonists to the forearm flexor muscles used so heavily in gripping the rock. The extensors are often disproportionately weak compared to the flexors, so regular strength training of this muscle group is vital to preventing injury.

Onset of pain is typically gradual, and will first appear after a hard day of climbing. Without treatment, the condition will progressively worsen to the point that climbing becomes prohibitively painful and even everyday tasks are hampered. Since such a severe case often requires a six-month (or longer) rehabilitation period away from climbing, it's paramount that you take the necessary steps to mitigate this injury early on.

The treatment protocol for lateral epicondylitis is basically the same as that described above for medial epicondylitis. Time away from climbing is mandatory—very few people successfully climb through elbow tendonitis of either kind. Use of anti-inflammatory medication and icing is helpful during the initial period of pain and inflammation, though these should never be used to allow continuation of climbing.

As pain and swelling subside, daily use of the stretching exercises outlined earlier is absolutely necessary to begin the rehabilitation process. Use a heating pad for a few minutes before stretching and ice the elbow for ten to fifteen minutes afterward. Gradually add in the dumbbell exercises for strengthening the forearm muscles (see "Medial Epicondylitis") and add weight incrementally over the course of a few weeks.

In mild cases of epicondylitis, you may be able to progress through this rehabilitation and begin a slow return to climbing in six to eight weeks. A counter-force brace worn just below the elbow may be beneficial upon beginning a slow return to climbing.

As stated earlier, severe episodes may take six months or more to eliminate and rehabilitate, so commit to the treatment process as early as possible. A surgical solution should be viewed as a last resort, when this conservative treatment repeatedly fails. The most popular procedure is to simply excise the diseased tissue from the tendon, then reattach the tendon to the bone. Eighty-five to 90 percent of patients recuperate in three months, 10 to 12 percent have improvement but some pain during exercise, and only 2 to 3 percent have no improvement (Auerbach 2000).

Shoulder Injuries

The shoulder joint takes lot of punishment from climbing, especially in those obsessed with "V-hard" bouldering, steep terrain, and sport-specific training. A variety of injuries can occur, ranging from tendonitis or a tear of the rotator cuff to partial or complete dislocations of the ball-and-socket joint of the shoulder. Given the complexity of the shoulder joint, however, a diagnosis can be difficult and may require expert consultation or an MRI to detect small tears of the rotator cuff and other subtle injuries.

SHOULDER INSTABILITY

The most common shoulder injury I've seen in climbers seems to center on development of a loose or unstable shoulder. More than one climber I know developed shoulder instability apparently from far too many hours hanging on a fingerboard or from long-term, overzealous stretching of the upper body. Climbing on overhanging routes day after day, and hard bouldering and training without adequate rest and antagonist-muscle training, can also lead to loose shoulders. No matter the mechanism, constant stretching of the ligaments and tendons and a growing muscular imbalance will make the shoulder joints susceptible to dislocation and injury. This may eventually lead to a debilitating injury and, possibly, the need for a surgical solution.

Dr. Joel Rohrbough has worked with many climbers and believes that a partial dislocation known as subluxation is the most common injury among climbers. This injury produces instability of the shoulder joint and manifests with pain from deep within or in back of the shoulder (Rohrbough 2001). In most cases the ball portion of the shoulder joint is levered forward during extreme movements with the elbow located behind the plane of the body. Furthermore, the force of the levering motion on the shoulder joint increases when the arm is extended with the elbow out (or back), as in grabbing a high gaston hold or making a long reach on overhanging rock.

Fresh shoulder injuries should be treated with the two-phase process of resting until pain diminishes and then use of rehabilitative exercises to strengthen the rotator cuff muscle group. Climbing activity must be markedly reduced or eliminated while you engage in the rehabilitative process, and you should also avoid any overhead motion or other activity that causes pain in the shoulder. Anti-inflammatory medicine and ice applied twice daily are useful in reducing initial pain and swelling.

The common course of therapy begins with gentle stretching and strengthening of the shoulder, but with no exercises above the level of the shoulder. Perform the four exercises from the "Shoulder Rehab Exercises" on pages 163 and 164 every other day, and gradually increase the weight from one pound to five pounds over about a five-week period. Gradually, you can introduce some basic push-muscle exercises (see Chapter 6) that strengthen the antagonist muscles. Decrease resistance on or eliminate completely any exercise that is too painful. Of course, rehabilitation is best guided by a professional physical therapist, and may take anywhere from two to six months before reintroducing climbing activities.

Unfortunately, a significant number of people with shoulder injuries ultimately require a surgical solution. The procedure may include removal of damaged tissue, repair of minor tears, or surgical tightening of affected ligaments and tendons. Surgery will be followed with long-term physical therapy; given a successful outcome, climbing activity may resume in six to twelve months.

Exercise: **Shoulder Rehab Exercises**

Perform the shoulder rehabilitation exercises three or four days per week. Be sure to perform each exercise on both sides of the body (with both arms).

- **Dumbbell Internal Rotation**

  Lie on your side with your bottom arm in front of your waist and a pillow under your head to support your neck. Hold a one-pound dumbbell in the hand of your bottom arm and position the arm so the forearm is perpendicular to your body. Keeping your upper arm motionless, bring the weight up to your body and hold for a moment before lowering it back to the floor. Perform the full range of motion with a ninety-degree angle between your forearm and upper arm. Do three sets of twenty slow, controlled repetitions. Gradually add weight, in one-pound increments, over the course of a few weeks.

- **Dumbbell External Rotation**

  Lie on the floor in the same position described in the previous exercise; this time, however, place a rolled-up towel under your upper arm. Hold a one-pound dumbbell in your upper hand and, while keeping your upper arm against the side of your body, let your forearm hang across the body so the elbow is bent at a ninety-degree angle. Now raise the weight toward the ceiling until it's parallel to

Dumbbell Internal Rotation

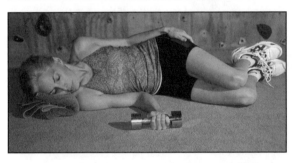

1. Lie on your side with your bottom arm in front of your waist.

2. Bring the weight up to your body.

Dumbbell External Rotation

1. Lie on the floor and let your forearm hang across your body.

2. Raise the weight toward the ceiling until it's parallel to the ground.

Bent-Over Arm Raise

1. Assume a bent-over position.

2. Lift your arm up to your side until it's parallel to the floor.

Bent-Over Arm Kickback

1. Assume a bent-over position.

2. Lift the dumbbell behind you until it's in position next to your hip.

the ground and hold for a moment before lowering the weight down to the starting position. Do three sets of twenty slow, controlled repetitions. Gradually add weight, in one-pound increments, over the course of a few weeks.

- **Bent-Over Arm Raise**
With one leg slightly ahead of the other, assume a bent-over position with your upper body supported by a bent arm braced onto the knee of the forward leg. Holding a light dumbbell in the opposite hand, lift your arm up to your side until it's parallel to the floor. Hold for a moment and lower slowly to the starting position. Keep your elbow straight throughout the range of motion. Do three sets of ten to fifteen repetitions.

- **Bent-Over Arm Kickback**
Assume the same bent-over position as in the previous exercise, but this time lift the dumbbell behind you until it's parallel to the floor and in a position next to your hip. Hold here for a moment and return to the starting position. Maintain a straight arm throughout the range of motion. Do three sets of ten to fifteen repetitions.

Knee Injuries

Injury to the knee is a relatively new phenomenon in climbing that correlates directly to the proliferation of indoor and sport climbing. New climbing techniques like the drop-knee weren't popularized until the 1990s, but this is now a hallmark move of the steep indoor and outdoor climbs that are so prominent today. Repeated use of this drop-knee, especially under high force load, can tear the specialized cartilage in the knee called the meniscus (Stelzle 2000).

MENISCUS TEAR

Meniscus is a tough, fibrous type of cartilage that sits between the ends of the femur and tibia (see **Figure 10.5**). The menisci serve primarily as shock absorbers between the ends of the bones to protect the articulating surfaces (McFarland 2000). There are two separate C-shaped meniscal cartilages in the knee, one on the inner half of the knee (the medial meniscus) and the other on the outer half (the lateral meniscus). A partial or total tear of a meniscus can occur during forced rotation of the knee while the foot remains in a fixed position. In climbing, these tears most often occur in severe drop-knee positions, which produce inside rotation of the knee under pressure. They can also result from high steps in a full hip turnout position and jumping off highball boulder problems.

A small meniscus tear can develop gradually from repeated use of these climbing moves, or a tear may occur suddenly. Some tears involve only a small portion of the meniscus, while others produce a bucket handle, or complete separation of a piece of cartilage. Symptoms can range from mild pain and no visible swelling to severe pain and swelling and reduced mobility (McFarland 2000). Many meniscal tears cause popping, clicking, and locking of the knee in certain positions.

Not all meniscus tears cause big problems. A minor tear in the thick outer portion of the meniscus may be able to repair itself given fairly good blood supply. Also, use of the supplement glucosamine sulfate (see "Arthritis" for more info) is believed to support the formation of new cartilage and may enhance the healing process. In minor cases, symptoms will

Figure 10.5 **Meniscus Tear**

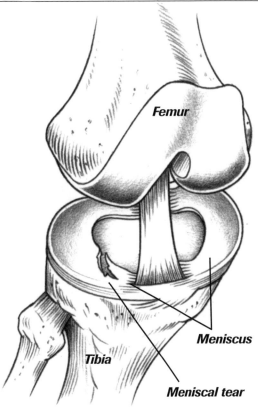

The meniscus can tear when the knee is forced to rotate while the foot remains in a fixed position. A severe drop-knee move or a twisting jump off a boulder problem can cause this injury.

disappear on their own; persistent pain that affects daily activities or produces significant pain in certain climbing positions may require surgery, however.

Arthroscopic surgery is very successful in relieving pain and restoring full function to the injured knee. The goal of arthroscopic surgery is to preserve as much of the meniscus as possible so as to decrease the chance of future arthritis (McFarland 2000). Tears on the outer margin of the meniscus are more amenable to repair, since they have greater blood flow compared to the thin, inner margin of the meniscus. Tears in the thin portion of the meniscus are typically excised; entirely detached pieces of cartilage are removed.

Recovery from arthroscopic surgery is rapid. The procedure is generally performed as outpatient surgery, followed by three to seven days of rest, ice packs, and elevating the limb. Crutches are often used during the first postoperative week, though weight can be placed on the injured leg as can be tolerated. Most patients return to work in less than a week, and other normal activities can be added during the second and third week after surgery.

Physical therapy may be beneficial, but is not required for fit individuals who can begin a gradual return to physical activity after two or three weeks. A full return to training activities and climbing typically takes two to three months.

Preventing Injuries

This chapter began by quoting studies that place your odds—as an avid rock climber—of getting injured as at least at three to one. Therefore, it seems appropriate that we conclude this tome with an attempt at lowering those odds!

First, abstinence is the only preventive measure that is absolute. Climbing is a stressful sport, and injury may be unavoidable. Still, I estimate that you can lower the risk by at least 50 percent if you follow all the preventive measures outlined below. Undoubtedly, some of these guidelines fly in opposition to the modus operandi of many climbers. By now, however, you are familiar with the thread weaving throughout this book: "To outperform the masses, you must do things that they do not do."

Ten Rules for Preventing Overuse Injuries

Detailed below are ten strategies for lowering your exposure to overuse injuries. Clearly, there will be situations that demand breaking one or more of these rules. By climbing and training in accordance with these guidelines most of the time, however, you will likely decrease your risk of injury and never, or only rarely, join the injured mass of climbers.

1. **Focus on technique training over strength training.** Many overuse injuries result from too much of a focus on strength training too early in an individual's climbing career. As advised throughout this book, it's fundamental to develop a high level of technical competence before jumping full bore into sport-specific training. Not only does good technique help you reduce stress on your fingers and shoulders, but it also helps maximize economy of movement and, thus, increases apparent strength on the rock.

Remember that two to four days per week of climbing will naturally produce rapid gains in sport-specific strength in beginners. Because tendons strengthen at a slower rate than muscles, novice climbers are not exempt from injury risk. With little experience, these new climbers have not yet developed the keen sense needed to distinguish "good pain" from "bad pain." The number of climbers who become injured during their first year or two in the sport—as they quickly progress from, say, 5.5 to 5.10 (or higher)—is alarming. Therefore, awareness, maturity, and a prudent approach to training are vital traits that must be fostered in all enthusiastic climbers.

Finally, it's important to avoid the added stress of using highly specific training tools, like a fingerboard or campus board, during the first year of climbing. After that, these activities can be added gradually as part of an intelligent, well-planned training for climbing program.

2. **Regularly vary the type of climbing.** Varying the type and magnitude of climbing stressors on the body is a highly effective way of lowering your exposure to injury. For instance, alternating consecutive weekends of climbing between sport and traditional routes naturally varies the type of specific strains placed on the body. Likewise, regularly changing the focus of weekday climbing and training activities—for example, alternating among bouldering, roped gym climbing, and general training—prevents any single system from being overly stressed. This practice of constantly mixing things up is the essence of cross-training applied to climbing.

3. **Use prophylactic finger taping in the most stressful situations and after injury.** This subject

was covered in length earlier in the chapter, but it's worth underscoring here—supportive taping of the finger tendon pulleys helps lower the force load placed on the tendons and may help prevent injury. Still, prophylactic taping is not something you should use every day and on every climb. Subjecting the finger tendons and annular pulleys to gradually increasing levels of stress is what will make them stronger and able to function under higher and higher loads in the future. The use of taping *all the time* could have a negative impact on the long-term strength of this system.

Reserve use of prophylactic taping techniques for workouts or climbs that you expect will push the envelope of what your tendons have previously experienced. For instance, taping would be a wise measure for attempting a hardest-ever route, any climb known to possess injurious hold types (one-finger pockets, extreme crimps, and the like), or high-intensity training techniques such as campus or HIT training. Of course, individuals recovering from recent finger injuries should tape their fingers during the early stages of returning to climbing.

4. **Proceed cautiously through dangerous moves.** An important sense to develop is that of knowing and managing movement through inherently dangerous moves or sequences. In recognizing that you are entering a dangerous sequence (say, a one-finger lock with poor feet) and in sensing that you are near injury on a move, you are empowered to either disengage from the move or cautiously manage through the sequence as expeditiously as possible. Clearly you need experience in such situations in order to develop this sense, but you can foster this important skill by knowing your body and the sensations you feel on various types of movements.

As a final note, a climber will often escape injury on the first attempt or pass through some heinous move, then get injured by attempting or rehearsing the painful move repeatedly. This is obviously a very unintelligent approach—no single route is worth getting injured and, possibly, laid up for months over. Bottom line: If you find yourself climbing into a move that feels overly painful or injury-scary, simply lower off and find a better route to enjoy.

5. **Don't climb to exhaustion.** There is nothing I enjoy more than occasionally maximizing a day of climbing fun by pulling down right into the evening twilight. As a regular practice, however, this is a prescription for injury. This chapter covered a range of overuse injuries that are largely caused by accumulated stress beyond what the body is capable of handling—that's why they call them *overuse* injuries!

Knowing when to say when is one of the subtle climbing skills that you can't learn from a book or video, but only through experience. Obviously, the best strategy is to err on the side of ending climbing early in the day versus right after you feel that finger tweak. The chapter on strength training hammered home the idea that quality training stimulus is far more important that the quantity of training. In strength training, less is often more.

When climbing, the right decision on when to call it a day is much less clear, since you want to maximize climbing fun without getting injured. In this situation only you can decide what's right for you. Don't be swayed into another burn on a strenuous route if you are approaching exhaustion and think your climbing technique will not be up to snuff. Keep in mind that many injuries occur late in the day, when you are tired and climbing sloppily.

One rule of thumb you might adopt is to call it quits early when planning to climb again the very next day or if you are already on your second day of climbing. In this way, you will limit undue accumulation of stress. Conversely, when sandwiching a single day of climbing between two rest days, you can feel better about packing in as many climbs as possible before dark.

6. **Don't climb or train more than four days per week.** This is another rule right out of Chapter 7, "Personal Training Programs." In most cases it's counterproductive to climb and train more than a total of four days per week. Consequently, if you are climbing four days a week on the rock, in the gym,

or both combined, you should do no other sport-specific training during the three remaining days of the week. Even with three days rest out of seven, your body will struggle to repair the microtraumas incurred to the tendons and muscles during your four climbing days. For this reason, it is wise to incorporate a training cycle that provides a complete week off every so often. This is valuable catch-up time for your biological climbing machine!

In a pure strength- and power-training program (such as in focused off-season training), you may only be able to train two or three days per week while resting four or five. Earlier in this chapter I presented several studies that indict overtraining (or under-resting) as one of the most common causes of overuse injury. Don't set yourself up for failure by succeeding at overtraining. Listen to your body, and when in doubt, favor over-resting.

7. **Always warm up and cool down.** Anyone with experience in traditional sports knows firsthand the importance of a proper warm-up and cooldown. Unfortunately, I have observed more than a few climbers who just tie in and start climbing without any preparatory warm-up activity, stretching, or submaximum climbing.

All that's needed for a good warm-up is to break a light sweat by jogging, hiking, or riding a bike for five to fifteen minutes. Follow this with some light stretching exercises, as described in Chapter 6. Start your climbing for the day by doing a series of easy boulder problems or a route or two that is much easier than you might want to get on. This minor inconvenience is a worthy investment in avoiding injury and maximizing your performance later in the day.

A brief cool-down is also beneficial since it will loosen up tight muscle groups and enhance the recovery process. In particular, stretching and a few minutes of light aerobic activity help maintain increased blood flow and speed dispersion of lactic acid accumulated in the most fatigued muscles.

8. **Maintain muscle balance by training antagonist muscle groups.** Training the antagonist muscles is one of the most overlooked—and most vital—parts of training for climbing. Muscle imbalances in the forearms, shoulders, and torso are primary factors in many of the overuse injuries covered in this chapter. If you are serious about climbing your best and preventing injury, then you must commit to training the antagonist muscles twice per week.

The time and equipment involved is minimal. All of the antagonist-muscle exercises described in Chapter 6 can be performed at home with nothing more than a couple of dumbbells. As for the time commitment, it's less than twenty minutes, twice per week. I advise doing these exercises at the end of your weekday climbing or sport-specific workout. Keep the weights light, and do every single exercise outlined for the antagonist muscles of the upper body and forearms, as well as the handful of exercises for the core muscles of the torso.

9. **Use periodization to vary your training schedule.** Many sports scientists consider periodization to be the gold standard for interweek planning of an effective and optimal strength-training program. As described in Chapter 5, periodization involves a premeditated variation in workout focus, intensity, and volume, which in the long term produces a maximum training response. Periodization may also reduce the risk of overuse injury, since the training focus and intensity changes every few days or weeks.

In a highly stressful sport like climbing, the most valuable aspect of periodization may be the intermittent rest phases or breaks away from all sport-specific activity. Chapter 7 advised use of the 4-3-2-1 cycle for most intermediate and elite climbers. Use of this training cycle provides one full week of rest out of every ten-week mesocycle, for systemic recovery and to blunt long-term accumulation of overuse stress. In the yearlong macrocycle it is advised to take one full month off from climbing-related stresses. These breaks away from climbing go a long way toward allowing the slow-to-adapt tendons and ligaments to catch up to the gains in muscular strength. It's also a healthy break for your mental muscle!

10. **Make getting proper rest and nutrition a top priority.** Getting proper rest and nutrition seems like an obvious rule for a serious athlete, but I'm often surprised by the bad dietary and sleep habits possessed by some very serious climbers. Fortunately, I have noticed improvement and increased awareness about rest and nutrition issues in recent years. No doubt the better-informed and more disciplined climbers are performing closer to their ultimate potential and with fewer injuries.

The chapters "Performance Nutrition" and "Accelerating Recovery" provide many useful strategies to employ as you increase the priority placed on these subjects. If you use most of these strategies, most of the time, I am confident that you will outperform the masses and reduce your risk of overuse injuries.

Certainly an occasional late night out or free day of eating and drinking whatever you like won't hurt (in fact, it's a great reward after a hard tick!). Still, consistent lack of sleep and poor nutrition slow recovery between workouts and days of climbing, and undoubtedly make you more vulnerable to injury. Most important is good nutrition and a solid eight to nine hours of sleep in the day or two following an especially hard workout or day(s) of climbing. Remember that training and recovery are opposite sides of the same coin—if you put the effort into training optimally, then it would be a waste not do everything in your power to recovery optimally as well.

Jeff Batzer showing no handicap as he tops out on **Upper Refuse,** *Cathedral Ledge, New Hampshire.*

PHOTO BY ERIC J. HÖRST

Afterword

The power of climbing is awesome. The simple act of moving over stone can change your day, and it can change your life. Climbing takes you to places you have never been before—breathtaking vistas that few humans ever see and deep into the very core of your being. In this way climbing helps us discover who we are and gives us the gift of insight into our true potential and what really is possible in our lives. Many "flatlanders" never gain this insight, and worse yet, far too many people around the world will never have the opportunity to experience the wonder of climbing (or any other pleasure-seeking activity) because they spend each day of their lives just trying to get by. From this perspective, I trust you will agree that in simply being able to go climbing and pursue self-actualization, we are better off than the majority of people on this planet. Regardless of your current disposition, vow to live each day with an attitude of gratitude. Look for ways to brighten the day of everyone you meet, and consider contributing some time or money to aid those who are less fortunate. I invite you to check out some of my favorite charities listed below. Share some of your climbing power with the world!

- *www.MakeAWish.org*
- *www.RedCross.org*
- *www.WorldVision.org*

Appendix A

Training Charts

Use the two blank training charts on the following pages to track your training progress. The Training and Climbing Macrocycle will enable you to set annual training objectives and seasonal climbing goals as well as record your actual progress. You can use the chart to plan your training for the four seasons, target specific types of training, track the number of days you train, and record your achievements throughout the year. In contrast, the Energy–Emotion Levels chart will allow you to track your physical energy and emotional mind-set hour by hour throughout the day. You can use this chart to observe patterns, avoid negative triggers, modify your emotional state, and better manage your energy and outlook for optimal performance.

Training and Climbing Macrocycle

Name/Year												
				Training Objectives and Seasonal Climbing Goals								
Month	**Jan**	**Feb**	**Mar**	**Apr**	**May**	**Jun**	**Jul**	**Aug**	**Sep**	**Oct**	**Nov**	**Dec**
Week	1 2 3 4 5	6 7 8 9	10 11 12 13	14 15 16 17 18	19 20 21 22	23 24 25 26	27 28 29 30 31	32 33 34 35	36 37 38 39	40 41 42 43 44	45 46 47 48	49 50 51 52

Training Focus
- Climbing/endurance
- Max. strength and power
- Anaerobic endurance
- Rest

Total number of days per week of finger training or climbing
7
6
5
4
3
2
1

Benchmark achievements and notes

Energy–Emotion Levels

Name: _____   Date: _____

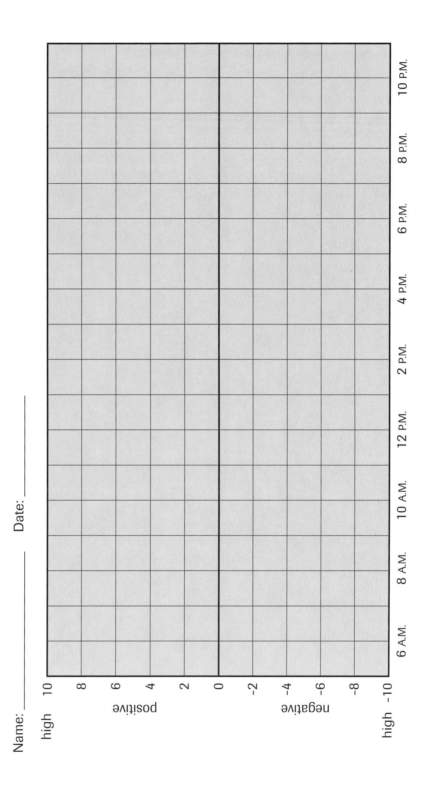

Appendix B

Self-Assessment Test Comments & Training Tips

The Self-Assessment Test in Chapter 2 covers physical strength, mental focus, and techniques and tactics. Taking the test should help you to gauge your overall strengths and weaknesses and pinpoint some specific areas for improvement. If you gave yourself a score of three or lower on any of the questions, you've identified weak spots that should be targeted for training. Here is a brief comment on each of these common problems as well as some specific tips for improving your climbing performance. For more in-depth information on any of these topics, see the chapters referenced below.

1. If your footwork deteriorates during the hardest part of the climb, you might be focusing on the lack of good handholds instead of zeroing in on crucial footholds (often the key to unlocking hard sequences).

    TIP: When the going gets tough, focus on your feet! (See Chapter 3.)

2. If your forearms balloon and your grip begins to fail, you are probably overgripping the holds and/or climbing too slowly.

    TIP: On near-vertical walls, relax your grip and place maximum weight over your feet. When the wall angle is overhanging, the number one rule is to climb fast from one rest to the next. (See Chapter 4.)

3. If you have difficulty stepping onto critical footholds during hard sequences, lack of flexibility or weak hip flexor muscles is the likely problem.

TIP: Begin daily stretching for a minimum of ten minutes and practice high steps in a gym setting. (See Chapter 6.)

4. If you find you get anxious and tight as you head into crux sequences, normalized breathing is the key to reducing tension and anxiety.

    TIP: Before starting up a climb, close your eyes and take five slow, deep breaths (each breath should take at least ten seconds). Try to maintain steady breathing as you climb. Take three more slow, deep breaths at each rest position and before you begin the crux sequence. (See Chapter 3.)

5. If your biceps pump out before your forearms, it usually means you're hanging out with bent arms. Straight-arm positions are fundamental to good climbing technique.

    TIP: Whenever possible, hang "by the bone" and not with flexed arm muscle. Straight-arm positions are especially important when placing gear, shaking out, or pausing to decipher the next sequence.

6. Do you have difficulty hanging on small, necessary holds? Although poor body positioning can make small holds even harder to use, it's likely that your contact strength (grip) needs work.

    TIP: Spend more time training on steep walls and gym cave areas, and go bouldering more often. Some limited fingerboard and hypergravity training is also recommended for intermediate and advanced climbers. (See Chapter 6.)

7. If you fail on sequences you know by heart, you might be making the common mistake of trying or inventing new sequences during a redpoint attempt.

   TIP: When you find a sequence that works, it's usually best to stick with it. Counter any mid-climb thoughts of trying a new sequence with the definitive belief that you already know (and can do) the best sequence.

8. If you stall at the start of crux sequences, you might be suffering from paralysis by analysis.

   TIP: When faced with a crux sequence, visualize two possible sequences, and then immediately try the one that looks more promising. Once you commit to a sequence, go for it! Only one thing should be on your mind—getting to the next good hold (or rest) as fast as possible.

9. Do you climb three or four days in a row? Unless you are one of those genetically gifted extreme outliers, climbing or training on three or four consecutive days is a practice that will lead to overtraining, injury, and a drop in performance.

   TIP: In this case, less is more. Switch to a two-day-on, one-day-off (or two-day-off) schedule and you will be training smarter and climbing harder!

10. Sewing-machine leg is common in the tight, anxious climber.

    TIP: Lengthen your warm-up and begin working some of the relaxation exercises described later in this text. (See Chapter 3.)

11. If you pump out on overhanging climbs, you should be aware that the pump clock starts running when you leave the ground. You might not be too weak to climb the route, just too slow!

    TIP: Practice climbing more quickly on known (wired) routes and when redpointing. Foster a watchful eye that's on the lookout for creative rests that might stop the clock for a few moments. (See Chapter 4.)

12. Do you get out of breath when you climb? Rapid breathing while climbing results from excess tension, irregular breathing, or poor aerobic fitness.

    TIP: Concentrate on maintaining relaxed, normal breathing while you climb. Also, consider engaging in some aerobic training (preferably running) three to four days per week. Build up to a maximum of four, twenty-minute runs per week. (See Chapter 6.)

13. If you begin thinking about how you might fail on a route before you even start, you should know that belief gives birth to reality. If the thought of failing crosses your mind, you likely will.

    TIP: Before you start up a climb, always visualize yourself successfully climbing the route from bottom to top. (See Chapter 3.)

14. Do you miss hidden holds on routes? Tunnel vision is a common cause of failure, especially during on-sight climbing.

    TIP: Scope the route from a few different vantage points before leaving the ground. As you climb, keep an open mind for hidden holds—the key hold always seems to take a little extra effort to locate. If a route feels really hard for its grade, chances are there's a good handhold or foothold escaping your view. (See Chapter 4.)

15. If you have difficulty hanging on to small holds or pockets, keep in mind that open-hand grip strength is crucial. Expert climbers favor it, while beginner climbers avoid it.

    TIP: While training and bouldering, force yourself to use the open-hand grip at least 50 percent of the time. Most intermediate and advanced climbers can significantly improve open-hand grip strength through use of HIT workouts. (See Chapter 6.)

16. It's common to grab onto gear rather than risk a fall trying a hard move. Assuming the potential fall is safe, always go for the move instead of grabbing gear or hanging on the rope. The bad habit of grabbing gear is easy to develop and very hard to break. Plus, you'll never learn where your true limit is if you give up in this way.

    TIP: Counter any thought of grabbing gear with the belief that there is absolutely a good hold just a few moves above you (there probably is!).

17. If much of your body weight is hanging on your arms, you might not be placing your weight (center of gravity) over your feet.

    TIP: Invest more time practicing technique and body positioning. Focus on keeping your crotch and hips in near the wall (except on slabs) and experiment with moves where you turn one hip or the other to the wall. Some flexibility training may be beneficial, too.

18. Intense soreness after only one day of cragging means that your training volume and intensity are not congruent with your outdoor climbing goals.

    TIP: Step up your indoor training and always try for two solid training days during the workweek.

19. Do you have difficulty visualizing yourself successfully climbing the route? All peak performers acknowledge the importance of visualization.

    TIP: Get into the habit of climbing each route in your mind's eye at least twice before giving it a real go. (See Chapter 3.)

20. If you think you cannot reach key holds on difficult routes, you should be aware that this is the oldest excuse in this sport. Funny thing is, some great short climbers never use this excuse! The reason—there is almost always a technical solution or intermediate hold to be discovered that will solve apparent reach problems.

    TIP: Try a move twenty different ways and you'll almost always find one that works!

21. If your feet cut loose and swing out on overhanging routes and roofs, it's possible that poor footwork and body positioning are responsible for the swinging feet syndrome. More often, however, it commonly results from weak core muscles (torso).

    TIP: Perform the core-muscle exercises, described in Chapter 6, at least twice weekly. Also, spend more time in a bouldering cave working on your steep-wall footwork and body position.

22. If you get distracted by activity on the ground, remember that while climbing your focus must be aimed upward, not down toward the ground. If less than 95 percent of your focus or attention is pointed toward the top of the climb, you don't have much of a chance of getting there.

    TIP: Clear your mind of what's happening on the ground. If you need confirmation that your belayer is paying attention, a simple "watch me" will do; then refocus on the move at hand. (See Chapter 3.)

23. It's common for beginning climbers to have difficulty reading sequences. Reading sequences comes from experience.

    TIP: Climb up to four days a week. Always try to figure sequences from the ground and "just say no" to beta (a real handicap to learning), except when climbing for performance.

24. Do you experience a deep flash pump on the first climb of the day? A flash pump results when you push your muscles too hard, too soon.

TIP: Lengthen your warm-up period, add more stretching and some sports massage, and always do a few increasingly difficult routes before attempting your project.

25. If you have more difficulty climbing when people are watching, remember that the pressure of needing to perform is entirely self-imposed. Therefore, it can be turned off as easily as you turn it on.

TIP: Commit to climb for yourself—for the challenge, adventure, and fun of it (all the reasons you got into climbing in the first place). Forget about the rest of the world, engage the process of climbing, and let the outcome take care of itself. (See Chapter 3.)

26. If your feet unexpectedly pop off footholds, take heart that this is a common problem, even among some advanced climbers.

TIP: Refocus your attention on your feet for a few weeks. Evaluate whether you carefully place your feet on the best part of a hold or simply drop them onto the biggest-looking part. Also, do you hold your foot position stationary as you stand up or does your shoe move on the hold? These are things you need to practice in a nonperformance setting. (See Chapter 4.)

27. Do you experience frequent elbow pain? There are two types of elbow tendonitis common to climbers. If you climb enough years, chances are you'll experience at least one of them.

TIP: Reverse wrist curls and forearm rotation exercises as well as regular forearm stretching will help prevent these problems. Perform three sets of reverse wrist curls (twenty-five reps with a five- to fifteen-pound dumbbell) and two sets of forearm rotation, three days per week, year-round. Stretch both sides of your forearms each day. (See Chapter 6.)

28. If you have trouble pushing yourself to the limit lead climbing a safe route, your problem is more likely mental than physical. Keep in mind that mental fortitude is as important as physical strength.

TIP: Practice pushing yourself a little farther into the discomfort zone (mental and physical) each week. This can be done in the gym and on safe routes at the crags. In time, you will instinctively push beyond your known limits when climbing on a personal-best route. (See Chapter 3.)

29. If you have difficulty finding midroute rest positions, you are missing the key to sending routes near your limit.

TIP: Creative practice (in a nonperformance setting) at finding funky rest positions and climbing experience at a wide range of crags will, in time, make finding "thank God" rests instinctual!

30. If your first attempt on a hard route is usually better than second or third attempts that day, you might lack endurance. Most climbers get three or more good tries on a project before experiencing diminishing returns. If you fatigue more quickly than this, lack of endurance is the likely culprit.

TIP: Climbing laps on training routes is a great way to improve endurance. Use an interval-climbing strategy in which you climb hard for five to ten minutes, then rest anywhere from five to twenty minutes, then repeat.

Appendix C

Fitness Evaluation & Questionnaire

Fitness Evaluation

This ten-part evaluation is strenuous. Perform a complete warm-up before proceeding, and rest extensively between tests. Take this fitness test annually to gauge your changes in conditioning for climbing. Please send me a copy of your initial test results so they can be included in an ongoing statistical study.

Test 1: One set maximum number of pull-ups. Do this test on a standard pull-up bar (or bucket hold on a fingerboard) with your palms away and hands shoulder width apart. Do not bounce, and be sure to go up and down the whole way.

Evaluation: Total number of pull-ups in a single set to failure.

Results: _____

Test 2: One repetition maximum pull-up. Do a single pull-up with a ten-pound weight clipped to your harness. Rest three minutes, then add ten more pounds and repeat. (If you are very strong, begin with a twenty-pound weight and increase at ten- to twenty-pound increments.) Continue in this fashion until you have added more weight than you can pull up.

Evaluation: The maximum amount of added weight successfully lifted for a single pull-up divided by your body weight.

Results: _____

Test 3: One-arm lock-off. Start with a standard chin-up (palms facing) then lock off at the top on one arm and let go with the other.

Evaluation: Length of time in the lock-off before your chin drops below the bar.

Results: Right arm _____ Left arm _____

Test 4: One set maximum number of Frenchies. Perform the exercise as described on page 95–96. Remember, each cycle consists of three pull-ups separated by the three different lock-off positions, which are held for five seconds. Have a partner time your lock-offs.

Evaluation: The number of cycles (or part of) completed in a single set.

Results: _____

Test 5: One set maximum number of fingertip pull-ups on a ¾-inch (19 millimeter) edge. Perform this exercise as in test 1 except on a fingerboard edge or doorjamb of approximately the stated size.

Evaluation: The number of fingertip pull-ups done in a single go.

Results: _____

Test 6: Lock off in the top position of a fingertip pull-up (¾-inch or 19-millimeter edge) for as long as possible.

Evaluation: Length of time in the lock-off until your chin drops below the edge.

Results: _____

Test 7: Straight-arm hang from a standard pull-up bar. Place your hands shoulder width apart with palms facing away.

Evaluation: Length of time you can hang on the bar before muscle failure.

Results: _____

Test 8: One set maximum number of sit-ups. Perform these on a pad or carpeted floor with your knees bent at approximately ninety degrees, your feet flat on the floor with nothing anchoring them. Cross your arms over your upper chest and perform each sit-up until your elbows touch your knees or thighs.

Evaluation: Number of sit-ups you can perform without stopping. Do them in a controlled manner—no bouncing off the floor.

Results: _____

Test 9: Wall split as described in the box in on page 74. Be sure that your rear end is no more than 6 inches from the wall.

Evaluation: Position your legs so they are equidistant from the floor and measure the distance from your heels to the floor.

Results: _____

Test 10: High-step stretch. Stand facing a wall with one foot flat on the floor with toes touching the wall. Lift the other leg up to the side as high as possible without any aid from your hands.

Evaluation: Measure the height of your step off the floor and divide it by your height.

Results: _____

Questionnaire

1. Name _____

   Address _____

   City/State/Zip _____

   Country _____

   E-mail address _____

2. Age_____ Sex_____

3. Height_____ Weight_____ Percent body fat (if known) _____

4. Previous sports background_____

5. Number of years climbing? _____

6. Preferred type of climbing (sport, trad, bouldering, big wall)?_____

7. Current on-sight lead ability (75 percent success rate at what level)? _____

8. Hardest redpoint (worked route)? _____

9. Are you currently doing sport-specific training for climbing? _____

   If so, which exercises do you use (circle): fingerboard, campus training, HIT, system wall, other?

   _____

10. Do you have a home climbing wall?_____

11. How often do you climb indoors (days per month)? _____

12. Do you belong to a climbing gym? _____ Which one? _____

13. Have you ever participated in a climbing competition?_____

14. Have you ever been injured while climbing or training for climbing? _____

    If so, describe. _____

15. Approximately how many days per year do you climb? _____

16. How many different climbing areas have you visited in the past twelve months? _____

17. What are your goals in this sport?_____

18. What chapter or part of *Training for Climbing* do you like best? _____

19. What subjects would you like to know about in a future edition?_____

    _____

    _____

20. What climbers would you like to see interviewed with regard to their training and climbing? _____

    _____

    _____

Please send a copy of your Fitness Evaluation and Questionnaire to the address below. Include a self-addressed stamped envelope and I'll send you a *Training for Climbing* sticker. Thank you!

Contact information:

Eric J. Hörst
P.O. Box 8633
Lancaster, PA 17604
www.TrainingForClimbing.com

Glossary

The following is a compilation of some of the technical terms and climbing jargon used throughout this book.

acclimatization—Physiological, adaptive responses to a new environment, such as high altitude, hot, and cold. *Acclimation* is acclimatization in an artificial environment.

active recovery—Restoration of homeostasis following vigorous exercise that involves continued light-intensity movement; facilitates faster recovery by enhancing lactate removal from the blood.

acute—Having rapid onset and severe symptoms.

adaptive response—Physiological changes in structure or function particularly related to response to a training overload.

adipose tissue—Body fat.

aerobic(s)—Any physical activity deriving energy from the breakdown of glycogen in the presence of oxygen, thus producing little or no lactic acid, enabling an athlete to continue exercise much longer.

aggro—Short for aggressive.

agonist—A muscle directly engaged in a muscular contraction.

anaerobic—Energy production in the muscles involving the breakdown of glycogen in the absence of oxygen; a by-product called lactic acid is formed resulting in rapid fatigue and cessation of physical activity.

anaerobic endurance—The ability to continue moderate- to high-intensity activity over a period of time; commonly called *power-endurance* or *power-stamina* by climbers, though these terms are scientifically incorrect.

anaerobic threshold—The workload or level of oxygen consumption where lactate production by the working muscles exceeds the rate of lactate removal by the liver; typically at 50 percent to 80 percent of maximum intensity of exercise, and in proportion to one's level of anaerobic-endurance conditioning.

anorexia—Pathological absence of appetite or hunger in spite of a need for food.

antagonist—A muscle providing an opposing force to the primary muscles of action (agonist).

antioxidants—Substances (vitamins and minerals) proven to oppose oxidation and inhibit or neutralize free radicals.

ape-index—Fingertip to fingertip distance (across your chest with arms out to each side) minus your height; a positive Ape-index is associated with above-average reach for a given height.

artery—A vessel that carries oxygenated blood away from the heart to the tissues of the body.

arthritis—Disease that causes inflammation, swelling, and pain in the joints.

arousal—An internal state of alertness or excitement.

ATP—Adenosine triphosphate; a high-energy molecule which is stored in the muscles in very small amounts. The body's ultimate fuel source.

atrophy—Gradual shrinking and deconditioning of muscle tissue from disuse.

back stepping—Outside edging on a foothold which is behind you while climbing a move with your side to the wall.

barndoor—Sideways swinging or uncontrolled turning of the body resulting from poor balance or body positioning.

basal metabolic rate—The minimum level of energy required to sustain the body's vital functions.

beta—Any prior information about a route including sequence, rests, gear, clips, etc.

biological value (BV)—A method for evaluating protein sources; a high BV protein source has a high percentage of nutrients actually absorbed from the human intestine as opposed to excreted.

blocked practice—A practice routine in which a specific task is practiced repeatedly, as in working a crux move or sequence.

bouldering—Variable practice of climbing skills performed without a belay rope at the base of a cliff or on small boulders.

campus (or campusing)—Climbing an overhanging section of rock or artificial wall with no feet, usually in a dynamic left hand, right hang, left hand (and so forth) sequence.

campus training—A sport-specific form of plyometric exercise, developed by Wolfgang Güllich at the Campus Center, a weight-lifting facility at the University in Nürnberg, Germany.

capillary—The tiny blood vessels that receive blood flow from the arteries, interchange substances between the blood and the tissues, and return the blood to the veins.

capillary density—Number of capillaries per unit area of muscle tissue. Capillary density increases, mainly in slow-twitch fibers, in response to aerobic training.

catabolic—A breaking down process in the body, as in muscle breakdown during intense exercise.

center of gravity—The theoretical point on which the total effect of gravity acts on the body.

chronic—Continuing over time.

concentric contraction—Any movement involving a shortening of muscles fibers while developing tension, as in the biceps muscle during a pull-up.

contact strength—Initial grip strength (and speed of gripping) upon touching a handhold.

cortisol—A hormone, released in response to emotional or exercise stress, that promotes fat utilization, inhibits inflammatory response, and facilitates breakdown of muscle proteins for energy.

cortisone—A synthetic form of cortisol used (injected) as an anti-inflammatory.

creatine phosphate (CP)—A high-energy phosphate compound stored in skeletal muscle and used to supply energy for brief, high-intensity muscle action.

crimp grip—The most natural (and stressful) way to grip a rock hold characterized by hyperextension of the first joint in the fingers and nearly full flexion of the second joint.

crux—The hardest move, or sequence of moves, on a route.

deadpoint—The high position in a dynamic movement where, for a moment, all motion stops.

detox—To shakeout, rest, and recover from pumped forearm muscles.

detraining—Reversal of positive adaptations to chronic exercise upon cessation of an exercise program.

drop knee—An exaggerated backstep, commonly used on overhanging rock, where the inside knee is dropped toward the ground resulting in a stable chimney-like position.

dynamic move—An explosive leap for a hold otherwise out of reach.

dyno—Short for dynamic.

eccentric contraction—Muscle action in which the muscle resists as it is forced to lengthen, as in the biceps during the lowering phase of a pull-up.

electrolyte—A substance which, in solution, is capable of conducting electricity. Certain electrolytes are essential to the electrochemical functioning of the body.

endurance—Ability to perform physical work for an extended period of time. Cardiovascular endurance is directly related to VO_2 Max, whereas muscular endurance is influenced by circulation and available oxygen.

enzyme—A protein molecule that aids chemical reactions.

epicondylitis—Inflammation of the tendon origins of the forearm flexors (medial) or extensors (lateral) near the elbow.

ergogenic—Performance enhancing.

estrogen—The sex hormone that predominates in females, but also has some functions in males.

extension—A movement which moves the two ends of a jointed body part away from each other, as in straightening the arm.

fast-twitch fibers—Muscle fiber type that contracts quickly and is used mostly during intense, powerful movements.

flagging—A climbing technique in which one foot is crossed behind the other to avoid barndooring and to improve balance.

flash—To climb a route first try without ever having touched the route, but with the aid of beta.

flash pump—A rapid, often vicious, muscular pump resulting from strenuous training or climbing without first performing a proper, gradual warm-up.

flexion—A movement that brings the ends of a body part closer together, as in bending the arm.

G-tox—A technique which uses gravity to help speed recovery from a forearm pump. It involves alternating, every five to ten seconds, the position of the resting arm between the normal hanging at your side position and a raised-hand position above your shoulder.

glycogen—Compound chains of glucose stored in the muscle and liver for use during aerobic or anaerobic exercise.

glycemic index (GI)—A scale which classifies how the ingestion of various foods affects blood-sugar levels in comparison to the ingestion of straight glucose.

Golgi tendon organ—Sensory receptors located between the muscle and its tendon that are sensitive to the stretch of the muscle tendon produced during muscular contraction.

gripped—Extremely scared.

hangdogging—Climbing a route, usually bolt to bolt, with the aid of a rope to hang and rest while practicing the sequence.

heel hook—Use of the heel on a hold, usually near chest level, to aid in pulling and balance.

homeostasis—The body's tendency to maintain a steady state despite external changes.

honed—In extremely good shape; with low body fat.

hormone—A chemical secreted into the bloodstream to regulate the function of a certain organ.

hyperemia—Increased blood flow in the working muscles during exercise or as a result of deep sports massage.

Hypergravity Isolation Training (HIT)—A highly refined and specific method of training maximum finger strength and upper-body power by climbing on identical finger holds (isolation) with greater than body weight (hypergravity). Also known as Hörst Isolation Training.

hypertrophy—Enlargement in size (for example, muscular hypertrophy).

insertion—The point of attachment of a muscle to a distal or relatively more movable bone.

insulin—A hormone that decreases blood glucose level by driving glucose from the blood into muscle and fat cells.

interval training—A method of anaerobic endurance training that involves brief periods of intense training interspaced with periods of rest or low-intensity training.

isometric—Muscular contraction resulting in no shortening movement of the muscle.

kinesiology—The scientific study of human movement.

kinesthetic—The sense derived from muscular contractions and limb movements.

killer—Extraordinarily good, as in a killer route.

lactic acid—Acid by-product of the anaerobic metabolism of glucose during intense muscular exercise.

lactic acid system—Energy pathway used in high-intensity activity over a short duration.

lean body weight—The weight of the body, less the weight of its fat.

ligament—Fibrous tissue that connects bone to bone, or bone to cartilage, to hold together and support the joints.

lunge—An out-of-control dynamic move; an explosive jump for a far-off hold.

macronutrients—Basic nutrients needed for energy, cell growth, and organ function (carbohydrates, fat, and protein).

manky—Of poor quality, as in a manky finger jam or a manky protection placement.

maximum strength—The peak force of a muscular contraction, irrespective of the time element.

micronutrients—Noncaloric nutrients needed in very small amounts, as in vitamins and minerals.

modeling—A learning technique where an individual watches, then attempts, a skill as performed properly by another person.

motor learning—Set of internal processes associated with practice or experience leading to a relatively permanent gain in performance capability.

motor skill—A skill where the primary determinant of success is the movement component itself.

motor unit—A motor neuron, together with a group of muscle cells stimulated in an all-or-nothing response.

muscular endurance—The length of time a given level of power can be maintained.

on-sight—When a route is climbed first try and with absolutely no prior information of any kind.

open-hand grip—The less-stressful finger grip involving only slight flexion of the finger joints.

osteoarthritis—A joint disease of older persons, in which cartilage in the joints wears down and there is bone growth at the edges of the joint.

overload—Subjecting a part of the body to greater efforts (intensity or volume) than it is accustomed to in order to elicit a training response.

overtraining—Constant severe training that does not provide adequate time for recovery; symptoms include increased frequency of injury, decreased performance, irritability, and apathy.

overuse—Excessive repeated exertion or shock that results in injuries such as inflammation of the muscles and tendons.

plyometric—An exercise that suddenly preloads and forces the stretching of a muscle an instant prior to its concentric contraction, as in dynamic up-and-down campus training.

power—A measure of both force and speed (speed = distance x time) of a muscular contraction through a given range of motion. Power is the explosive aspect of strength. (Technically the term finger power is meaningless since the fingers normally don't move when gripping the rock).

pronation—The inward turning of a body part, as in turning the forearm inward and the palm face down.

psyched—Raring to go or very happy.

pumped—When the muscles become engorged with blood due to extended physical exertion.

random practice—A practice sequence in which tasks from several classes are experienced in random order over consecutive trails.

recommended dietary allowances (RDA)—Quantities of specific vitamins, minerals, and other nutrients needed daily that have been judged adequate for maintenance of good nutrition. Developed by the Food and Nutrition Board of the National Academy of Science.

recruitment—The systematic increase in the number of active motor units called upon during muscular contraction.

redpoint—Lead climbing a route bottom to top in one push.

reminiscence effect—The phenomena of enhanced motor skill and performance after an extended time-off period from climbing and training.

schema—A set of rules, usually developed and applied unconsciously by the motor system in the brain and spinal cord, relating how to move and adjust muscle forces, body positions, etcetera, given the parameters at hand, such as steepness of the rock, friction qualities, holds being used and type of terrain.

sharp end—The lead climber's end of the rope.

shred—To do really well, or to dominate.

skill—A capability to bring about an end result with maximum certainty, minimum energy, and minimum time.

slow-twitch fibers—Muscle fiber type that contracts slowly and is used most in moderate-intensity endurance activities such as easy to moderate climbing or running.

sport climbing—Usually refers to any indoor or outdoor climbing on bolt-protected routes.

spotter—A person designated to slow the fall of a boulderer, with the main goal of keeping the boulderer's head from hitting the ground.

stabilizer muscle—A muscle that is stimulated to help anchor or stabilize the position of a bone.

strength—The amount of muscle force that can be exerted; speed and distance are not factors of strength.

strength endurance—See *anaerobic endurance*.

supination—Rotation of the forearm outward and palm upward.

tendonitis—A disorder involving the inflammation of a tendon and synovial membrane at a joint.

tendon—A white fibrous cord of dense connective tissue that attaches muscle to bone.

trad—Short for a traditional climb (or climber) that requires natural protection placements.

training effect—A basic principle of exercise science which states that adaptation occurs from an exercise only in those parts or systems of the body that are stressed by the exercise.

transfer of learning—The gain or loss in proficiency on one task as a result of practice or experience on another task.

tweak—To injure, as in a tweaked finger tendon.

variable practice—Practice in which many variations of a class of actions are performed; opposite of blocked practice.

vein—A vessel which returns blood from the various parts of the body back to the heart.

visualization—Controlled and directed imagery that can be used for awareness building, monitoring and self-regulation, healing, and most important, as mental programming for good performances.

VO$_2$ max—Maximal oxygen uptake, as in the measurement of maximum aerobic power.

wired—Known well, as in a wired route.

working—Practicing the moves on a difficult route via toprope or hangdogging.

Suggested Reading

Ament, Pat. (1977,1998) *Master of Rock*. Mechanicsburg, PA: Stackpole Books.

Armstrong, Lawrence E. (2000) *Performing in Extreme Environments*. Champaign, IL: Human Kinetics.

Brand-Miller, Jennie, et al. (1999) *The Glucose Revolution: The Authoritative Guide to the Glycemic Index*. New York: Marlowe & Company.

Burke, Edmund R. (1999) *Optimal Muscle Recovery*. Garden City Park, NY: Avery Publishing Group.

Colgan, Michael. (1993) *Optimum Sports Nutrition*. Ronkonkoma, NY: Advanced Research Press.

Covey, Stephen. (1989) *The Seven Habits of Highly Effective People*. New York: Simon & Schuster.

Csikszentmihalyi, Mihaly. (1990) *Flow: The Psychology of Optimal Experience*. New York: Harper Perennial.

Garfield, Charles A. (1984) *Peak Performance: Mental Training Techniques of the World's Greatest Athletes*. New York: Warner Books.

Goddard, Dale, Neumann, Udo. (1993) *Performance Rock Climbing*. Mechanicsburg, PA: Stackpole Books.

Hörst, Eric J. (1997) *How to Climb 5.12*. Guilford, CT: Globe Pequot Press/Falcon Publishing.

Hörst, Eric J. (2003) *Mental Wings: A Seven-Step, Life-Elevating Program for Uncommon Success*. www.MentalWings.com.

Long, John. (1993) *How to Rock Climb!* Guilford, CT: Globe Pequot Press/Falcon Publishing.

Meagher, Jack. (1990) *Sports Massage*. New York: Station Hill.

Orlick, Terry. (1990) *In Pursuit of Excellence*. Champaign, IL: Human Kinetics.

Sagar, Heather Reynolds. (2001) *Climbing Your Best*. Mechanicsburg, PA: Stackpole Books.

Schmidt, R. A. (1991) *Motor Learning and Performance: From Principles to Practice*. Champaign, IL: Human Kinetics.

References

Chapter 1

Ament, Pat. (1977, 1992) *Master of Rock*. Lincoln, NE: Adventure's Meaning Press.

Barss, Stephanie J. (1997) "Physiological attributes of recreational rock climbers." A master's thesis presented to the faculty of Western Washington University.

Bloomfield, J., Ackland, T. R., Elliot, B. C. (1994) *Applied Anatomy and Biomechanics in Sport*. Carlton, Victoria, Australia: Blackwell Scientific Publications.

Ericsson, K. A., Krampe, R. T., Tech-Rsmer, C. (1993) "The role of deliberate practice in the acquisition of expert performance." *Psychological Review* 100(3): 363–406.

Fox, P. W., Hershberger, S. L., Bouchard, T. J. (1996) "Genetic and environmental contributions to the acquisition of a motor skill." *Nature* 384: 356–358.

Goddard, Dale, Neumann, Udo. (1993) *Performance Rock Climbing*. Mechanicsburg, PA: Stackpole Books.

Güllich, W., Kubin, A. (1986) *Sportklettern Heute: Technik, Taktik, Training*. München, Germany: Bruckmann.

Hörst, Eric J. (1994) *Flash Training*. Evergreen, CO: Chockstone Press.

Hörst, Eric J. (1997) *How to Climb 5.12*. Helena, MT: Falcon Press/Globe Pequot.

Mermier, C. M., Janot, J. M., Parker, D. L., Swan, J. G. (2000) "Physiological and anthropometric determinants of sport climbing performance." *Brit J Sports Med* 34(5) (Oct): 359–365.

Seiler, S. (2000) "Limits to performance." *Sportscience* 4(2).

Watts, P. B., Martin, D. T., Durtschi, S. (1993) "Anthropometric profiles of elite male and female competitive sport rock climbers." *J Sport Sci* 11(2) (Apr): 113–117.

Chapter 3

Covey, Stephen. (1989) *The Seven Habits of Highly Effective People*. New York: Simon & Schuster.

Feltz, D., Landers, D. (1983) "The effects of mental practice on motor skill learning and performance." *Sport Psych* 5.

Garfield, C. (1984) *Peak Performance*. New York: Warner Books.

Kubistant, T. (1986) *Performing Your Best*. Champaign, IL: Leisure Press.

Levinson, W. (1994) *The Way of Strategy*. Milwaukee, WI: ASQC Quality Press.

Chapter 4

Knudson, D. V., Morrison, C. S. (1997) *Qualitative Analysis of Human Movement*. Champaign, IL: Human Kinetics.

Schmidt, R. A. (1991) *Motor Learning and Performance: From Principles to Practice*. Champaign, IL: Human Kinetics.

Chapter 5

Adams, K., O'Shea, J., O'Shea, K., Climstein, M. (1992) "The effect of six weeks of squat, plyometric, and squat-plyometric training on power production." *Applied Sport Sci Res* 6.

Bloomfield, J., Ackland, T. R., Elliot, B. C. (1994) *Applied Anatomy and Biomechanics in Sport*. Carlton, Victoria, Australia: Blackwell Scientific Publications.

Bloomfield, J., Fricker, P., Fitch, K. (1992) *Textbook of Science and Medicine in Sport*. Carlton, Victoria, Australia: Blackwell Scientific Publications.

Chu, Donald A. (1996) *Explosive Power & Strength*. Champaign, IL: Human Kinetics.

Kaneko, M., Fuchimoto, T., Toji, H., Suei, K. (1983) "Training effect of differing loads on the force-velocity relationship and mechanical power output in human muscle." *Scand J Sport Sci* 5.

O'Shea, K., O'Shea, J. (1989) "Functional isometric weight training: Its effect on dynamic and static strength." *J Applied Sport Sci Res* 3.

Tidow, G. (1990) "Aspects of strength training in athletes." *New Studies in Athletics* 1.

Watts, P., Newbury, V., Sulentic, J. (1996) "Acute changes in handgrip strength, endurance, and blood lactate with sustained sport rock climbing." *J Sports Med Physical Fitness* (Dec).

Chapter 6

Bell, G., Peterson, S., Quinney, A., Wenger, H. (1989) "The effect of velocity-specific strength training on peak torque and anaerobic rowing power." *J Sports Sci* 7.

King, J., et al. (2001) "A comparison of high intensity vs. low intensity exercise on body composition in overweight women." American College of Sports Medicine Annual Meeting.

Sölveborn, Sven-A. (1985) *The Book About Stretching*. Japan Publications.

Wilmore, J. (1983) "Body composition in sport and exercise: Directions for future research." *Med Sci Sports Exercise* 15.

Chapter 7

Bloomfield, J., Ackland, T. R., Elliot, B. C. (1994) *Applied Anatomy and Biomechanics in Sport*. Carlton, Victoria, Australia: Blackwell Scientific Publications.

Davis, B., Elford, J., Jamieson, K. (1991) "Variation in performance in simple muscle tests at different phases of the menstrual cycle." *J Sports Med Physical Fitness* 31.

Wilmore, J. (1974) "Alterations in strength, body composition and anthropometric measurements consequent to a ten-week weight training program." *Med Sci Sports* 5.

Chapter 8

Brilla, L. R., Conte, V. (1999) "A novel zinc and magnesium formulation (ZMA) increases anabolic hormones and strength in athletes." *Sports Med, Training Rehab J* (Nov).

Duchaine, Daniel. (1996) *Bodyopus*. Carson City, NV: Xipe Press.

Graham, T. E., et al. (1998) "Metabolic and exercise endurance effects of coffee and caffeine ingestion." *J Appl Physiol* 85: 883–889.

Horswill, C. A. (1995) "Effects of bicarbonate, citrate, and phosphate loading on performance." *Int J Sport Nutrition* 5: S111–119.

Kelly, G. S. (1997) "Sports nutrition: A review of selected nutritional supplements for endurance athletes." *Alt Med Rev*.

Linderman, J. K., Gosselink, K. L. (1994) "The effects of sodium bicarbonate ingestion on exercise performance." *Sports Med* 18: 75–80.

McBride, J. B., et al. (1998) "Effect of resistance exercise on free radical production." *Med Sci Sports Exercise* 30 (1).

Nissen, S., Panton, L., et al. (1996) "Effect of HMB supplementation on strength and body composition of trained and untrained males undergoing intense strength training." *FASEB J* 10A: A287.

Nissen, S., Sharp, R., et al. (1996) "Effect of leucine metabolite HMB on muscle metabolism during resistive exercise training." *J Appl Physiol* 81: 2095–2104.

Pasman, W. J., et al. (1995) "The effect of different dosages of caffeine on endurance performance time." *Int J Sports Med* 16: 225–230.

Robergs, R. A. (1991) "Nutrition and exercise determinants of post-exercise glycogen synthesis." *Int J Sport Nutrition*.

Schoffstall, J., et al. (2001) "Effects of dehydration and rehydration on the one-rep maximum bench press of weight-trained males." *J Strength Cond Res* 15.

Spriet, L. (1995) "Caffeine and performance." *Int J Sport Nutrition* 5: S84–99.

Toubro, et al. (1993) "Safety and efficacy of long-term treatment with ephedrine, caffeine and an ephedrine/caffeine mixture." *Int J Obes* 17 (1): S69–72.

Vukovich, M., et al. (1997) "Effect of HBM on VO_2 peak and maximal lactate in endurance-trained cyclists." *Med Sci Sports Exercise*.

Williams, Melvin H. (1989) *Beyond Training*. Champaign, IL: Leisure Press/Human Kinetics Publishing.

Kreider, R. B., et al. (1992) "Effects of phosphate loading on metabolic and myocardial responses to maximal and endurance exercise." *Int J Sports Nutrition* 2.

Meagher, Jack. (1990) *Sports Massage*. New York: Station Hill Press.

Monedero, J., Donne, B. (2000) "Effect of recovery interventions on lactate removal and subsequent performance." *Int J Sports Med* (Nov.)

Niles, T. S., et al. (1997) "The effects of carbohydrate-protein drink on muscle glycogen resynthesis after endurance exercise." *Med Sci Sports Exercise* 29 Suppl 5.

Richter, E. A., et al. (1984) "Enhanced muscle glycogen metabolism after exercise." *Amer J Physiol* 246.

Rupp, J. C., et al. (1983) "Effect of sodium bicarbonate ingestion on blood and muscle pH and exercise performance." *Med Sci Sports Exercise* 15.

Watts, P. B., Daggett, M., Gallagher, P., Wilkens, B. (2000) "Metabolic response during sport rock climbing and the effects of active versus passive recovery." *Int J Sports Med* (Apr).

Williams, R. B., et al. (1982) "Type A behavior and elevated physiological and neuroendocrine responses to cognitive tasks." *Science* 29 (Oct): 218.

Chapter 9

Bloomfield, J., Ackland, T. R., Elliot, B. C. (1994) *Applied Anatomy and Biomechanics in Sport*. Carlton, Victoria, Australia: Blackwell Scientific Publications.

Bompa, Tudor O. (1983) *Theory and Methodology of Training*. Dubuque, IA: Kendall/Hunt Publishing Co.

Burke, Edmund R. (1999) *Optimal Muscle Recovery*. Garden City Park, NY: Avery Publishing Group.

Coyle, E. F., Coggan, A. R. (1984) "Effectiveness of carbohydrate feeding in delaying fatigue during prolonged exercise." *Sports Med* 5.

Dinan, T. G., et al. (1994) "Lowering cortisol enhances growth hormone response in healthy individuals." *Acta Physiol Scand* 151(3) (Jul).

Chapter 10

Auerback, David, M. (2000) *Tennis Elbow/Lateral Epicondylitis*. Southern California Orthopedic Institute. www.scoi.com.

Bach, Allan W. (1999) "Finger joint injuries in active patients." *Physician Sportsmedicine* 27(3).

Bannister, P., Foster, P. (1986) "Upper limb injuries associated with rock climbing." *Brit J Sports Med* 20.

Bollen, S. R. (1988) "Soft tissue injuries in extreme rock climbers." *Brit J Sports Med* 22.

Crouch, D. M. (1998) "Finger tips: the key to treating finger injuries is knowing what ails you." *Rock & Ice* 84.

Doran, D. A., Reay, M. (2000) "Injuries and associated training and performance characteristics in recreational rock climbers." In *The Science of Rock Climbing and Mountaineering*. Champaign, IL: Human Kinetics Publishing.

Gabl, M., Lener, M., Pechlaner, S., Lutz, M., Rudisch, A. (1996) "Rupture or stress injury of the flexor tendon pulleys? Early diagnosis with MRI." *Handchir Mikrochir Plast Chir* 28 (Nov).

Gabl, M., Rangger, C., Lutz, M., Fink, C., Rudisch, A., Pechlaner, S. (1998) "Disruption of the finger flexor pulley system in elite rock climbers." *Am J Sports Med* 26(5) (Sep–Oct).

Jebson, Peter, Steyers, J. L., Curtis, M. (1997) "Hand injuries in rock climbing: Reaching the right treatment." *Physician Sportsmedicine* 25(5).

Klauster A., et al. (2002) "Finger pulley injuries in extreme rock climbers: depiction with Dynamic Ultrasonography." *Radiology* (222) (3): 755–61.

Lewis, R. A., Shea, O. F., Shea, K. G. (1993) "Acute carpal tunnel syndrome: Wrist stress during a major climb." *Physician Sportsmedicine* 21(7).

Lin, G. T., et al. (1989) "Functional anatomy of the human digital flexor pulley system." *J Hand Surg Am* 14.

Lin, G. T., et al. (1998) "Biomechanical analysis of flexor pulley reconstruction." *J Hand Surg Brit* 14.

Lister, G. D. (1979) "Reconstruction of pulleys employing extensor retinaculum." *J Hand Surg Am* 4.

Marco, R. A., Sharkey, N. A., Smith, T. S., Zissimos, A. G. (1998) "Pathomechanics of closed rupture of the flexor tendon pulleys in rock climbers." *J Bone Joint Surg Am* 80(7) (Jul).

McAlindon, T., et al. (2000) "Glucosamine and chondroitin for treatment of osteoarthritis." *JAMA* 283: 1469–1475.

McFarland, Edward G., et al. (2000) *Patient guide to knee arthroscopy*. Johns Hopkins Department of Orthopaedic Surgery. www.hopkinsmedicine.org.

Moutet, F., Guinard, D., Gerard, P., Mugnier, C. (1993) "Subcutaneous rupture of long finger flexor pulleys in rock climbers." *Ann Chir Main Memb Super* 12(3).

Nirschl, Robert P., Kraushaar, Barry S. (1996) "Assessment and treatment guidelines for elbow injuries." *Physician Sportsmedicine* 25(4).

Reginster, J. Y., et al. (2001) "Long-term effects of glucosamine sulfate on osteoarthritis progression: A randomized, placebo-controlled clinical trial." *Lancet* 357(9252) (Jan 27).

Robinson, Mark. (1988) "Fingers: Get a grip on injury prevention and treatment." *Climbing* (Aug).

Robinson, Mark. (1993) "Snap, crackle, pop: Climbing injuries to fingers and forearms." *Climbing* (Jun–Jul).

Robinson, Mark. (1993) "The elbow: Understanding a common sore subject." *Climbing* (Apr).

Rohrbough, Joel. (2000) "'Pop'' goes your climbing season." *Climbing* (Nov).

Rooks, M. D. (1997) "Rock climbing injuries." *Sports Med* 23.

Seiler, J. G., Leversedge, F. J. (2000) "Digital flexor sheath: Repair and reconstruction of the annular pulleys and membranous sheath." *J S Orth Assn* 9(2).

Seiler, J. G., et al. (1995) "The flexor digitorum longus: an anatomic and microscopic study for use as a tendon graft." *J Hand Surg Am* 20.

Stelzle, F. D., Gaulrapp, H., Pforringer, W. (2000) "Injuries and overuse syndromes due to rock climbing on artificial walls." *Sportverletz Sportschaden* 14(4) (Dec).

Warme, W. J., Brooks, D. (2000) "The effect of circumferential taping on flexor tendon pulley failure in rock climbers." *Am J Sports Med* 28 (Sep–Oct).

Wright, D. M., Royle, T. J., Marshall, T. (2001) "Indoor rock climbing: Who gets injured?" *Brit J Sports Med* 35(3) (Jun).

Index

A

A2 ring finger taping method, 157
abdominal crunch exercise, 100, 101
abdominal stretch, 76
accomplished climber workout, 116,
    118–19
    anaerobic endurance and, 118, 119
    antagonist muscle training and,
        118, 119
    core muscle training and, 118, 119
    grip strength and, 118, 119
    lock-off and, 118
    mental technique and, 118, 119
    motor learning and, 118, 119
    nutrition and, 118
    pull power and, 118, 119
    rest and, 118, 119
    sport-specific strength training and,
        118, 119
achievement curve, 8
Action Directe, 8, 92
active rest, 143, 145, 149
adenosine triphosphate (ATP), 139
aerobic energy production, 58
aerobic training, 61, 66–67, 71
    beginner-level workout and, 116,
        117
    bouldering and, 106
    elite climber workout and, 121
    female issues and, 121
    goals of, 106
    sport climbing and, 106
agonist muscle training, 54, 56
    female climbers and, 121
algae, 136
All Sport, 133, 145
Allen, Tori, 122
alpine climbing, 11, 66, 106, 114
    aerobic training and, 106, 107

big wall climbing and, 106, 107
electrolytes and, 133
fat and, 126
nutrition and, 125, 130
anabolic steroids, 149
anaerobic endurance (A-E) training,
    65, 66
    accomplished climber workout and,
        118, 119
    elite climber workout and, 120
    lactic acid and, 65, 66, 139
    mesocycle training schedule and,
        111–12, 113
    protocol (B) and, 89
    System Training (B) and, 85
anaerobic energy production, 57–58
anaerobic threshold, 57–58, 62, 65,
    66, 139, 144
androstenidione (aka andro), 136
annular pulley, 154, 155, 158, 159,
    167
    crimp grip and, 155, 158
    injury treatment and, 156–57, 167
    surgery and, 156–57
ANSWER Sequence, 33, 34–35
antagonist muscle training
    accomplished climber workout and,
        118, 119
    beginner-level workout and, 116,
        117
    bench press and, 105
    dips and, 105–6
    elite climber workout and, 120, 121
    female climbers and, 121
    forearm rotation exercise and, 103
    hand and forearm exercises and,
        102–3
    injury prevention and, 168
    muscle description and, 54
    push ups and, 105

reverse wrist curl exercise and, 103
shoulder injury and, 162
shoulder press and, 104–5
antioxidants, 131, 148
aquaman exercise (A), 99, 100
arm
    positions of, 78–79
    stretch of, 73
arthritis, 159–60
arthroscopic surgery, 165–66
Atkins diet, 128
ATP-CP
    creatine and, 135
    fatigue and, 139
    recovery and, 141
    system of, 57, 58, 61, 90
attitude, 27, 32, 34, 35, 45, 149
autonomous stage learning, 43
avulsion, 158, 159
awareness, 34
axis of rotation, 5–6, 57

B

Bachar, John, 3
Bachar Ladder (B-), 4, 97–98
back extension exercise (A), 99–100
backstepping, 41, 44, 47
Balance Bars, 134, 144
Basic Rockcraft (Robbins), 3
beginner-level workout, 116–17
    aerobic training and, 116, 117
    antagonist muscle training and,
        116, 117
    body composition and, 116, 117
    mental training and, 116, 117
    nutrition and, 116, 117
    sport-specific training and, 117
    supercompensation and, 116, 117
bench press, 105

beta hydroxy-beta-methylbutyrate (HMB), 135–36
bicep stretch, 72
big-wall climbing, 106, 107, 114
 electrolytes and, 133
biological value (BV), 132, 133
blocked practice, 47, 48, 49
blood glucose
 carbohydrates and, 139–40
 fatigue and, 139–40
 recovery and, 141
body composition, 70, 71, 106, 116, 117
body fat, 70, 71
 female issues and, 121
bouldering (A), 2, 8, 9, 11, 30, 44, 45, 48–49, 50
 anaerobic endurance and, 84, 65, 66
 aerobic training and, 106
 ATP-CP and, 57, 139
 campus training and, 90
 carbohydrates and, 134
 central fatigue and, 140
 cool down and, 89
 core muscle training and, 98
 effective training and, 83
 effectiveness of, 47
 elite climber workout and, 120
 fast twitch muscle fibers and, 55
 fat and, 126
 forearm pump and, 90
 gym membership and, 114
 home wall and, 114
 Hypergravity Isolation Training and, 86
 indoor training and, 84
 junior climbers and, 122, 123
 medium-term recovery and, 144
 mesocycle training schedule and, 112
 nutrition and, 125, 130
 outdoor training and, 84
 periodization training and, 60
 power training and, 64–65, 84
 shoulder injury and, 162
 skill practice and, 84
 strength training and, 62, 63, 64, 66, 84

 target training and, 114
"bowstringing," 154, 155, 157, 158
breathing, 26, 33, 34–35, 39, 50
Bridwell, Jim, 2–3
Brown, Katie, 5
B-scale grading system, 8
"buddy taping," 156, 158, 159

C

calcium, 132
calf stretch, 76
calorie deficit, 70–71
camming device, 8
campus board, 67, 80, 84, 90,115. *See also* campus training.
 ATP-CP and, 139
 creation of, 91
 plyometric training and, 91
Campus Center, 4
campus training, 4, 9, 55, 61, 65, 90
 central fatigue and, 140
 double dynos and, 92
 feet-on and, 65
 finger taping and, 167
 injury and, 152, 153
 laddering (B) and, 91
 lock-offs and, 92
 mesocycle training schedule and, 112
 neurological adaptation and, 93
campusing. *See* laddering.
capacity, absolute maximum, 56
capillary density, 61, 65
carbohydrates
 blood glucose and, 139–40
 bouldering and, 134
 cragging and, 134
 daily requirements of, 129–30
 fuel sources and, 133–34
 function of, 128
 glycemic index (GI) and, 128, 129, 134
 glycogen and, 139
 long-term recovery and, 148
 medium-term recovery and, 144, 145
 performance nutrition and, 128–30, 131

 types of, 128
carpal tunnel syndrome, 159
centering, 32, 34, 39
central fatigue, 137, 140
chalking, 33
chest stretch, 72
chitosan, 136
cholesterol, 127
chondroitin, 160
"chunking down," 48, 50
circuit training, 59
Clark, Dr. Kristine, 130
Climber's elbow, 160
climbing
 history of, 1
 requirements for, 1
climbing gyms, commercial, 4, 53, 109, 114
coenzyme Q10, 136
cognitive stage learning, 42
Collins, Jim, 3
comfort zone, 25, 31
commitment, 13, 41
community wall, 115
competition, 48, 49
 elite climber workout and, 120
 macrocycle training schedule and, 113
 preparation for, 38
complex training, 67, 111
 elite climber workout and, 120
concentric contraction, 54, 59, 64, 65, 93
concentric strength, 49
conditioning exercises
 difficulty level of, 69, 76
confidence, 23, 25, 32, 36, 37, 42, 44, 50
contact strength, 62
core muscle training (A)
 abdominal crunch (A) and, 100
 accomplished climber workout and, 118, 119
 aquaman (A) and, 99, 100
 back extension (A) and, 99
 bouldering and, 98
 female climbers and, 121
 front lever (B/C) and, 98, 100–101
 hanging knee lift (B) and, 100–101

side hip raises (A) and, 99
straight-arm flag and, 98
traversing and, 98
upper-trunk extension (A) and, 99–100
cortisol, 149
cortisone injection, 161
counterforce bracing, 161, 162
course corrections, 18, 22
crack climbing, 41, 44, 48
cragging
carbohydrates and, 134
fat and, 126
medium-term recovery and, 144
nutrition and, 125, 130
cramps, 140
creatine, 134–35
loading of, 135
creatine phosphate, 139
creativity, 44–45, 51
crimp grip, 48, 54, 59, 77, 79, 86
annular pulley injury and, 155, 158
arthritis and, 159–60
full-crimp grip and, 81, 85, 87
half-crimp grip and, 77, 81, 84, 85, 87
medium crimp grip and, 82
overhanging crimp ladder and, 80
overhanging crimpfest route and, 45
small crimp grip and, 82
cross-fiber friction, 146–47
cross-through, 48
cross-training, 59, 166
cruciform pulley, 154
crux move, 14, 32, 48
ATP-CP system and, 57
fast twitch muscle fibers and, 55
lactic acid and, 57
training and, 81
crux sequence, 48, 50
curiosity, 14, 45

D

dangling-arm shakeout, 142, 143
deadpoint, 41, 44, 47
one-arm traversing training (B)

and, 89–90
deep two-finger pocket, 82
dehydration, 130
delayed-onset muscle soreness, 140
Designer Whey Protein, 132
detraining principle, 58, 61
dip exercise
chair and, 105–6
stair and, 105–6
direct-pressure strokes, 147
disinhibition, 56, 64
DOMS. *See* delayed-onset muscle soreness.
double dynos (C), 92
double stag stretch, 75
down pull, 78, 85
downclimbing route, 49
drop-knee technique, 47, 165
Dynamic Ultrasonography, 155
dyno throws, 62

E

early training techniques, 2, 3
eccentric contraction, 54, 64, 65, 79, 91, 93, 98
eccentric strength, 49
elbow
counterforce bracing and, 161, 162
lateral epicondyle tendonitis of, 161–62
medial epicondyle tendonitis of, 160–61
rest and, 156
taping and, 161
electrolytes, 133
elimination drill, 49
elite climber workout, 116, 119–21
aerobic training and, 121
anaerobic endurance training and, 120
antagonist muscle training and, 120, 121
bouldering and, 120
competition and, 120
complex training and, 120
indoor climbing and, 120
mental training and, 119

Mental Wings and, 120
nutrition and, 120
planning and, 120
self-assessment and, 119
sport-specific strength training and, 119, 120, 121
strength training and, 119, 120
supercompensation and, 120, 121
embarrassment, 31–32
emotions
alteration of, 30
control of, 27–28, 30
Energy-Emotion Matrix and, 28
evaluation of, 28, 29, 30, 174
energy bars, 128, 134, 144, 145, 148
glycemic index (GI) and, 134
energy production, 57–58
Energy-Emotion Matrix, 28
engram. *See* schemas.
epinephrine, 149
ergogenic effect, 136
ergogenic supplements, 132
evaluation, 9
extended grip. *See* open-hand grip.

F

failure, 23, 31
falls, 31, 50
fast twitch muscle fiber (FT), 54, 55, 57, 64, 67
fat
alpine climbers and, 126
daily requirements for, 126
functions of, 126
long-term recovery and, 148
menstruation and, 126
performance nutrition and, 125, 126–27, 128, 131
sources of, 127
types of, 127
"fat whackers," 136
fatigue, 38, 44, 137–40
accumulation of metabolic by-products and, 137, 139
anaerobic endurance training and, 139
ATP-CP and, 139

blood glucose and, 139–40
central, 137, 140
cramps and, 137, 140
dehydration and, 130
depletion of muscle fuel and, 137, 139
glycogen and, 134, 139
lactic acid and, 57–58, 65, 139
low blood glucose and, 137, 139
massage and, 147
microtraumas and, 137, 140
rest and, 61
System Training and, 84
fear, 44, 30–32
control of, 30–32
embarrassment and, 31–32
failure and, 31
falls and, 31
pain and, 31
feet off-climbing, 65
feet skidding, 14
female issues
aerobic training and, 121
agonist muscle training and, 121
antagonist muscle training and, 121
body fat and, 121
calcium and, 132
core muscle training and, 121
grip strength and, 122
hypertrophy and, 122
iron and, 132
menstruation and, 122
mental training and, 122
sport-specific strength training and, 121, 122
Fig Newtons, 134
finger
anatomy of, 154–55
annular pulley injury and, 155, 158–59, 167
arthritis and, 159–60
avulsion and, 158, 159
"bowstringing" injury and, 154, 155, 157, 158
carpal tunnel syndrome and, 159
collateral ligament sprains and, 159
crimp grip and, 159–60
Dynamic Ultrasonography and, 155

flexibility training and, 80
injury of, 152, 153, 154
injury treatment and, 156–57, 158, 159, 160
positioning and, 76–77
rest and, 156
stretches of, 72–73
surgery and, 156–57, 159
taping methods for, 157–58, 159, 166–67
tendon rupture and, 158, 159
tendonitis and, 158
Finger rolls, heavy (B+), 92–93, 94
fingerboard, 4, 8, 9, 56, 60, 61, 66, 80, 115
central fatigue and, 140
endurance training and, 83
hangs and, 64
injury and, 152, 153
moving hangs and, 83
neurological adaptation and, 93
pyramid training and, 82–83
training and, 81, 82
fingertip
exercises for, 86
fingertip pull-ups (A+) and, 2, 81
pyramid training (B) and, 82–83
repeaters training (B) and, 82
First Touch game, 48–49
fitness training, 9, 10–11
campus training and, 9
fingerboard and, 9
fitness v. skill and, 10
free-weights and, 9
hypergravity and, 9
running and, 9
stretching and, 9
Flash Training (Hörst), 4
flashing, 9, 50
flexibility training, 71, 72
finger and forearm training and, 80
lower-body stretches and, 73–76
upper-body stretches and, 72–73
focus, 23, 44, 49
creation of, 38
drills and, 39
practice and, 38–39
foot

footwork and, 14, 49
placement of, 48
popping off holds and, 14
weighting of, 48
foot flags, 51
force production rate, 62
forearm
flexibility training and, 80
G-Tox recovery technique and, 142–43
rotation exercise of, 103–4
stretches for, 72–73
Frenchies exercise, 64, 81, 95–96
froggie stretch, 75
front lever, 2
exercise (B/C) for, 100, 102
fuel sources, 133–34

G

gamma oryzanol, 136
Gaston move, 51, 79, 84, 85
shoulder and, 162
Gatorade, 129, 133, 134, 145
genetics, 4, 5, 6, 7
GHB, 136
Gill, John, 1–2, 3, 8, 81, 97, 98, 109
glucosamine sulfate, 160, 165
glycemic index (GI), 128, 129, 134
energy bars and, 134
long-term recovery and, 148
medium-term recovery and, 144–45
glycogen, 129, 134, 139
carbohydrates and, 139
medium-term recovery and, 144, 145
nutrition and, 139
recovery and, 141, 142, 143
goals
importance of, 13
long-term (mega) and, 13, 19, 21
medium-term and, 19, 21
setting, 18–21, 43
short-term and, 19, 20, 50
Goldstone, Richard, 2
golf, 5, 42, 45, 47
golfer's elbow, 160
Golgi tendon organ, 56

grade explosion, 8
grading systems, 8
Graham, David, 5, 6
Gravitron, 65
Griffiths, Laura, 123
grip strength, 5, 6, 59, 62, 63
    accomplished climber workout and,
        118, 119
    female climbers and, 122
    ratio to body mass and, 7
grip-relax repeating sequence (GRRS),
    81–82
growth hormone, 149
G-Tox forearm recovery technique,
    142–43
Gullich, Wolfgang, 4, 8, 23, 65, 92

H

hand pronator exercise. *See* forearm
    rotation exercise.
hangdogging, 8, 9, 44, 48
hanging knee lift exercise (B), 100,
    101
Harding, Warren, 3
heel hook, 44, 51
high repetition training, 66
high-stepping, 51, 71
Hill, Lynn, 3, 27, 51
Hindenbergian forearm pump, 65
hip flexors, 100
hip turns, 47
HMB. *See* beta hydroxy-beta-methyl-
    butyrate.
hold recognition, 49
Holloway, Jim, 3
homeopathic supplements, 136
home-wall climbing, 83, 114, 115
hormones
    profiles of, 5, 6
    release of, 149
Hörst, Lisa Ann, 42
How to Climb 5.12 (Hörst), 4, 30, 42,
    48
Huber, Alex, 5, 6
Huber,Thomas, 5, 6
hydrogenated oils, 127, 128
hyperemia, 146
Hypergravity Isolation Training (HIT)
    (B/C), 67

anaerobic endurance protocol (B)
    and, 89
central fatigue and, 140
effectiveness of, 85–86
finger taping and, 167
grips and, 87–89
HIT Strip, 87, 88, 89
HIT system and, 56
HIT workout and, 60
maximum strength protocols
    (B+/C) and, 86–89
sample workouts for, 87–89
tips for, 88
hypergravity training, 9, 56, 57, 60,
    63–64, 67, 80, 111
    mesocycle training schedule and,
        112
hypertrophy, 56–57, 64, 65, 93
    female climbers and, 122
hypogravity, 65

I

impact force, 65
improvement
    course correction and, 18
    Cycle of Improvement and, 18, 22
    gear and, 53
    goal setting and, 18
    rate of, 45
    taking action and, 18, 22
individualization training principle,
    58, 59
indoor climbing wall, 4, 47, 49,
    84–84, 120. *See also* climbing
    gyms, commercial; home-wall
    climbing.
    injury and, 152, 153, 165
    junior climbers and, 122, 123
injury, 38
    ability and, 152, 153
    back and, 152
    "bowstringing," 154, 155, 157, 158
    campus training and, 152, 153
    causes of, 152–53
    indoor walls and, 152, 153
    medical attention and, 154
    overuse and, 151–53
    rest and, 156, 160, 161, 162
    sport-climbing and, 152, 153

strength-training and, 161, 162
stretching and, 161, 162
types of, 151–52
wrist and, 152
injury, elbow, 152, 153
    counterforce bracing and, 161, 162
    lateral epicondyle tendonitis and,
        161–62
    medial epicondyle tendonitis and,
        160–61
    rest and, 160, 161, 162
    taping and, 161
injury, finger, 152, 153, 154
    arthritis and, 159–60
    avulsion and, 158, 159
    carpal tunnel syndrome and, 159
    collateral ligament sprains and, 159
    crimp grip and, 159–60
    fingerboard and, 152, 153
    rest and, 156
    rupture and, 158, 159
    surgery and, 156–57, 159
    taping methods for, 157–58, 159,
        166–67
    tendonitis and, 158
    treatment of, 156–57, 158, 159,
        160
injury, knee, 152, 153
    arthroscopic surgery of, 165–66
    meniscus tear of, 165–66
injury prevention, 166–69
    antagonist muscle training and, 168
    caution and, 167
    conservative finger taping and,
        166–67
    cooling down and, 168
    cross-training and, 166
    dehydration and, 130
    exhaustion and, 167
    good technique and, 166
    massage and, 146
    nutrition and, 169
    periodization and, 168
    rest and, 167–68, 168, 169
    sport-specific training and, 166
    strength-training and, 167
    stretching and, 168
    supercompensation and, 148
    variation principle and, 166

warming up and, 168
injury, shoulder, 152, 153
    rehab exercises for, 163–64
    subluxation of, 162
    surgery and, 162
inosine, 136
instruction, one-on-one, 41
interday recovery. *See* recovery, long-
    term.
internal self-talk, 14, 27, 50, 51
interval training, 58, 66, 71, 80–81
    mesocycle training schedule and,
        112
intraclimb recovery. *See* recovery,
    short-term.
intraday recovery. *See* recovery,
    medium-term.
introspection, 14
iron, 132
isometric contraction, 54, 59, 64, 96

J

Jacobson, Edward, 32
"jersey finger," 158–59
junior climbers, 121
    bouldering and, 122, 123
    fun and, 122, 123
    indoor climbing and, 122, 123
    mental training and, 122, 123
    skill training and, 122, 123
    sport climbing and, 122, 123
    sport-specific training and, 122, 123
    strength training and, 122, 123
    training of, 122, 123

K

Kauk, Ron, 3
Ketogenic diet, 128
knee, 152
    arthroscopic surgery of, 165–66
    meniscus tear and, 165–66
kneebar technique, 51

L

lactic acid, 106, 139
    active rest and, 149

anaerobic endurance training and,
    139
fatigue and, 139
lactic acid system and, 57–58, 65
massage and, 145–46
recovery and, 141, 142, 143
rest and, 139
lactic acid buffering supplements
    recovery and, 143, 144
laddering, 91
layoff
    skills and, 10–11
learning curve, 45
LeMenestral, Antoine, 5, 6
LeMenestral, Marc, 5, 6
lever length, 5
Levinson, William, 31
local endurance, 5
lock-offs, 84, 89
    accomplished climber workout and,
        118
    arm angles exercise (B+) and, 96
    Frenchies (A+) and, 95–96
    one-arm (B+) and, 80, 96–97
    palms away exercise (B+) and, 96
    palms inward exercise (B+) and, 96
    steep-wall exercise (B) and, 96
    training and, 59, 64, 94–98
    uneven-grip pull-ups exercise (B)
        and, 96
Long, Jim, 3
lunges, 51, 59, 65, 67
    central fatigue and, 140
    one-arm lunges (B) and, 65, 89–90

M

macrocycle training schedule, 113–14
    competition and, 113
    rest and, 113
macronutrients, 125, 127, 130
magnesium, 131–32
massage, 144–45, 148
    recovery and, 143
    strokes for, 146, 147
Master of Rock, 3
McCarthy, Jim, 2
MCTs, 136

Meagher, Jack, 146
menstruation, 122, 126
mental training, 9, 23–39, 41
    attitude and, 27
    beginner-level workout and, 116,
        117
    breathing and, 26
    comfort zone and, 25
    confidence and, 25
    detached self-image and, 25
    elite climber workout and, 119
    female climbers and, 122
    importance of, 6, 7
    internal self-talk and, 14, 27
    junior climbers and, 122, 123
    peak performance zone and, 26
    positive influence and, 25
    process-orientation and, 27
    quality of thinking and, 23
    relaxation and, 27
    risk and, 25
    rituals and, 26
    strategies for, 50–51
    tension and, 26
    visualization and, 9, 25–26
Mental Wings, 9, 23, 50–51, 120
mesocycle training schedule, 111–13
    anaerobic endurance training and,
        111–12, 113
    bouldering and, 112
    campus training and, 112
    complex training and, 112
    hypergravity training and, 112
    interval training and, 112
    power training and, 111, 112, 113
    rest and, 112, 113
    schemas and, 111
    strength training and, 111, 112,
        113
microcycle training schedule, 110–11
micronutrients, 130–31
    minerals and, 131–32
    vitamins and, 130–31
microtraumas, 140, 147, 160, 168
    recovery and, 141
milk, 133
mitochondrial density, 61
modeling, 41

monounsaturated fatty acids, 127
motor learning, 41, 42
    accomplished climber workout and,
        118, 119
    autonomous stage and, 43
    cognitive stage and, 42
    definition of, 42
    motor stage and, 42–43
    neural adaptation and, 55–56
    relaxation and, 50
    schema and, 43–44
    skill transference and, 45
Motor Learning & Performance
        (Schmidt), 42
motor stage learning, 42–43
motor unit, 55, 67
    synchronization of, 56
moving hangs (B), 83
multipitch climbing, 66, 106
    gym membership and, 114
    home wall and, 114
    target training and, 114
multipitch routes, 11
multisensory learning
    verbal beta and, 51
muscle
    description of, 147
    muscular system adaptation and,
        56–57, 60, 63
    stress points of, 147
muscle fiber
    fast twitch (FT) and, 54, 55, 57, 64,
        67
    growth of, 56–57
    motor units and, 55, 67
    recruitment and, 55, 67
    slow twitch (ST) and, 54, 55, 64, 67
    types of, 5, 6
muscle glycogen, 62, 70–71
muscle movement
    agonist and, 54
    antagonist and, 54
    concentric contraction and, 54, 64
    eccentric contraction and, 54, 64
    isometric contraction and, 54, 64
    stabilizer and, 54
musculotendinous junction, 56

N

narrow pinch grip, 82
nervous system fatigue, 140
neural system adaptation, 55–56, 63
    plyometric training and, 65
neuromuscular adaptation
    campus training and, 93
    fingerboard training and, 93
    recovery and, 141
Next Proteins, 132
Nicole, François, 5, 6
Nicole, Frederic, 5, 6
nonjudgment, 51
nutrition, 9, 70–71, 106, 116, 117
    accomplished climber workout and,
        118
    elite climber workout and, 120
    glycogen and, 139
    injury prevention and, 169
    long-term recovery and, 148
    macronutrients and, 125, 127, 130,
        131
nutrition, performance, 125–36
    carbohydrates and, 128 –130, 131
    fat and, 125, 126–27, 128, 131
    micronutrients and, 130–31
    protein and, 125–26, 131, 132
    sports supplements and, 130,
        131–36
    water and, 130

O

OKG, 136
Olympic Training Village, 3
O'Neal, Shaquille, 6
one-pitch sport routes, 11
on-sight ascent, 9, 29, 37, 38, 43, 49
open-hand grip, 54, 59, 77, 79, 81
    position of, 84, 85, 86, 87
    double dyno training and, 92
open-grip finger position, 48
overgripping, 14, 32
overtraining syndrome, 60–61

P

pain, 31

passive rest, 143
peak performance zone, 26, 35, 43
Penn State Center for Sports
        Medicine, 130
performance
    genes and, 5, 6, 7
    performance triad and, 5, 23
    practice and, 5, 6, 7
Performance Rock Climbing (Goddard), 4
periodization, 60, 168
Phos Fuel, 144
phospholipids, 126
pinch grip, 51, 54, 59, 77, 78, 85, 86,
        87, 88
plyometric training, 4, 56, 65
    campus board and, 90, 91
    complex training and, 67
    heavy finger rolls and, 93
    one-arm deadpoint traversing (B)
        and, 90
    one-arm lunges and, 90
pocket climbing, 48
pocket holds, 88
polyunsaturated fatty acids, 127
positive attitude, 23, 25, 30, 50
posture, 30, 35, 39, 59
power, 62
    mesocycle training schedule and,
        111, 112, 113
    training for, 64
PowerBar, 134
premature fatigue, 14
problem solving, 50, 51
process v. outcome orientation, 25,
        27, 31, 32, 35, 48, 50
progressive overload training princi-
        ple, 58, 60, 63
Progressive Relaxation Sequence, 32,
        33, 147
protein
    beta hydroxy-beta-methylbutyrate
        (HMB) and, 135–36
    biological value (BV) and, 132, 133
    daily requirements for, 126, 132
    functions of, 125
    long-term recovery and, 148
    medium-term recovery and, 145

performance nutrition and, 125–26, 131, 132
    sources for, 126, 132
    whey, 132, 133
protein powders, 132–33
pull muscles, 61
pulldowns, 56, 84
    pulldown machine and, 66
pull-ups, 4, 59, 61, 66
    central fatigue and, 140
    ATP-CP and, 139
    power training and, 65
    weighted pull-ups and, 57, 60, 64, 89
pull-ups, training, 94–98
    Frenchies (A+) and, 95–96
    heavy pull-downs (A+) and, 95
    lat pull-downs (A/B) and, 94
    power pull-ups (B) and, 95
    pull-up intervals (A) and, 95
    30 second pull-ups (A) and, 95
pump doubling, 49
push-ups, 105
pyruvate, 136

R

recovery, 137–49
    acceleration of, 10, 137
    central fatigue and, 140
    curve of, 140
    lactic acid and, 141
    microtraumas and, 141
    rebuild and, 141–42
    recharge and, 141
    refuel and, 141
    stretching and, 71
    water and, 141
recovery, long-term
    active rest and, 149
    attitude and, 149
    carbohydrates and, 148
    delayed-onset muscle soreness and, 141
    fat and, 148
    glycemic index (GI) and, 148
    massage and, 146, 148
    microtraumas and, 147

neuromuscular adaptation and, 141
    nutrition and, 148
    protein and, 148
    stretching and, 148
    supercompensation and, 141, 148
recovery, medium-term
    blood glucose and, 141
    bouldering and, 144
    calorie consumption during climb and, 144–45
    carbohydrates and, 144, 145
    cragging and, 144
    energy bars and, 144
    glycemic index (GI) and, 144–45
    glycogen and, 141, 144, 145
    hyperemia and, 146
    massage and, 144, 145 47
    protein and, 145
    refueling strategies for, 145
    relaxation and, 144, 147
    stretching and, 144, 145, 146, 147
    water and, 144
recovery, short-term
    active rest and, 143
    ATP-CP and, 141
    dangling-arm shakeout and, 142, 143
    efficient climbing and, 142
    glycogen and, 142, 143
    G-Tox and, 142–43
    hydration and, 143–44
    lactic acid and, 142, 143, 144
    massage and, 143
    passive rest and, 143
    Watts study and, 143
recruitment, muscle fiber, 55, 67
redpoint ascent, 9, 29, 37, 38, 42, 43, 48, 49, 50
refueling strategies, 145
relaxation, 27, 39, 42, 48
    ANSWER Sequence and, 34–35
    creativity and, 51
    differential relaxation and, 33–34
    learning and, 44, 50
    progressive relaxation and, 32, 33
    Progressive Relaxation Sequence and, 32, 33
    recovery and, 147

Reminiscence Effect, 112, 140
rest, 9, 58, 60–61, 80
    accomplished climber workout and, 118, 119
    finger injury and, 158
    Hypergravity Isolation Training and, 86–87, 89
    individualization and, 59
    injury and, 156, 160, 161, 162
    injury prevention and, 167–68, 168, 169
    lactic acid and, 139
    macrocycle training schedule and, 113
    mesocycle training schedule and, 112, 113
    microcycle training and, 111
    muscular adaptation and, 60
    relaxation positions and, 33, 34
    supercompensation and, 60–61
reverse side pull, 79, 85
reverse wrist curl exercise, 103
risk, 25
ritual, 26
Robbins, Royal, 3
Robinson, Dr. Mark, 42, 44, 77, 93, 157
Rock & Ice, 158
Rohrbough, Dr. Joel, 157, 162
rope climbing exercise (B-), 97–98
rotator cuff, 162
running, 11
rupture, 158

S

sacrifice, 19, 20, 21
SAID Principle (specific adaptation to imposed demand), 11, 66, 106, 114
schemas
    definition of, 43
    development of, 43–44, 45, 46, 47
    mesocycle training schedule and, 111
Schmidt, Dr. Richard, 42
selenium, 132, 148
self-assessment, 13–22

action and, 18
conditioning exercises and, 69
course correction and, 18
Cycle of Improvement and, 18, 22
elite climber workout and, 119
evaluation of test scores, 17
goal setting and, 18–19
importance of, 13, 14
mind map for, 18
test of, 15–16
test comments and training tips,
    177–80
self-image, 25
serratus muscle, 100
shallow three-finger pocket, 82
shallow two-finger pocket grip, 82
shark cartilage, 136
Sharma, Chris, 5, 6, 27, 51
Shawagunks, 2, 3
shoulder
    injury, 162–64
    rehab exercises for, 163–64
    rest for, 162
    shoulder press exercise, 104–5
    stretch for, 72, 73
    subluxation and, 162
    surgery, 162
side hip raise exercise (A), 99
side pulls, 48, 49, 51, 85
skills
    acquisition of, 45
    autonomous stage learning and, 43
    cognitive stage learning and, 42
    confidence and, 44
    discipline and, 44
    drills and, 47–49
    fitness and, 10
    junior climber training and, 122,
        123
    motor learning and, 41, 42–43
    performance and, 46, 47
    practice of, 9, 10–11, 14, 41
    self-assessment and, 46
    transference of, 45, 59, 66
    weaknesses and, 46
Skinner, Todd, 3, 92, 93
sleep, 148–49, 169
sloper, 82

slow twitch muscle fiber (ST), 54, 55,
    64, 67
smiling, 30, 35
sodium bicarbonate, 144
sodium phosphate, 144
solution orientation, 50
specific adaptation to imposed
    demands. See SAID Principle.
specificity training principle, 58, 59
speed training, 49, 64–65
spinal twist, 75
splinting, 156, 159
splits, 74
sport climbing, 66
    gym membership and, 114
    home wall and, 114
    injury and, 153
    junior climbers and, 122, 123
    knee injury and, 165
    target training and, 114
Sportklettern Heute (Gullich), 4
sport-route, 30
sports drinks, 135
    electrolytes and, 133
    fuel sources and, 133–34
Sports Massage (Meagher), 146
sports massage. See massage.
Sports Medicine, 153
sports supplements, 131–36
    beta hydroxy-beta-methylbutyrate
        (HMB) and, 135–36
    creatine and, 134–35
    energy bars and, 134
    ineffective products and, 136
    protein powders and, 132–33
    sports drinks and, 133–34
sport-specific strength training, 53,
    56, 66, 70, 109
    accomplished climber workout and,
        118, 119
    arm positions and, 78–79
    beginner-level workout and, 117
    central fatigue and, 140
    elite climber workout and, 119,
        120, 121
    female issues and, 121, 122
    finger positions and, 76–77
    fingertip exercises and, 81–82

injury prevention and, 166
junior climbers and, 122, 123
shoulder injury and, 162
stabilizer, 54, 56
stemming, 71
stick game, 48
sticking, 62, 65
straight-arm hangs (A), 80–81, 81, 83
    endurance test of, 6
strategy, 41
strength, concentric, 49
strength deficit, 56
strength, eccentric, 49
strength protocol (B+/C), 86–89
strength training, 9, 10–11, 23, 41
    bouldering and, 63, 64
    complex training and, 67
    creatine and, 134–35
    definition of, 62
    disinhibition and, 56, 64
    elite climber workout and, 119, 120
    endurance training v., 61, 62
    fitness v. skill and, 10
    grip and, 54
    injury and, 161, 162
    injury prevention and, 167
    junior climbers and, 122, 123
    maximum ability and, 63
    mental technique and, 14
    mesocycle training schedule and,
        111, 112, 113
    motor learning and, 55–56
    motor unit synchronization and, 56
    muscular failure and, 53–54
    muscular power and, 62
    muscular system adaptation and,
        56–57, 63
    negative impact of, 10
    neural system adaptation and,
        55–56, 63
    recovery and, 137
    System Training (B) and, 85
    technical skills and, 14
stretching, 9, 144, 145, 146, 147, 148.
    See also flexibility training.
    injury and, 161, 162
    injury prevention and, 168
    lower-body, 73–76

range of motion and, 71
upper-body, 72–73
subluxation, 162
supercompensation, 60–61, 67,
    86–87, 89, 116, 117
    creatine and, 135
    elite climber workout and, 120, 121
    long-term recovery and, 148
    recovery and, 141
surgical tubing, 2
Swiss finger taping method, 157
System Training (B), 84–85
    anaerobic endurance and, 85
    forearm pump and, 90
    Hypergravity Isolation Training
        and, 85, 86
    strength training and, 85

T

taping methods, 157–58, 159, 166–67
target thinking, 9
target training, 114
technical skills, 6, 7, 23
technology, 8
tendon insertions, 5, 6
tendonitis, 158
    lateral epicondyle tendonitis and,
        161–62
    medial epicondyle tendonitis and,
        160–61
tennis elbow, 161
tension, 26, 32, 33–34, 35
testosterone, 136
toproping, 48, 49
torso stretch, 73
touches. *See* lock-offs.
tracking, 49
training
    definition of, 8
    variables of, 6, 7
training program
    accomplished climber workout and,
        116, 118–19
    beginner-level workout and,
        116–17
    blank charts, 173
    competition and, 110

elite climber workout and, 116,
    119–21
    motivation and, 110
    nutrition and, 9–10
    recovery acceleration techniques
        and, 9–10
    rest and, 9–10
    weakness' targeted for, 110
    workout manipulation and, 110
    workout schedule and, 110–14
trans fatty acids, 127
travel, 9
traversing
    core muscle training and, 98
    one-arm, 65, 67
    training, 47–48
tricep stretch, 73
Troyer, Vern, 6
Twinlab, 144
two-finger grip, 87, 88
two-finger pocket hold, 86

U

underclinging, 47, 48, 49, 51, 78–79,
    84, 85
uneven-grip pull ups (B), 55, 96
upper back stretch, 73
upper-body power, 5
upper-trunk extension exercise (A),
    99–100

V

vanadyl sulfate, 136
variable practice, 47
variation training principle, 58, 60,
    82, 94, 111
    injury prevention and, 166
verbal beta, 51
vertical jump increase, 67
visualization, 9, 23, 25–26, 33, 50
    associated visualization, 36–37
    future success and, 37
    competition and, 38
    disassociated visualization, 36
    fatigue and, 38
    injury and, 38

safety and, 37
self-confidence and, 36–37
training and, 35–36
vitamin C, 131, 132, 148
vitamin E, 131, 132, 148
voluntary force, maximum, 56

W

water, 128–30, 134, 143, 144
Way of Strategy, The (Levinson), 31
webbing loop, 59
whey protein, 132, 133, 145
Woods, Tiger, 45
workout schedule
    macrocycle and, 113–14
    mesocycle and, 111–13
    microcycle and, 110–11

X

X finger taping method, 157

Y

Yaniro, Tony, 3, 61
Yosemite Camp Four, 2–3

Z

zinc, 131–32
ZMA supplement, 132
Zone diet, 128

About the Author

An accomplished climber for more than twenty-five years, Eric J. Hörst has ascended cliffs all across the United States and Europe. Driven by his passion for adventure and challenge, he has established more than 400 first ascents, primarily on his home cliffs in the eastern U.S.

A student and teacher of climbing performance, Eric has personally helped train hundreds of climbers, and his training books and concepts have spread around the world to climbers in more than forty countries. He is widely recognized for his innovative practice methods and training tools, and he has been a training products design consultant for Nicros, Inc., since 1994.

Eric is also known as the author of the popular *Flash Training* (Falcon, 1994) and *How to Climb 5.12* (Falcon, 1997); both books have foreign translations available in parts of South America and Europe. He has written more than two dozen magazine articles on the subject, appeared on numerous TV broadcasts, and his techniques have been featured in magazines such as *Climbing, Rock & Ice, Outside, Men's Health, Muscle Media,* and *Men's Journal,* among others. Eric's Web site is www.TrainingForClimbing.com; visit here for the latest information on climbing performance, or to schedule a personal consultation, training seminar, or speaking engagement.

Eric currently lives in Lancaster, Pennsylvania, with his wife, Lisa Ann, and his sons, Cameron and Jonathan.

Eric Hörst on **Welcome to Conditioning *(5.12d/5.13a)*, Fern Buttress, Endless Wall, New River Gorge, West Virginia.**

PHOTOGRAPH BY **STEWART GREEN**

ACCESS: It's every climber's concern

The Access Fund, a national, non-profit climbers organization, works to keep climbing areas open and to conserve the climbing environment. Need help with closures? land acquisition? legal or land management issues? funding for trails and other projects? starting a local climbers' group? CALL US! Climbers can help preserve access by being committed to Leave No Trace (minimum-impact) practices. Here are some simple guidelines:

- **ASPIRE TO "LEAVE NO TRACE"** especially in environmentally sensitive areas like caves. Chalk can be a significant impact on dark and porous rock—don't use it around historic rock art. Pick up litter, and leave trees and plants intact.

- **DISPOSE OF HUMAN WASTE PROPERLY** Use toilets whenever possible. If toilets are not available, dig a "cat hole" at least six inches deep and 200 feet from any water, trails, campsites, or the base of climbs. *Always pack out toilet paper.* On big wall routes, use a "poop tube" and carry waste up and off with you (the old "bag toss" is now illegal in many areas).

- **USE EXISTING TRAILS** Cutting switchbacks causes erosion. When walking off-trail, tread lightly, especially in the desert where cryptogamic soils (usually a dark crust) take thousands of years to form and are easily damaged. Be aware that "rim ecologies" (the clifftop) are often highly sensitive to disturbance.

- **BE DISCRETE WITH FIXED ANCHORS** *Bolts are controversial and are not a convenience*—don't place 'em unless they are *really* necessary. Camouflage all anchors. Remove unsightly slings from rappel stations (better to use steel chain or welded cold shuts). Bolts sometimes can be used proactively to protect fragile resources—consult with your local land manager.

- **RESPECT THE RULES** and speak up when other climbers don't. Expect restrictions in designated wilderness areas, rock art sites, caves, and to protect wildlife, especially nesting birds of prey. *Power drills are illegal in wilderness and all national parks.*

- **PARK AND CAMP IN DESIGNATED AREAS** Some climbing areas require a permit for overnight camping.

- **MAINTAIN A LOW PROFILE** Leave the boom box and day-glo clothing at home—the less climbers are heard and seen, the better.

- **RESPECT PRIVATE PROPERTY** Be courteous to land owners. Don't climb where you're not wanted.

- **JOIN THE ACCESS FUND** To become a member, make a tax-deductible donation of $35.

The Access Fund
Preserving America's Diverse Climbing Resources
P.O. Box 17010
Boulder, CO 80308
303.545.6772 • www.accessfund.org